WINNING VOLLEYBALL

WINNING VOLLEYBALL

Third Edition

ALLEN E. SCATES

UCLA Head Coach
Most Successful Coach in Collegiate Volleyball History
NCAA Volleyball Champions, 1970, 1971, 1972, 1974, 1975, 1976, 1979, 1981, 1982, 1983
Head Coach, U.S. Olympic Volleyball Team, 1972
Head Coach, U.S. Pan American Team, 1971
Coached USVBA Champions, 1965, 1967, 1974

Wm. C. Brown Publishers
2460 Kerper Blvd.
Dubuque, Iowa 52001

Library of Congress Catalog Card Number: 83–26567

ISBN 0–697–06351–8

Printed in the United States of America
10   9   8   7   6   5   4   3   2   1

To my loving wife, Sue
Thank you for your patience.

Contents

II   TEAM PLAY

III   SPECIAL GROUPS

IV   ORGANIZATION

Preface

Volleyball is played in 140 countries using standard international rules. Volleyball is a physically demanding game with plays and patterns that rival basketball for intricacy and imagination. The NAIA, NCAA, and NJCAA have all adopted volleyball as a championship event. In 1975, volleyball became the first professional team sport where men and women competed together.

This book is the complete guide for the player, teacher, and coach who want a comprehensive insight into the many changes in fundamentals, tactics, and strategy that have occurred in volleyball during the last few years. It is the most readable, well-illustrated book on American volleyball. Unless specifically noted, this book is designed for both male and female players.

Six of the thirteen chapters are devoted to helping the beginner master the latest fundamental techniques used at all levels of competition. A new chapter on charts and statistics for use in designing practices and game strategy has been added for teachers and coaches. Step-by-step learning sequences and drills are included to improve performance. Hundreds of easy-to-follow sequence and action photographs of All-American and Olympic men and women clearly illustrate techniques. The coverage of the serve, pass, set, spike, block, and individual defensive techniques gives everyone from the prospective player to the established coach insight into the basic principles required for successful play. These fundamental techniques should not be considered too advanced for the average player.

Detailed sections are presented on coaching, duration and intensity of practice sessions, selection of offense and defense, and scouting and game plans. All standard offenses and defenses and serve reception patterns are covered. This material is more advanced than any text being offered by American authors. It is a necessity for serious students of the game. After studying this book, the reader should be qualified to become a teacher or coach at any level of play.

ACKNOWLEDGMENTS

I wish to express my thanks to the contributing photographers: Richard Mackson; Norm Schindler; Stan Troutman; Tom Leja; Dr. Leonard Stallcup; Terry O'Donnell; Gary Adams; Bob Van Wagner; Bruce Hazelton of *Event Concepts*; Lurline K. Fuji; Andy Banachowski; Stan Abraham; Bud Fields; Ron Haase of *Event Concepts*; Brian Kamper; and Gordon Elser.

Special appreciation is also extended to the past and present members of the UCLA Volleyball Team, the men and women of the United States Volleyball Association, and the students of the Beverly Hills School District. My thanks also go to Patt Koehler and Nancy Rodriquez who typed this major revision.

This book is dedicated to the memory of Harry E. Wilson and Dodge Parker.

Allen E. Scates
Los Angeles, California

Introduction

ORIGIN AND DEVELOPMENT

In 1895 William G. Morgan, a YMCA physical director in Holyoke, Massachusetts, devised the game of volleyball (first called mintonette) by stringing a lawn tennis net across a gym at a height of 6 ft. 6 in. and using the inside of a basketball for a ball.[1] The game was invented to provide an activity for middle-aged businessmen that was competitive, fun, and not too strenuous. In 1896 Morgan put on a demonstration for a conference of YMCA physical directors at Springfield, Massachusetts, and Professor Alfred T. Halstead of Springfield College renamed the game *volleyball*.[2] Mr. Morgan's volleyball rules were published in 1897 in the *Handbook of the Athletic League of YMCAs of North America*.[3] During the next several years, YMCA physical directors introduced the game throughout the United States and in many foreign countries. In 1913, volleyball was included in the Far Eastern Games at Manila by Elwood S. Brown, the International YMCA Secretary. In 1916 the *Spaulding Volleyball Rule Book* was published at the request of the YMCA, and the NCAA was invited to help promote the game. In 1916 it was estimated that 200,000 persons in the United States played volleyball.[4] During World War I, "more than 16,000 volleyballs were distributed in 1919 to the American Expeditionary Forces alone."[5]

[1]Harold T. Friermood, "Volleyball Reflections," in the *1970 Official Volleyball Guide* (Berne, Indiana: United States Volleyball Association, 1970), pp. 144–49.
[2]*Ibid.*

[3]See Harold T. Friermood (ed.), *When Volleyball Began: An Olympic Sport* (Berne, Indiana: United States Volleyball Association, 1966). A complete reproduction of the *1916 Spaulding Volleyball Guide* and selected highlights of the sport of volleyball.
[4]See Friermood, "Volleyball Reflections."
[5]See Friermood (ed.), *When Volleyball Began.*

The United States Volleyball Association (USVBA) was formed in 1928, and the previously closed National YMCA Championship became open to teams from other organizations. The first senior championship for men 35 years or older also began in 1928.

Members of the United States Armed Forces often stretched a rope or net between supports and played volleyball during rest periods in World War II. The sight of American soldiers playing volleyball helped the sport's growth and worldwide popularity.

It was estimated that within two years after the close of the war the number of volleyball players doubled and some five to ten million participants were active in the United States alone.[6]

The International Volleyball Federation (FIVB) was formed in 1947 with the USVBA as a charter member. In 1948 the USA volleyball team made a goodwill tour of Europe. The USVBA sponsored separate college and women's divisions in the 1949 championships held in Los Angeles. The University of Southern California won the Collegiate Division and Houston, Texas, won the Women's Division competition.[7] Los Alamitos Naval Air Station won the first Interservice Volleyball Championship held at Columbus, Ohio, in 1952.[8] Volleyball was included in the 1955 Pan American Games in Mexico City. Mexico won and the USA placed second. In 1964 volleyball took a monumental step forward when it was included in the Olympic Games held in Tokyo, Japan.

In 1969 the National Association of Intercollegiate Athletics (NAIA) adopted volleyball as an official NAIA championship event and held its first tournament at George Williams College in Downers Grove, Illinois. In 1970 the National Collegiate Athletic Association (NCAA) and Division of Girls and Women's Sports (DGWS) held national championships. The Association for Intercollegiate Athletics for Women (AIAW) was formed in 1971 by the DGWS to provide leadership for women's intercollegiate athletic programs and to conduct all championship events formerly conducted by the DGWS.

The first AIAW Junior College/Community College Championship was held at Miami Dade Community College in 1973. In 1974 the National Junior College Athletic Association (NJCAA) held its first volleyball championship at Schoolcraft College in Livonia, Michigan. In 1981 the NCAA conducted its first volleyball championship for women. All national collegiate sports governing bodies now conduct championship events in volleyball.

THE MODERN GAME

The status of volleyball has increased tremendously since it was adopted as an Olympic sport in 1964. That sensational performance of the 1964 Gold Medalist Japanese Women's team opened the door to mass exposure of the sport via television, film, and tours of foreign teams throughout the world.

The 1964 Japanese women used the greatest individual and team defenses known to the game. They perfected the

---

[6]See Carl M. McGowan (ed.), *It's Power Volleyball* (Berne, Indiana: United States Volleyball Association, 1968).

[7]Harold T. Friermood, "Cumulative Record of Volleyball Championship Winners," in the *1969 Official Volleyball Guide* (Berne, Indiana: United States Volleyball Association, 1969), pp. 105–21.

[8]See Friermood, "Volleyball Reflections."

rolling dig, which enables them to go to the floor and retrieve a hard-hit spike and then roll to their feet in time for the next play. Japanese men perfected the spectacular *diving save,* which provided even greater court coverage and made their defense the model for several years.

Volleyball was slow to develop in this country because of its image as a game that was not strenuous in which a ball was lobbed back and forth across a low net. Today the game of "power" volleyball demands a player who can dive, sprawl or roll to the floor to recover his opponent's attack and jump high above the net to block or spike a moving ball into his opponent's court. Power volleyball requires more organization of team strategy than recreational volleyball. The athlete playing power volleyball must master the individual skills of the game in order to perform with quickness, alertness, coordination, and stamina in complex playing situations.

During the past decade, new standards of volleyball training and performance have emerged to test the speed, strength, endurance, and coordination of the best athletes. The sport has assumed a position of importance in the eyes of students and athletic departments throughout the country.

A majority of the better teams are using quick combination offenses which feature a variety of sets and spikes designed around fast patterns of attack. There is increased emphasis on the defensive techniques of diving and rolling to the floor to dig or retrieve balls; these tactics, in turn, have led to longer rallies.

Volleyball is a universal game easily adapted to the needs and abilities of all participants. For younger players, the net can be lowered, and for recreational and coeducational play, rules can be modified. Volleyball appeals to people of all ages at different levels of skill.

Volleyball is played in 140 countries and about 30 countries recognize the game as a major sport. In the United States, volleyball is the most popular team participant sport and is a popular spectator sport as well. The game is very popular in East Europe and the Far East. In the last few years our USA Women's Team has emerged as one of the top three teams in the world. Our men have the strongest collegiate program in the world and are also ranked in the top three with the USSR and Brazil. Young players in Eastern Europe participate in 100 to 150 international matches before they become a starter on the national team. Japan and the USSR host 60 to 70 international matches a year.

I

FUNDAMENTALS

1

Serving

A well-developed serve puts the opposing team on the defensive. Accurate placement, unpredictable movement, and high velocity of the ball—or a combination of these factors—are crucial elements for an effective serve. Varsity players should be able to deliver their strong serves to their opponents' court in at least nine out of ten attempts. In Olympic competition, there is less than a 5 percent chance of scoring an ace on the serve.

In the 1976 Olympics, the Polish Gold Medalist Men's Team served 1,063 times and made 35 aces (3.29%), while making 46 errors (4.33%). The Japanese Women Gold Medalists served 449 times with 12 aces (2.67%), while making 13 errors (2.9%).

In 1978 college play, the UCLA Men's Team attempted 1577 serves with 106 aces (6.7%) and 105 errors (6.65%) in league competition. Most coaches should be satisfied when their team has more service aces than errors.

TYPES OF SERVES
USED IN COMPETITION

The underhand serve is still used by many players participating in recreational volleyball in this country. Athletes participating in "power" volleyball, where a refined application of team strategy and individual skills are required, overwhelmingly prefer the overhand floater serve. Europeans participating in power volleyball once favored the round house and overhand spin, although the majority have switched to the overhand floater serve. Many of the Oriental teams still use a sidearm floater serve.

In the first series of international competition the serve was the only fundamental part of the game in which American teams consistently outperformed European teams. The improved technique of the forearm pass used by Europeans has negated the slight serving advantage that the Americans once enjoyed. United States national

3

a.　　　　　　　　　　　　　　**b.**

Figure 1-1 *The Serve.* The server tosses the ball above and in front of her serving shoulder and transfers her weight to her front leg before contacting the ball. (Tom Leja)

teams have not experienced any great difficulty receiving the fast and predictable round house and overhand spin serves of the Europeans. Consequently, our players have not used these serves.

The team whose members use a variety of serving styles will have a definite advantage when playing against a team whose servers all use the same style. When a team is trying to pass hard overhand spin serves, roundhouse floater serves, and overhand floater serves they will not be able to get in a passing groove and their passing may become erratic. Servers on the same team should also vary their serving positions to further confuse the opposition. Some players should serve from the endline while others serve ten or twenty feet behind the endline to confuse the passers timing.

SERVING RULES

The service area is located in the right third of the court behind the end line. The server cannot touch the lines bounding this area or the floor outside the service area until the ball is contacted. However, the server's arm or body may be extended in the air over or beyond these lines. If the playing area does not extend to a minimum depth of 6 ft. beyond the end line, the server is allowed to step into the court to whatever distance is necessary to provide the minimum service area.

With the hand, fist, or arm, the server hits the ball over the net into the opponents' area of the court. The right back player on the serving team is the first server of the game. This player continues to serve until his team commits a foul or the game is completed. If a member of the serving team commits a foul, a side out is called by the referee, and the ball is awarded to the opposing team, whose members rotate clockwise one position to the position of server. The player rotating from the right front position is always the next server.

UNDERHAND SERVE

Beginning players should learn the underhand serve first. If overhand serves are allowed, beginners will commit many serving and passing errors which will make play boring due to a lack of activity. With underhand serves, there will be better passes and more rallys. Beginners will get greater exercise and become emotionally involved. The underhand serve is the easiest to learn

and control. It requires very little strength in comparison to the other serves and can be mastered by most elementary school children. The weak or uncoordinated child should be allowed to serve in front of the serving line during games and gradually move back to the regulation 30-ft. serving line as his skill and confidence improve.

The server places her left foot forward and bends both knees slightly. She takes a long backswing with her striking arm and contacts the ball below its midline with the heel of her hand (if the hand is open) or with the heel and knuckles (if the hand is closed). If the server prematurely takes her eyes off the ball, she may contact the ball above its midline and serve into the net. The server's weight shifts from the back leg to the forward one at the moment of contact. The ball is tossed and hit in the air. When the player tosses the ball it should

a.

b.

Figure 1-2 *The Underhand Serve.* Striking the ball on its right side will cause it to travel to the server's left or cross court (*a*). Notice that the player's serving arm follows-through at a slight angle (*b*). When the ability to strike the ball on its right or left side has been mastered, the position of the player's body can remain the same, regardless of where he intends to direct the ball. (Los Angeles City Unified School District)

not go higher than the chest. Follow-through occurs in the direction of flight.

When follow-through does not occur in a straight line, i.e., when the armswing is across the body or away from the body, the ball travels past the side lines and out of bounds.

OVERHAND SERVE

Overhand Floater Serve

The overhand floater serve, which has no spin, moves in an erratic path as it approaches the receiver, making it difficult for the opponent to pass. To achieve the desired floating action, the hand and forearm move together as a whole; there is only a momentary point of contact and very little follow through. When the ball is contacted near the center with a straight movement of the hand, it will have a spinless flight. Due to the air pushing against the ball, it will travel with a "wiggle" type of motion, rising, dropping, or moving from side-to-side like a knuckleball in baseball. At recent major domestic championships, the overwhelming majority of the serves were overhand floater serves.

If the floater serve does not have any "action" or wiggle-type movement of the ball, the server has usually hit the side of the ball, snapped the wrist, or used too much follow-through. The majority of servers hit the ball with the heel of the hand. Some, however, strike the ball with the heel of the hand and closed fingers or a closed fist. Players generally prefer to bend their arm slightly on contact. For additional power, most servers take a short step forward with their foot just prior to contact.

In Figure 1-3, Olympian Patti Bright holds the ball about shoulder height, directly in line with her back foot. Her feet are in a stride position and her weight is evenly distributed. She tosses the ball about 3 ft. in the air, above and in front of her right shoulder. Her right arm extends from a cocked position to contact the ball a few inches below its midline with the heel of her hand. Patti is short; therefore, she fully extends her right arm upon contact with the ball so that it will travel in a low trajectory and still clear the net. Notice that her wrist is stiff and that there is little follow-through.

Overhand Spin Serve

The overhand spin serve results in a fast dropping action, which gives the opposition less time to react. Although quite effective when used against inexperienced competition, better players find the flight of the ball very predictable (due to its spinning action) and usually have little trouble in passing the serve. It is difficult for most servers to control the spin serve, and it is not popular with coaches because of the increased chance of a serving error.

Very few players in this country have developed the accuracy and speed needed to score frequently with this serve in important competition. During the early 1960s, Tom Vogelsang developed an overhand spin serve using a spike jump which was effective in beach doubles competition. Currently, members of the Brazilian and Canadian Men's Team are utilizing the jump overhand spin serve in major international matches. This trend will probably continue because the jump allows the server to direct the ball in a lower trajectory, making it more difficult to pass.

To serve an overhand spin, the right-handed player places his left foot in front and stands in a stride position. He tosses the ball about 4 ft. in the air (one foot higher

a.   b.   c.

d.   e.

Figure 1-3 *Overhand Floater Serve.* Olympian Patti Bright demonstrates the overhand floater serve. (Los Angeles City Unified School District)

Figure 1-4 *Overhand Spin Serve.* This serve results in a fast dropping motion that gives the passer less time to react. The legendary Gene Selznick prepares to contact the ball slightly on its right side to impart a curving motion. (Dr. Leonard Stallcup)

than the toss for the floater). The server's left arm should be fully extended as his right arm, hand held open, cocks behind his head. Shoulders rotate so that the left shoulder faces the net and weight is on the back foot. As the ball starts to descend, the shoulders twist forward, and the elbow leads the way as the arm begins to straighten. The ball is contacted in the center of the lower midsection. The heel of the server's hand first contacts the ball, and then the wrist snap rolls his hand over the ball, imparting a topspin as weight shifts to the forward foot.

The server may contact the ball on the left or right side, causing the ball to curve. Right-handed players usually strike the ball on the right side because it is a natural motion and is easily learned.

ROUND-HOUSE SERVE

In 1960 the Japanese Women's team introduced the round-house floater serve in international competition at the World Volleyball Championships in Brazil. Because their opponents did not have an opportunity to practice receiving the hard, fast-floating action of this serve, it was an instant success. After the Japanese Women's team won the Gold Medal in the 1964 Olympic Games in Tokyo, they made numerous tours in the United States to compete against our top women players. After attempting to field the superior serves of the Japanese for six years, the United States National Women's Team began a serious attempt to copy their serving technique during practice for the 1970 World Volleyball Championships in Bulgaria.

In 1969 a Japanese student, Toshi Toyoda, arrived in the United States to study and to play volleyball at UCLA. He came with a mastery of the round-house floater serve and was the most effective server in the 1969 and 1970 USVBA National Championships. In 1969 he was one of the few men at the USVBA Championships to use the round-house floater; in 1970 a few more players began to use the round-house floater but had not yet perfected it.

Round-House Floater Serve

The round-house floater serve is effective because of its unique dropping and side-to-

a.	**b.**

Figure 1-5 *Toss for Round-House Serve.* As the player tosses the ball, he leans over his back leg, extending his serving arm downward. His arm moves in a windmill motion, contacting the ball directly over the hitting shoulder. (The Ealing Corp.)

side movement. Although it is becoming more popular, few players in the United States have mastered this serve, so there has been little opportunity to practice receiving it.

Better players are reluctant to try a new serving style because they are forced to endure a temporary loss of serving effectiveness while struggling to learn the new technique. Until the round-house floater serve becomes common in this country, it will remain an effective serve in local, regional, and national competition. Because it can be delivered with great force and with a dropping side-to-side movement that has

proven unpredictable to receivers, more players should try this technique.

To accomplish the round-house floater serve, the player stands with his body perpendicular to the net, feet shoulder-width apart, and knees slightly flexed. He tosses the ball about 3 ft. in the air, slightly in front of and above his forward shoulder. During the toss, his body leans backward as both legs bend. His hitting arm swings upward from the area of his right knee in a fully extended windmill motion. As the ball starts to descend, he shifts his weight forward and extends his legs. He contacts the ball with the heel of his hand, directly

a.

b.

c.

d.

e.

Figure 1-6 *Round-House Floater Serve.* All-American Toshi Toyoda prefers to move far behind the endline so that he can contact the ball with great force and still direct it into the opponents' court. (The Ealing Corp.)

above the right shoulder. (If the ball is contacted *behind* the shoulder, it usually has a high trajectory and travels out of the opponents' court. If the ball is contacted *in front of* the shoulder, it usually travels in a very low trajectory and hits the net.)

The weight of the player's body should be supported by his front leg when the ball is hit. After contact, the server pivots on his front foot and faces the net, ready to move to his defensive assignment.

Round-House Spin Serve

The round-house spin serve, used by several male members of Asian and European teams, is a very fast serve that drops rapidly but cannot be directed with the same accuracy as the overhand floater serve. Once the ball leaves the server's hands, the receivers can predict its flight: thus, members of our national men's teams have passed this serve well and have not attempted to copy the round-house spin serve.

The outstanding difference between the round-house spin serve and the round-house floater lies in the technical execution of contacting the ball with the striking hand. For the spin serve, the ball is struck with the entire cupped hand in the same manner as the overhand spin serve.

To increase the power and speed on the spin serve, the server can toss the ball high in front of him and run to the ball to contact it. A quick rotary movement of the arm and hand and the momentum of the body impart a tremendous amount of speed to the ball.

SERVING DRILLS

In serving drills and in competition, varsity players should be able to serve to a specific

Figure 1-7 *Round-House Spin Serve.* Contact is first made below the midline of the ball with the heel of the hand. As the wrist snaps forward, the palm and fingers impart a topspin to the ball, making it drop. The arm follows through in the direction of the flight. (Andy Banachowski)

area of the court nine times out of ten, and serve without error nineteen out of twenty times.

To facilitate serving to specific spots, it is best to divide the court into the six areas that are universally used in all countries. Once the players become familiar with the zones of the court, it becomes easy for the coach to give precise signals to the server during drills and competition. Players should practice serving to all six areas on the court. In competition, there are tactical reasons for serving to each area and it would

.

give a coach great flexibility if the players had the capability to pinpoint their serves.

Serving practice should be held at the beginning, middle and end of practice sessions to simulate game conditions when players are fresh, tired or exhausted. For variety some coaches recommend four drills that call for accurate serves interspersed with intense exercises. In drill one, players can block, spike or dig, then serve and repeat the drill. The player blocks in area two, runs off the net to the backcourt spiking line to dig or dive for a ball hit by the coach and then goes to the backline to serve two balls to area six and three. He then repeats the drill.

In the second drill, the player blocks in area two and then runs off the net for an approach and spikes a set delivered from area three before serving two balls to area one and six. In the third drill, the player blocks in area two, dives for a ball thrown by the coach in area three and then quickly recovers and spikes a set delivered by the coach to area two. He then runs to the service area and serves to area two and four.

In the fourth drill, the player serves the ball to area five and runs to area one to dig the ball hit by the coach. After digging the ball back to the coach, the player dives for the coach's dink shot in area two, returning the ball to the coach. The player recovers and sets a ball thrown by the coach to area four and returns to the serving area.

When serving to targets on the floor, the court should be cleared of receivers and the players divided along the end lines of the available courts so they can serve back and forth across the net. When the ball lands out of bounds, the player recovering the serve should signal how far the ball landed out of bounds so the server can adjust the force or direction of the serve. The server should always serve from the serving area

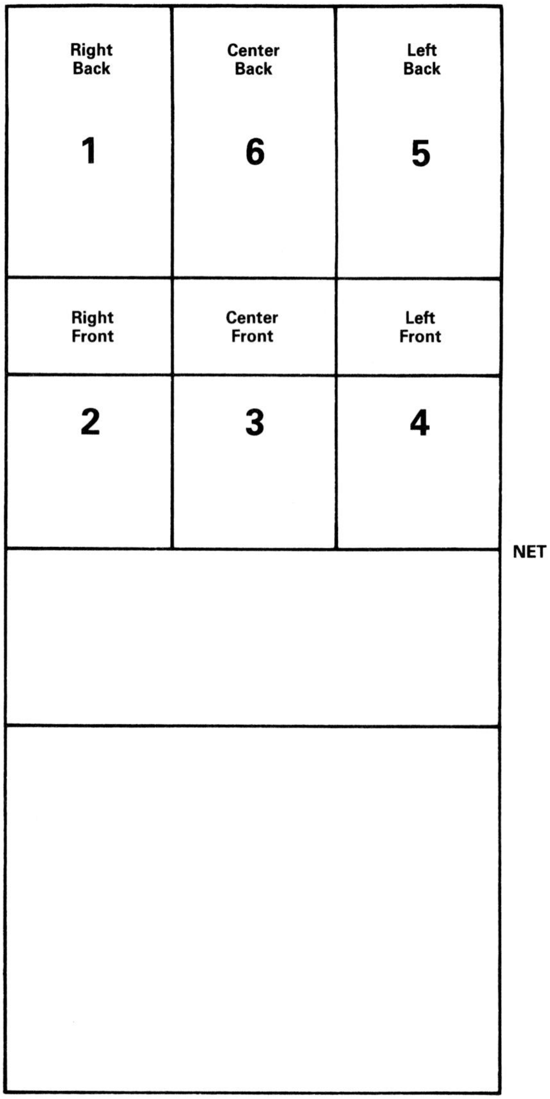

Right Back 1	Center Back 6	Left Back 5
Right Front 2	Center Front 3	Left Front 4

NET

Diagram 1-1 *Areas of the Court*

behind the court. When practicing line serves, each player might have a partner who stands on the opposite side of the net serving the ball back and forth from any position behind the end line. The best position to serve crosscourt is near the sideline. When serving down the line, the best position is 9 ft. from the sideline.

Since serving is probably the dullest fundamental to practice, it is motivating to make the drills competitive by placing towels, chairs, or other markers on the floor for players to hit. The coach can keep a practice serving chart to record the players' scores. Players should not ease up when using targets but deliver their toughest serves during all drills.

It is often beneficial to combine serving and receiving drills. Each player should receive from 50 to 100 serves during every practice session. If the drill is server-oriented, the receiver can be placed in position at the discretion of the server. For example, if the server wishes to serve cross court, the receiver takes the right-front or right-back position.

A simple game can provide competition between two players by allowing the receiver to score one point each time the ball is passed to a designated target area and by giving a point to the server each time the receiver fails to pass the ball accurately. Balls that are served out—into the net or away from the receiver's area—are scored for the receiver. At UCLA we add a blocker who attempts to stuff low serves back into the server's court. These blocks are scored for the receiver.

A similar server-receiver game incorporates some of the pressure that occurs during actual competition. To win this game, either the server or the receiver must score three straight points. For example, if the server has two points and the receiver has passed the ball perfectly, the receiver takes the lead, 1 to 0. As soon as the opponent scores, the other player's score automatically returns to 0.

A third player can be added to act as the passing target for the receiver. When one of the players wins, the third player exchanges positions with the winner and the loser remains in the same position. In this manner, the weakest player gets the added work that is needed to improve performance. It is surprising how readily a coach can detect from such a simple game which performers will do well in pressure situations.

The most time-consuming, although effective, way for the server to practice is to direct serves against the type of actual team-receiving formation that will be faced in competition. Weaknesses inherent in the formation can be pointed out to the server and attacked.

SERVING TACTICS

Players should serve to score a point, not only to put the ball into play. The serve should be directed to a player who: 1) is a weak receiver; 2) has just made an error; 3) is a substitute; 4) is upset over the last play; or 5) is tense. The server should aim for a spot that is: 1) in the seam of receiving responsibility between two players; 2) open; or requires the best attacker to receive the ball or alter the approach. Another tactic is to pick a key player and to constantly serve to that player in an attempt to wear him out.

The serve should be extra strong when the server's team is far ahead or behind in scoring; in the beginning or near the end of a game; and when the server's team has not scored for a long period of time. The serve following a time out, a substitution, or a serving error by a teammate should be served easy to ensure that there will be no serving error. The serve following should be strong.

2

Passing

Passing simply refers to the act of hitting the ball to another teammate. Typically, a player passes the ball to a teammate who sets it for the spiker to hit into the opponents' court. Occasionally, the pass is spiked or dinked to confuse the opponents' block. A passer in highly competitive or power vollleyball should attempt to receive the serve or the spike in an underhand manner in order to strike the ball with both forearms simultaneously.

FOREARM PASS

Nearly all service receptions are fielded by the forearm pass method because of the referee's strict interpretation of what constitutes a thrown ball in the overhand position. At one time, the forearm pass was only used to receive serves by players who had "bad hands" and did not want to risk a rule infraction, or by players who were not in position to use the overhand pass. The restrictions placed on the serving area, removal of the serving screen (created by the server's teammates who stood in front of him to block the view of the receiver), and new techniques for the forearm pass have enabled players to use the forearm pass with better accuracy than with the overhand pass. In fact, directives from the International Volleyball Federation and United States Volleyball Association encouraging the return of the overhand pass were not heeded by players and coaches.

The forearm pass is also used to handle low balls and spikes. When used to recover the opponents' attack, it is called a *dig*. Up to 70 percent of a female high school team's practice can be devoted to this fundamental technique. (The defensive technique of digging will be covered in Chapter 6 along with the *dive* and *roll*.)

15

Figure 2-1 *Forearm Bump Pass.* The forearm pass is the recommended way to pass a serve to the setter. The ball is hit off the forearms. (Richard Mackson)

FOOTWORK AND BODY POSITION

Every coach looks for size when selecting squad members, but size without quickness will be neutralized by a well-trained, fast-moving, opposition. Quickness and coordination are the most important physical assets in receiving the serve, in digging, and in setting. In order to pass the ball accurately, players must take small, quick steps while maintaining a low center of gravity. For all passing techniques, the player's weight should be evenly distributed on the inside balls of the feet and the heels should be off or barely touching the floor. The feet should be placed wider apart than the shoulder width, with one foot set slightly ahead of the other. Knees should be bent at a 90° angle for smaller players and at a smaller angle for taller players. Hips are bent at approximately 90° and the back is straight. The elbows are held in front of the knees and the knees are bent forward in front of the toes. The hands are held in front and apart about waist high, and the weight is forward. The head should be held upright.

Most of the footwork in serve reception and digging is to the side. The two patterns of movement are the side step and the crossover and run step.

Figure 2-2 *Waiting for the Serve.* While anticipating the serve, the player's body should be in a low position, with their feet more than shoulder width apart and eyes on the server. (Gordon Elser)

Side Step

The side step is performed by sliding the lead foot laterally and following it with the trailing foot. The steps are small and quick, with the trailing foot moving to within 6 in. of the forward foot. When the player arrives at the desired area, the front foot hits the floor first and points in the direction of the intended pass. It is very important to maintain a low body position in order to stop with good balance. The stop is made with the lead foot slightly forward and the trailing foot closing the gap between the feet to approximately shoulder-width.

After this movement is perfected without the ball, the coach should lob the ball to the left and right of the player and receive a return pass from him. When moving to the left or right, the passer's lead foot should face the coach before the ball is contacted. The coach or partner should feint in several directions before releasing the ball to enable the passer to make slide steps in different directions before receiving the ball.

Crossover and Run Step

The crossover and run step is used to cover greater distances when moving laterally. The crossover and run is accomplished with the inside foot as the passer takes as many successive running steps as necessary to approach the desired area. When the player has time to stop and pass, the front foot should hit the floor first and point in the general direction of the target area. The trailing or outside foot completes the movement as it swings in front of the planted foot and points directly at the target area. The feet are approximately shoulder-width apart, in a stride position.

HAND POSITIONS

The ball *must not* be played with the open palms in the underhand position because the referee will call a foul. There is no written rule prohibiting the use of the open hand in underhand play, but the universal interpretation of officials is that the ball cannot be clearly hit using this technique.

a.

b.

Figure 2-3 *Clenched Fist for Passing.* The fist is clenched with the thumbs placed parallel and on top of the index fingers (*a*). The remaining fingers are wrapped around the closed fist (*b*). (Lurline K. Fujii)

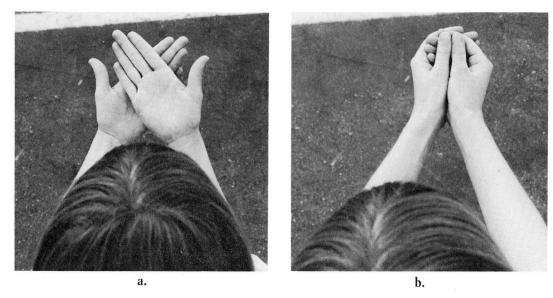

a.   b.

Figure 2-4 *Curled Fingers for Passing.* The hands are held open, with the palms facing upward (*a*). The fingers are then curled and the thumbs held parallel to create a flat surface (*b*). (Lurline K. Fujii)

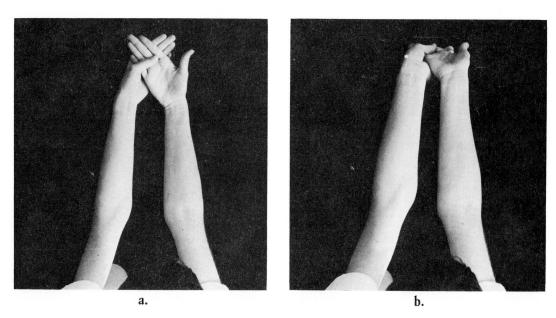

a.   b.

Figure 2-5 *Thumb Over Palm for Passing.* The thumb of the bottom hand is folded over the top hand (*a*). Hands are pointed toward the floor in order to rotate the forearms outward and to create a soft rebounding surface (*b*). If the ball is contacted by the hands in this position, rather than by the forearms, the referee may call a thrown ball. (Lurline K. Fujii)

Figure 2-6 *Interlaced Fingers for Passing.* The interlaced fingers prevent the arms and hands from flying apart on contact to help insure a favorable rebounding surface. This method is rapidly gaining popularity. (Richard Mackson)

The hands should be clasped in a manner that is comfortable and effective for the individual player. Beginning players readily learn the popular *clenched-fist* position. This hand position presents a good rebounding service for balls that cannot be reached with the forearms and must be struck with the hands.

The *curled-finger* position allows for more of an outward rotation of the forearms. The *thumb-over-palm* position enables the player to achieve a maximum outward rotation of his forearms, which creates a soft rebounding service. This position should not be used by most men since their wide shoulder structure usually prevents them from bringing their forearms close together to form a favorable rebounding surface.

The newest technique used for joining the hands is the interlaced finger position in which the palms are put together and the fingers interlaced to prevent the hands from breaking apart on contact with the ball. This is used by the USA and Russian Women's Team and various college women's teams that have all team members using the same method for every technique.

ARM POSITIONS

At the 1956 World Games in Paris, the American team displayed good control with the "bump" pass. Other national teams preferred to squat low or roll to the floor when making an overhand pass and only "bumped" the serve when it was impossible to use the overhand method.

About 1960, Japanese women began receiving the serve on their wrists and forearms with amazing accuracy. They would keep their elbows locked upon contact.

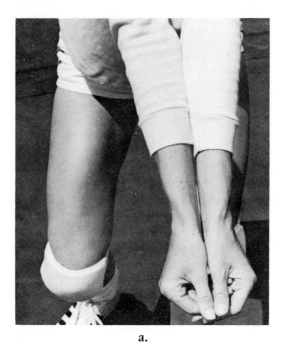
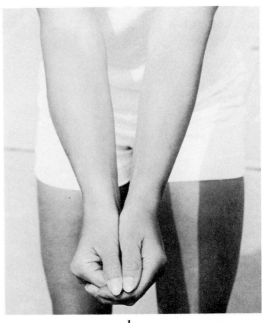

a.   b.

Figure 2-7 *Contact Area.* Some players are flexible enough to create an ideal rebounding surface in the area from their wrists to elbows (*a*). Others must be satisfied to extend their arms and hold them close together and to contact the ball on the lower forearm or wrist (*b*). (Los Angeles City Unified School District)

Within a few years all countries began to use the forearm pass to receive serves.

In the early 1960s the term "bump" was still used to describe all serves passed in the underhand manner. By 1965 most of the players contacted the ball on their forearms instead of with their wrists and hands. Prior to contact, elbows should be completely extended and rotated outward, exposing the flat inner surface of the forearms. Thumbs and wrists should be pointed toward the floor. Although the arms are extended before contact, they must not be rapidly moving forward when receiving a hard serve or last split second lateral adjustment of the arms will not be possible. Lateral movement is a necessity when re-

ceiving hard floater serves that travel in an unpredictable path. The split second lateral adjustment of the arms is difficult if the arms are too rigid; extended but relaxed arms are what often make the difference between an average and an outstanding passer. The arms must move slowly forward to absorb or cushion a rapidly moving ball for longer contact and greater control. After absorbing the shock of the ball, the arms continue forward in a direct line towards the target area. The ball should contact the soft internal part of the forearms about half way between the wrist and the elbow.

The speed and movement of the arms depend on the speed of the approaching ball and the distance the pass must travel.

a.   **b.**

Figure 2-8 *Arm Movement.* Upward coordinated movement of legs and arms is important when the ball is moving slowly. There should be little upward movement when receiving fast serves; if there is, the pass will travel too far. The ball should contact both forearms simultaneously. (The Ealing Corp.)

PASSING TECHNIQUES

Players who are successful serve receivers anticipate the flight of the ball and quickly position their body in its path before contact. The body is lowered or raised so that the ball can be contacted between the legs. The receiver leans slightly forward with the back straight, arms fully extended, and elbows rotated outward to form a soft rebound surface with the forearms. The player should try to watch the ball before, during, and after contact.

Poor serve receivers do not watch the ball as long as their more accurate teammates. They twist their waist instead of moving their feet to receive the ball between the legs and are forced to bat at the ball with their arms. Probably the most

common error is standing up to pass the ball, rather than passing it from a low position. Squatting should be practiced. American players naturally react to low balls by lowering themselves from the waist instead of lowering their bodies with their legs, as is the custom of the Asians.

Follow-through of the arms and knees depends on the speed of the approaching serve and the intended placement of the ball. If the ball moves over the net slowly or must be passed a long distance, the player's arms and legs should move upward as contact is made, which gives greater impetus to the flight of the ball.

Generally, hard overhand floater serves requires little follow-through. Teams that run a fast offense to confuse the block often try to use quick low passes that gets to the

Figure 2-9 *Japanese Low Pass Technique.* The pass travels in a fast, low arc. To achieve a low trajectory, the ball is contacted with the arms pointing toward the floor and the back held straight. Notice that all players are watching the serve receiver in case they may have to help out with a bad pass. (Dr. Leonard Stallcup)

setter before the opposing blockers have a chance to observe the attack patterns of the spikers. Asian teams consider the pass and dig to be the most important part of the offense and spend over 50 percent of their practice time passing serves and spikes. Instead of passing the ball above the net, they concentrate on passing in a low trajectory into the path of the oncoming setter. This pass is particularly advantageous in a fast attack.

MOVING TO THE BALL

Good footwork greatly enhances the likelihood of an accurate pass. Players must move quickly toward the flight of the ball. Backcourt receivers should stand close to the backline so they will not have to move backward to receive the ball. When players reach the receiving area, they should plant

Figure 2-10 *Screw-Under Pass.* The passer executes a screw-under step to position the upper part of her body behind the ball just prior to contact. Beginners rarely are capable of making this split-second adjustment and usually rely on a lateral arm movement to compensate for poor body position. (Richard Mackson)

a.   b.   c.

Figure 2-11 *Changing Direction.* Changing direction with the elbow-lock technique is recommended to provide greater control over the ball and to enable the forearms to remain in contact with the ball for a longer period of time. Prolonged contact with the ball is maintained by lateral rotation of the body and arms. Lateral rotation of the body should only be used to pass a slow-moving ball. (The Ealing Corp.)

their feet and pivot toward the target with their outside foot ahead and pointed toward the setter.

If the ball is to one side, the receiver may position his body behind the ball by taking a long slide step and squatting on the sliding leg while extending the other leg. This maneuver has become known as the *screw under step.*

Changing Direction

When passing a slow-moving ball from a lateral position, prolonged contact and better control of the ball can be maintained by rotating the upper body toward the target area while the ball is being passed (see Figure 2-11a,b,c). Players should not twist their waists when receiving a serve or hard-driven spike.

Figure 2-12 *Low Lateral Pass.* The inside shoulder dips forward to turn the interior part of the forearms toward the ball. The player leans toward the ball with a lateral tilt, and with his weight over his front leg. (Stan Troutman)

Figure 2-14 *One-Arm Pass.* The one-arm pass is frequently used in competition, but often neglected in practice sessions. With this technique, contact with the ball can be made with the forearm, the wrist, or the fist. (Richard Mackson)

Figure 2-13 *High Lateral Pass.* Often players must extend their legs completely to orient the interior part of the forearms toward the ball to pass at shoulder height. (Richard Mackson)

LATERAL PASS

The passer must reach laterally to contact the ball when there is not enough time to position his body for the regular forearm pass. When both arms are used, this technique is called a *lateral pass.*

ONE-ARM PASS

When the ball is too far away to contact with the lateral pass, a one-arm pass, or dig, is used. The dig is an attempt to recover a spiked ball with a one- or two-armed pass.

Volleyball lore tells us that the term *dig* originated from beach play. Players would scoop low balls inches from the sand, using their fists and a bent elbow. Today, most players use the forearm to contact the ball whenever possible. The fist is used on balls that are harder to reach.

BACKWARD PASS

The backward pass is often used by a backcourt player to recover balls hit off the top of the blocker's hands. Occasionally, players amaze their teammates by making perfect sets from the back line area or farther with this technique.

The elbow lock technique used in Figure 2-15 is recommended on high balls. On

lower backward passes the player should bend his elbows.

PASSING FROM UNUSUAL POSITIONS

During a game the player will often be called on to pass the ball from unusual positions. Players who have been thoroughly drilled to react to the ball do not hesitate to place themselves in whatever position necessary to pass the ball. To prevent injury, the player must maintain proper flexibility by performing stretching exercises to meet the strenuous demands of competition.

Figure 2-15 *Backward Pass.* Immediately before contact is made with the ball, the shoulders shrug upward and the player leans backward. (Richard Mackson)

Figure 2-16 *Passing a Low Ball.* The player drops into a full squatting position to field the ball. (Richard Mackson) ▼

3

Setting

The *set* is an overhand or forearm pass that places the ball in position for a spiker to attack it. The set is usually performed by a specialist called the *setter* who uses the overhand pass whenever possible. The overhand pass is a more precise method of delivering the set, and it gives the spiker a better opportunity to analyze the flight of the approaching ball. The fingers of both hands are used to contact the ball with the overhand pass. If the ball has not been clearly hit or has visibly come to rest, the setter has committed an error.

The basic offense employs two setters and four spikers. Beginning setters need speed, mobility, and anticipation to move quickly after the pass and deliver a normal set in a high arc that drops about 2 ft. from the net at either corner of the net.

Good setters require superior reactions and ball-handling skills to place the ball at any spot along the net at any height. Out-

standing setters possess the mental alertness and control to take advantage of the blocker's weaknesses and their spikers' strengths. They know the individual preferences of their spikers and are capable of watching the spiker's approach, the ball, and opposing blockers when moving into position to receive a good pass. They have the competitive spirit to bolster their teammates' play and to perform well in tense situations.

SETTER'S BODY POSITION

If the pass is close to the net, the traditional position for the setter is to turn the body sideways to the net with the knees bent and the arms up to prepare to contact the ball above the head as the ball crosses the center of the body, the hands contact the ball in front of the face and the ball is

Figure 3-1 *Basic Setting Position.* The setter positions herself directly in front of the ball and holds her hands about 6 in. in front of her face. The ball must be contacted simultaneously with the fingers and thumbs of both hands, or it will be ruled a fault. (Richard Mackson)

the approaching hitters and the flight of the pass. The Japanese use predetermined plays and know what spiker is going to receive the set if the pass is good. They use a one-setter system so the setter can devote many practice hours to perfecting this position.

FRONT SET

When the ball is passed, the setter must anticipate its flight and move quickly under it. He should be in a stationary, relaxed

Figure 3-2 *International Setting Position.* This position allows the setter a good view of the pass and the approaching spiker. He can look at the blockers just prior to contacting the ball. (Richard Mackson)

delivered directly forward or backward. This is the best position to teach beginning setters and is still used by most national teams.

The international setting position used by many foreign teams is more deceptive. When setters receive a good pass in this position, they face area five of their own court. The setter should stand with their inside foot forward with a slight backward lean of the hips when setting close to the net. This posture is better for delivering play sets to the quick hitters.

The Japanese system has the setter stand with his back toward the net. It is extremely difficult for the setter to watch the opponent's block but he has a clear view of

position when the ball arrives, with his feet in a stride position, shoulder-width apart. The foot closest to the net should remain flat on the floor until contact. The forward foot should also be closest to the net and point toward the antenna in area four. The setter's nose should be in line with the descending ball, and his hands should be cupped about 8 in. in front of his face prior to contact.

Beginners should be coached to keep the hands in front of the face. When the ball is about to be contacted, weight shifts over the front foot and the back foot rests on its toes. The setter should be directly behind the ball, his elbows close to the sides of his body, and his upper arms horizontal to the floor. His hands should be held approxi-

Figure 3-3 *Back to the Net Setting Position.* Deceptive setters can often catch blockers flat footed with this exciting style. (Richard Mackson)

Figure 3-4 *Setting a High Pass.* The ball's force causes the player's fingers to bend backward and come within 3 or 4 in. of his face (*a*). Index and middle fingers supply most of the force as the fingers and wrist spring forward (*b*). Smooth follow through helps to ensure a well-directed pass (*c*). (The Ealing Corp.) ▼

a.   **b.**   **c.**

a.　　　　　　b.　　　　　　c.

d.　　　　　　e.

Figure 3-5 *Setting a Low Pass.* The player's buttocks are close to the floor and his hands are held in front of his face. His back is straight and his weight is centered behind his back foot when the ball is contacted. He follows through with his arms as the ball is released. (The Ealing Corp.)

mately 6 in. in front of his head, wrists cocked and fingers spread. He contacts the ball mainly with the index and middle fingers and partly on the thumbs. The fingers absorb the flight of the ball much like a spring compressing and then extending forward. The wrist cocks back during the compression stage and then springs forward and releases the ball (Figure 3-4).

BACK SET

The back set is used to confuse the block. For this reason, the setter must be careful not to arch his back too soon because experienced middle blockers will "read" the play and get an early jump on the ball. The back set uses the same initial body position as the front set. The hands contact the ball

a.   b.   c.

Figure 3-6 *Back Set.* Contact is made above the forehead; the palms are held up and back throughout the release and follow-through. Olympian Patti Bright delivers the back set here. (Los Angeles City Unified School District)

Figure 3-7 *Long Back Set.* For most players, the long back set requires an exaggerated back arch and follow-through over the head. (Richard Mackson)

above the forehead and extend up as the back arches. The head should be raised as the arms follow-through.

LATERAL SET

The lateral set should be attempted in game conditions by superior ball handlers only. Average setters should employ the safe strategy of facing the direction to which they intend to set and using an occasional

back set to confuse the blocker. Generally, referees on the local level carefully scrutinize the lateral set, even though it is an established technique developed to complement the quick attack.

Some outstanding setters prefer to receive passes with their backs to the net and to deliver their sets laterally for greater deception. This technique allows the setter to keep his fingers on the ball for a greater period of time; consequently, the ball is placed with greater accuracy.

At this time, referees from other countries are more liberal in their interpretations of what constitutes a legal set. At the

Figure 3-8 *Lateral Set.* The ball is delivered laterally to freeze the block. (Richard Mackson)

high school level there are still a few referees who insist that the setter release the ball directly forward of or opposite to the direction in which he is facing. Successful setters are flexible enough to adapt their style to the philosophy of the referee on the stand. Generally, referees of regional and national status allow setters to use the lateral set, which makes the quick-hitter attack function so effectively. Some local referees still prefer the traditional front-and-back setting style, which limits deception considerably.

In Figure 3-9, the setter takes a long squatting step to the side with his right leg while extending his left leg. He lowers his body until his face is even with the ball's height (a). He then quickly pivots on his right foot as he releases the ball to the left so that his body, head, and arms are turned in the direction of the ball's flight (b). He extends his arms, wrists, and fingers as he releases the ball.

SETTING A DEEP PASS

When the pass is short of the target area, the setter must hurry to get behind the ball so the set will not have to be made on the run. Traditional strategy calls for the setter to face the corner of the net where the set will be delivered. Of course, two blockers will probably be waiting at that point before the setter touches the ball. Better setters learn to set the ball laterally to the other side of the net if the middle blocker leaves early in anticipation of a normal set.

Most beginners make a mistake when setting the type of pass shown in Figure 3-10. They try to set this kind of pass on the run instead of actually stopping slightly

a.   b.

Figure 3-9 *Low Lateral Set.* The low lateral set is difficult to execute because the player must pivot quickly on his squatting leg. (The Ealing Corp.)

Figure 3-10 *Long Set.* The setter has extended her whole body in order to gain enough power to deliver a long set. (Los Angeles Unified School District)

beyond the ball, thereby allowing contact to be made in a direct line between setter and target area. Notice how Patti Bright in Figure 3-10 has followed through by extending her arms and legs to ensure the proper height and distance of the set.

For greater power and distance, long passes or sets should be executed with the body in a forward leaning position. When setting at the net, the body should have a slight backward tilt.

a.

b.

Figure 3-11 *Jump Set.* The setter's hands have conformed to the surface of the ball just before contact (*a*). The setter's fingers are about to spring forward to release the ball (*b*). (Richard Mackson)

Figure 3-12 *Saving a Long Pass.* The setter prevents the ball from crossing the net into the opposition's block. (Richard Mackson)

JUMP SET

The jump set should be used everytime the ball is passed close to the net and the setter can make contact above the net. This confuses the block and gives the blockers less time to react to the attack. The setters in Figure 3-11 are using good technique in utilizing this skill.

The jump set is also used to place the setter in position to save a long pass that will drop over the net as illustrated in Figure 3-12. Setters must spend many hours practicing until they know their exact range above the net in attempting to jump set balls that would otherwise travel over the net. The coach must pass balls over the net

from different areas of the court, while the setters run from their various starting positions and attempt to jump set the ball to all attack positions along the net. A front row setter must learn when to hit, jump set or block the ball. After the fundamental technique of jump setting has been mastered, the coach should add attackers and blockers to the drill.

Better front court setters may jump in the air and decide to set or spike depending on the reaction of the opposing blocker; this is particularly effective with a very close pass as illustrated in Figure 3-13. The set-

Figure 3-13 *Confusing the Block.* The blocker is forced to jump with the front court setter or he will spike the ball unopposed. (Richard Mackson)

ters face the net and set the ball laterally to the attacker. This is a very difficult maneuver and takes outstanding control due to the increased likelihood of netting or throwing the set.

On a very close pass it is often impossible for the setter to set with two hands, so the setter must use one hand. In Figure 3-14a, the setter has contacted the ball with all his fingers of his right hand. It looks as if he is teeing it up for number twelve who is taking off to hit the ball as it leaves the setter's fingers. In Figure 3-14b the other setter is in a similar position and we see the spiker about to hit the ball after it has left the setter's fingertips.

STRATEGY

Setters should decide what type of setting strategy will best work against their opponents. They should know who are the strongest and weakest blockers on the opposing team and observe their blocking switches so that they are prepared in the event that continual setting in front of the weaker blocker is necessary. When the opposition is in the habit of stacking its strongest blockers on the star spiker, it may be advisable to set a less capable spiker against a weaker block.

Setters should be familiar with the referee's style as well as their opponents' style.

a.

b.

Figure 3-14 *One-Handed Set.* It is fairly common for setters to save errant passes into the net with a one-handed set to an attacker in zone three. (Stan Troutman)

Although most of the same rules should be in effect in all NCAA, USVBA, NAIA, AAU and other major organizational play, interpretation of those rules may vary considerably from one referee to another. Usually, the average setter is not overly concerned with the referee's interpretation of a thrown ball, since most of his sets are high and wide and are delivered in the traditional manner. Better players, capable of setting laterally and delivering the ball from a variety of body positions, are very concerned.

Better setters can cause blockers to move in the wrong direction or move too late to block effectively. Faking a back set by stepping backward but arching the back and thereby contacting the ball high above the forehead to deliver a front set is a technique used to deceive blockers. The opposite ploy is to step forward without arching the back and then delivering a back set. Another technique is to wait for the pass with the back to the net and set the ball laterally.

When beginners use these techniques, it is called bad form and a poor grasp of the fundamentals of setting. When expert setters use them and deliver the set cleanly and accurately, they are classified as players with an exciting and innovative style.

Good setting techniques are developed by learning to set the ball from every conceivable position. Training for the set is accomplished by having someone toss the ball to the setter from every possible angle and speed. In competition, about 40 percent of the passes are set while running, jumping, diving, or falling.

Several years ago a very talented setter who had developed his ability to set cleanly from off balance positions lost an important match for his team in the USVBA National Championships because he would not

Figure 3-15 *Setting While Falling.* Better setters can control the ball from a variety of positions. (Richard Mackson)

deliver the ball in the traditional manner demanded by the referee—that is, from in front of his face in the direction in which he was facing or directly opposite the way in which he was facing. He often set the ball laterally with his back to the net. His team would have won handily if he had delivered a normal set and allowed his spikers to provide the deception necessary to defeat the block by varying the spike. Deception is a good goal for the setter and worth striving for, but he must be flexible enough to quickly evaluate the limits the referee establishes for him and to change his style if necessary.

Figure 3-16 *Setting from the Right Side.* The area two spiker (No. 13 in left foreground) is delivering a high set to the outside attacker. (Stan Troutman)

Sets from the right back should normally be delivered in a high arc to the left front of the court, as shown in Figure 3-16. Smaller players may have to squat halfway to the floor and extend their legs in a synchronized motion upon contact to ensure the necessary height and distance for this type of set.

Since almost all balls that the spikers will set originate from the four corners of the court, the crosscourt setting drills in the following section should be used in the majority of practice sessions. When setting from the backcourt, the ball should be de-livered to an area about 5 ft. from the antenna and about 2 ft. from the net. The ball should be set high and have the illusion of dropping straight down from the ceiling. Low sets from the backcourt do not allow the spiker to look at the blockers.

TEACHING PROGRESSION

The following teaching progression has been used successfully with secondary school players:

1. Demonstrate the hand position for the overhand set. Instruct the players to *shape* their fingers around the volleyball at their feet. Have them remove their hands from the ball and place them 6 in. in front of the face with fingers remaining spread and elbows close to the body. Check each member of the group individually.

2. Divide the group into partners and have them face each other at a distance of 5 ft. Distribute one volleyball for every two people. Assign one partner as a tosser and the other as a volleyer. From a distance of 5 ft., demonstrate a two-hand underhand toss that falls in an arc on a partner's forehead. Instruct the volleyers to return the ball in an arc that will land on the tosser's forehead. Stress contacting the ball with a cocked wrist and extending the wrist forward when releasing. After pushing the ball forward the hands should not separate. After 10 tosses, partners should exchange roles. To provide motivation, the volleyer scores one point every time the pass drops in an arc over the tosser's head. The first partner to score 15 points wins.

3. Demonstrate a three-quarter squat, with the back held straight, and simulate an overhand pass. Stress keeping the hands in the "shape" of the ball. Have the class squat and simulate a pass while you verbally correct individual form. Repeat drill number 2, using a low underhand toss that drops at the waist.

4. Demonstrate the side step by instructing the tossers to lob the ball from side-to-side to make the volleyers take a lateral step to get behind the ball. Stress moving the outside foot ahead so the volleyer is facing in the direction of the set. Increase the difficulty by instructing the tosser to lob the ball so that the volleyer must take several side steps.

Figure 3-17 *Setting from a Squatting Position.* The setter's arms and wrists are extending as his fingers spring forward to release the ball. (The Ealing Corp.)

5. Demonstrate the technique for setting a low pass to either side. Take a long side step and squat on the same leg to the level of the toss while fully extending the other leg. Body weight is over the squatting leg. Body, head, and arms turn toward the tosser and simulate a set. Turn your back to the class and instruct them to move with you. Check individual form and then give each partner 10 tosses before changing roles. Stress the pivot and turn toward the tosser.

6. Instruct the partners to rally from a distance of 5 ft. Use all of the techniques in preceding drills 2 to 5 to keep the ball in play.

7. Increase the distance between partners to 10 ft. Show the class how to bend their legs and to extend them to gain additional power and distance in the set. Instruct the tosser to lob the ball in an arc that falls near the volleyer's head. Change roles after 10 tosses. Stress keeping the hands 6 in. in front of the face because power is lost when contact is made with extended arms.

8. Instruct the partners to rally from a sitting position at a distance of 5 ft. Stress moving the upper part of the body behind the ball by leaning laterally. Point out how difficult it is to set the ball when hands are not in front of the face.

9. Move partners to a standing position, 10 ft. apart. Instruct the tosser to lob the ball in a high arc anywhere within a 5-ft. radius of the volleyer. The volleyer must move quickly to get under the ball and face the setter before contacting the ball.

10. Divide the players into groups of three. Place them in a straight line at a distance of 5 ft. apart. Demonstrate the back set. Have the class simulate a back set. Stress contacting the ball in front of the body and carrying it above the head as the legs extend and the back arches. The arms and hands stay together until the follow through is completed. Players on the end should lob the ball to the middle player, who back sets it to the other tosser. The volleyer turns and repeats the drill. Rotate after 10 back sets. Increase the distance between players to 10 ft. and repeat.

11. After players learn the rudiments of the back set, they can be paired off once again and placed 10 ft. apart.

Figure 3-18 *Setting Laterally.* The lateral set is a common tactic used by better setters. (Richard Mackson)

Demonstrate how to set the ball about 5 ft. straight overhead, quickly make a half-turn, and back set the ball to the partner. The partner sets the ball overhead, pivots, and returns the back set. Stress a quick pivot and stationary body position before setting.

12. Demonstrate the lateral set by passing the ball about 5 ft. overhead, executing a quarter-turn, and setting the ball laterally to the partner, who will pass directly above the head, make a quarter-turn, and deliver a lateral set back to you. Stress moving the arms and body to the side as the ball is set (Figure 3-18).

13. Players squat and set from a low position; the bottom of the net is used to force a player into a low position. The player starts on the same side of the net as the coach and runs under the net to set a tossed ball. The player is forced into a low position and must use short, fast steps in order to turn and reach the ball in time to set it back to the coach.

Setting with One Ball to Two Players. *Start by overhand passing back and forth in a straight line.*

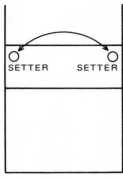

Diagram 3-1

Partners face each other in a straight line, shoulders at a right angle to the set. They set back and forth from a distance of 15 ft. As they warm up, the distance increases to 30 ft. Setting specialists should always drill by the net.

Return to the 15-ft. distance and set the ball laterally. Players drilling by the net should stand facing the net. Halfway through this drill, partners should change positions to practice setting to the left and right. Gradually increase the distance.

Partners once again stand facing each other, shoulders at a right angle to the net. They pass the ball 5-10 ft. directly overhead, turn halfway around so that their back is toward their partner, and set backwards. The partner passes to himself (i.e., straight up) and returns the back set. Gradually increase the distance to 30 ft.

Partners stand about 10 ft. apart. The tosser lobs the ball at a setter, aiming between the setter's knee and waist. The setter squats and delivers a 15-ft. set that drops in the area of the tosser's head. Increase the distance between partners.

The tosser lobs the ball from side-to-side at a distance of 10 ft. The setter takes short, fast slide steps to reach the area of the toss. Then he takes a long lateral step and squats on the outside leg, pivots, and sets to the tosser.

Crosscourt Set—Three Players. *Balls set from the backcourt should travel crosscourt so that the spiker can watch the approaching set. The setter starts in the standard backcourt defensive position that the team uses. The middle back position is a good one from which to drill because this area usually receives many balls that are deflected by the block. One of the spikers lobs balls to the backcourt, and the setter delivers the ball crosscourt. The spiker who receives the set can also practice by setting to the other spiker.*

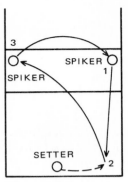

Diagram 3-2

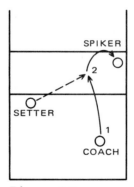

Diagram 3-3

Setting on the Run. *Although every setter should strive to contact the ball with his feet in a stationary position, it is necessary to make a great number of sets on the run. The following drill should be introduced during the first week of practice before poor techniques of setting on the run are allowed to develop. The coach lobs the ball 10-15 ft. in front of the setter so that the player can just manage to contact the ball using the overhand passing technique. If the setter is close to the spiker, he attempts to set the ball straight up in the air. The forward momentum of the setters body will cause the ball to travel in a forward arc. The great majority of sets delivered on the run travel too far because the setter attempts to set the ball forward.*

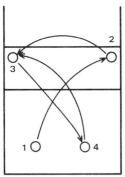

Crosscourt Set—Four Players. *When four players are used in the crosscourt setting drill, the ball is kept in continuous motion with the overhand pass.*

Diagram 3-4

Back Set. *Although most coaches prefer their spikers to set the ball in front of them, there are always situations that demand a back set. One player works on a 15-ft. set, the middle player on a back set, and the other player on a 30-ft. set. Rotate to all positions.*

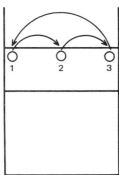

Diagram 3-5

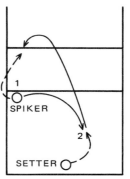

Diagram 3-7

Dig and Set. *The coach stands on a table and spikes the ball at either of the two backcourt players. The player who does not dig the ball must set it to one of the two spikers stationed at the corners of the net.*

Backcourt Set and Spike. *The spiker tosses the ball over his shoulder to the setter in the backcourt and approaches for the spike. A blocker or blockers may be added.*

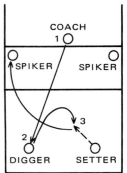

Diagram 3-8

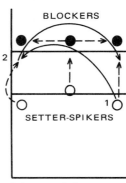

Diagram 3-9

Long and Short Back Sets. *The middle player delivers a back set from both directions. The setter can vary the distance between the spikers to practice back sets of varying heights and distances.*

Diagram 3-6

Decision Set. *This is a drill for advanced players. Three spikers start 10-12 ft. from the net and attack against three blockers. The object of the drill is to spike the ball against one blocker or no block, in the event the blocker does not jump. One spiker sets a teammate; if a two-man block forms in front of the spiker who has received the set, he must set one of his two teammates. If a spiker receives the second set, he must hit it over the net. This drill is very beneficial if spikers are learning the jump set. It can also be used with two attackers against three blockers.*

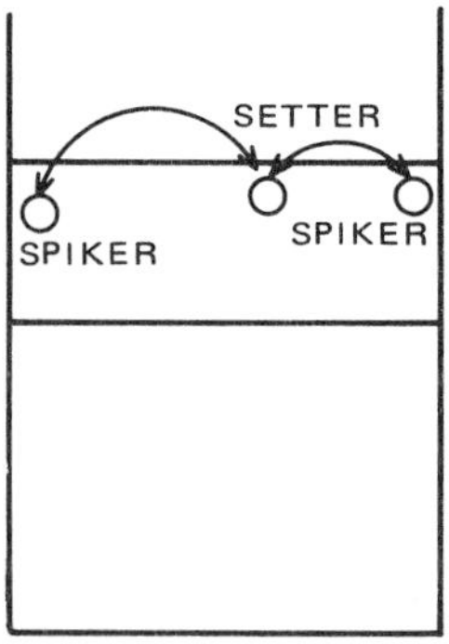

DRILLS FOR SETTING SPECIALISTS

All passes for setting drills should move the setter forward or laterally to simulate game situations.

The low position is difficult for setters to master. The setter must be very quick in order to run under the descending ball. This low position gives the setter extra time to deliver the ball to hitters who are late.

Short Back Set. *When a setting specialist is having difficulty with a particular set, the coach should develop a drill to practice overcoming the problem. The setter in the three-hitter attack should receive the set about 10 ft. from the right side line and face the left sideline. The setter who often neglects the spiker approaching down the right sideline needs extra practice on the short back set. The coach should pass balls to the setter from various positions on the court and evaluate the placement of each set. After the setter releases the ball, he must quickly turn and cover the spiker to field spikes that rebound off the block.*

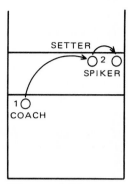

Diagram 3-10

Figure 3-19 *Low Position.* No. 6 has delivered a set from a low position to give the attacker time to get above the net. Blockers who wait for the set will be beaten by this ploy. This tactic is possible if the pass falls in an arc close to the net. (Richard Mackson)

Figure 3-20 *Short Back Set.* The setter is about to arch her back and extend her arms over her head to deliver the ball to the approaching spiker. (Richard Mackson)

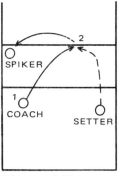

Jump Set. *Setters who master the jump set can greatly improve the effectiveness of their attack. The coach should attempt to lob balls 1 or 2 ft. over the net as the setter runs in from various court positions and attempts to save the pass by reaching above the net and setting the ball before it crosses the tape. Instruct the spiker to stand at various attack positions along the net.*

Diagram 3-11

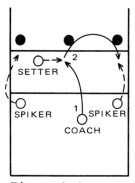

Spike or Set. *Better setters can jump in the air and, depending on the reaction of the opposing blocker, set or spike the ball. The coach should vary the height and distance of the pass. After the setter learns the fundamental technique of the jump set, the drill should be run against aggressive blockers.*

Diagram 3-12

Figure 3-21 *Jump Set.* The Japanese setter is in excellent position to deliver the ball in any direction as the Polish blockers await his decision. (Richard Mackson)

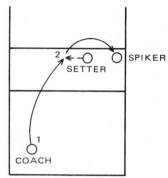

Diagram 3-14

Move Forward and Back Set. *Most setters are in the habit of setting forward when they run forward to line up the pass. Pass the ball well in front of the setter from various court positions and instruct the setter to deliver a back set.*

Figure 3-22 *Spike or Set.* The setter has approached the net with his body in a spiking position to force the opposing blocker to commit himself. The setter then sets to a teammate who now has only one blocker to defend against him. (Norm Schindler)

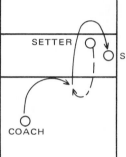

Diagram 3-15

Lateral Set. *When a setter must run behind the 10-ft. line to line up the pass, he can generally set the ball only in the direction he is facing. Good ball handlers can be taught to set laterally, however. The threat of a lateral set is important because it will force the middle blocker to stay "honest" and remain in the center of the court until the setter releases the ball. The coach passes the ball around the 10-ft. line from various areas of the court and instructs the setter to set laterally.*

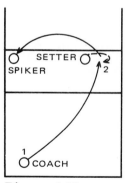

Diagram 3-13

Move Backward and Front Set. *Most setters deliver a back set when they take several steps backward to line up the ball. This frequently occurs when they are close to the side line. They must learn to deliver a front set under these conditions, with enough distance and height to reach the spiker on the other side of court. The coach should pass the ball behind the spiker from various positions on the court and instruct the setter to deliver a front set.*

Lateral Set Facing the Net. *When a low pass drops close to the net, the average setter must play the ball with the forearm pass. A setter with "good hands" can be taught to squat and face the net to set the ball laterally for best accuracy. The coach lobs low passes at various locations along the net.*

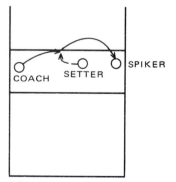

Diagram 3-16

Figure 3-23 *Move Forward and Back Set.* This is a good tactic for an experienced setter because the middle blocker is usually moving with the setter and will have difficulty changing direction to reach the spiker. (The Ealing Corp.)

Lateral Set with the Back Toward the Net. *The setter using a three-hitter attack should learn the lateral set, or the middle spiker will only receive the ball on a perfect pass. Pass the ball from various areas of the court while moving the setter off the net to force a lateral set to the middle attacker.*

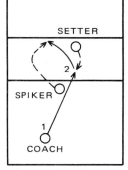

Diagram 3-17

Backcourt Dig and Set. *The simplest play for the middle-in player to make is a set to the corner spiker whom he is facing. The coach stands on a table and spikes to a backcourt digger. The middle-in player runs under the dig and delivers a front set to the end spiker.*

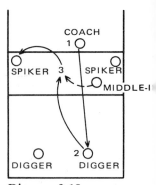

Diagram 3-18

Figure 3-24 *Lateral Set with the Back Towards the Net.* This set is very effective in defeating middle blockers. (Department of Photography and Cinema, The Ohio State University)

Dig and Set. *The next step is to allow the middle-in player to set any of the attackers.*

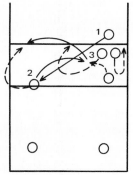

Diagram 3-19

Middle-In Sets to Off-Blocker. *The middle-in player has numerous opportunities to set balls looped over or deflected by the block. Often the only attacker who can get in position to spike on the quick change to offense is the former off-blocker. The coach stands on a table and dinks over the blockers. The middle-in player sets the dink to the off-blocker. The off-blocker can spike or set to another front court player.*

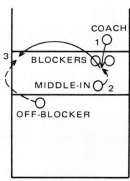

Diagram 3-20

Figure 3-25 *The Quick Set.* A successful completion of the quick, or one-set rests almost entirely upon the setter. He must place the ball directly in front of the attacker's shoulder for a successful play. (Norm Schindler)

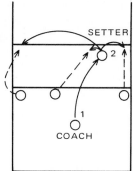

Diagram 3-21

Setting the Attack. *The setter must be familiar with the idiosyncrasies of the spikers he will be playing next to in actual competition. Long hours of practice are necessary to refine the attack that has been selected. Teams that use the middle-in defense must give extra setting practice to the players covering the area behind the block. This player is responsible for setting any balls that are dug when his team uses a three-hitter attack. The quick reactions and speed of the setter usually make him too valuable a digger to be assigned to the area behind the block. In fact, some coaches place a big, slow spiker behind the block on defense to keep him out of the way. If this player is expected to set when the team switches from defense to offense, much individual coaching attention with special drills is needed.*

4

Attacking

Spiking is the act of jumping in the air and hitting the ball from above the level of the net into the opponents' court. It is an offensive play that usually drives the ball into the opponents' court with great force. Spiking requires coordinating the jump and armswing in order to contact the moving ball. This process can be divided into the approach, take off, and contact.

An off-speed spike is accomplished by reducing the speed of the arm just prior to contacting the ball. This is an effective tactic when used infrequently and directed to a weakness in the defensive alignment.

The dink shot is a soft contact of the ball that is usually lobbed over the block.

The on-hand side of the court is the side on which the spiker contacts the ball with his predominant hand before it crosses in front of his body. For example, the left-front corner is the on-hand side for a right-handed spiker because the ball is contacted in front of the right shoulder. If the ball is set to the right front corner, it travels across the body to the right side before the spiker contacts the ball. This is known as the *off-hand spike*.

For the left-handed spiker, the on-hand and off-hand sides of the court are reversed—*off-hand* is the left front, *on-hand* is the right front.

APPROACH FOR THE SPIKE

The preliminary position for the left-front spiker is 8 to 12 ft. from the net, near the left side line.

Diagram 4-1 shows the following sequence: When the ball is passed close to the net on the spiker's side of the court, he must take a quick straight approach in order to receive a set that will travel a short distance (*a*). When approaching during a

49

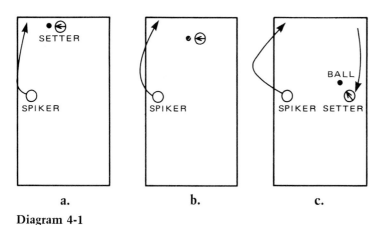

Adjusting the Approach to the Pass.
The spiker must antici-pate where the pass will be directed and who will set the ball as he begins the approach for the spike.

a.   b.   c.

Diagram 4-1

Figure 4-1 *Approach for the Spike.* The player covers a distance of 10–12 ft. in three or four steps. He gradually increases the speed of his approach as he nears his takeoff point. (The Ealing Corp.)

good pass, most spikers prefer to swing slightly outside the boundary line and approach the set at a slight angle so that they can keep the ball and blockers in view at the same time (b). When a poor pass is directed deep into the court, the primary setter usually cannot reach the ball and a backcourt player becomes the setter. In this situation the spiker should take a wide approach so that he can keep the player setting the ball in full view as he moves toward the net (c).

After the spiker reaches his preliminary position, he normally takes four steps *during his approach for the spike.* Coaches should teach the spiker a right, left, right, left sequence which comes naturally to most right-handed spikers. This approach opens the striking shoulder to the setter in area three and four, and is convenient for a fake X approach in area two when the spiker changes direction on his second step and pushes back toward the sideline with the left foot.

Spikers at all levels of competition commonly start their approach too soon. Often they run under the set and cannot see the blockers. Starting the approach too soon also requires the spiker to wait for the set after arriving at the net and to lose several inches off his vertical jump. To correct this situation, the coach can hold the spiker's shirt during practice and then release him at the last possible moment. After this drill is repeated numerous times, the habit of approaching too early should be corrected.

TAKEOFF

The pre-jump takeoff is similar to the hop a diver takes before leaving the diving board. The spiker starts the approach while the setter is lining up the pass and adjusts his speed to the flight of the ball.

The spiker then takes a one foot takeoff or pre-jump that directly leads into the two foot takeoff for the spike. If the spikers approach is late, the pre-jump will be low. If the spiker arrives on time the pre-jump will be higher. The spiker leans backward after the pre-jump to slightly counteract forward momentum and prevent broadjumping. The arms are extending backward preparing to move forward in a rotary motion to get the striking hand in position. The spiker should try to land simultaneously with both heels parallel; as the legs bend the weight is shifted to the balls of the feet, then the knees and ankles are contracted causing the spiker to leave the floor. Smaller players may bend their knees up to ninety degrees, but it is ineffective for larger players to do so. The pre-jump takeoff gives the player good body control but the overwhelming majority of players use the step-close takeoff because they believe it allows them to jump higher.

In the step-close takeoff, the spiker takes a long last step by jumping forward, contacting the floor first with the heel of one foot and then with the heel of the other foot; his weight then rolls from both heels to the toes as he takes off. When using this method, there is a tendency to broad jump when the spiker accelerates too quickly during the approach, or when he leans too far forward with the upper part of his body while preparing to jump. Spikers must keep their center of gravity behind the heels to successfully transfer their forward momentum into a high vertical jump.

The step-close takeoff approach is favored by men and women participating in open and collegiate volleyball in the United States. In both the pre-jump and step-close takeoff, arms are extended backward to ap-

Diagram 4-2 Pre-Jump Takeoff. *Advocates of this technique believe it gives the spiker better body control.*

Diagram 4-3 Step-Close Takeoff. *Most players prefer this technique because they believe it is faster and gives them a higher vertical jump.*

proximately shoulder height; they swing down and forward in an arc as the heels hit the floor during the last step. By the time the weight shifts to the toes, the arms should be swinging forward and up above the shoulders as the player's legs and ankles forceably contract, moving him into the air.

Occasionally, a player may approach a high pass or set and take off on the leg opposite his attacking arm to spike the ball. One-leg takeoff usually does not allow the spiker the desired balance and control; it is often used by the setter to surprise the block on the second touch of the ball. It is also used when the spiker does not have time to use a two-foot takeoff. The Japanese incorporate a one leg takeoff on some of their plays which utilize a sudden burst of speed to move away from the blocker. The USC's Women's Team uses the one leg takeoff to hit back one-sets.

A spiker who utilizes a quick approach will ensure a powerful impact of kinetic energy on the takeoff phase. The takeoff must be accomplished quickly and "explosively" for added inches in height. The height of the jump will then depend on the speed of the approach, a coordinated takeoff and strength.

Figure 4-2 *Heel-Toe Contact.* Whether the spiker uses the pre-jump or the step-close takeoff, a heel-toe contact will provide better body control and a higher vertical jump. (Los Angeles Unified School District)

CONTACTING THE BALL

During the ascent the player's hands reach head height, his back begins to arch and his legs bend backward at the knee. His left arm continues to rise until it reaches three-quarters to full extension above the shoulder. The right arm moves laterally above and behind the shoulder, and the hand is cocked behind the head. The body twists in the direction of the attacking arm and the left shoulder turns towards the net. The left arm and shoulder drops quickly as the right arm uncoils toward the ball, with the elbow leading the way. The striking shoulder elevates and the upper body torques toward the ball as the body snaps forward from the waist. At contact, the attacking arm is extended and the hand, either cupped or flat and stiff, is held open. As the wrist snaps forward, the heel and palm of the hand simultaneously contact the ball, followed by the fingers.

The ball should be hit above and in front of the attacking shoulder, slightly after the apex of the jump. After contact, the striking arm continues down and across the body.

Figure 4-3 *Drawn Bow.* The back is arched and the knees flexed in a reverse "C" or "drawn bow" to provide extra power to the spiker. (Bob Van Wagner)

Figure 4-4 *Elevated Shoulder.* The elevated striking shoulder allows the spiker to contact the ball higher in the air. (Bud Fields)

As the feet touch the floor, legs bend to absorb the impact.

For greater power, better jumpers have time to arch the back and flex the legs at the knee joints to create a "drawn bow" effect. They powerfully contract the stomach and hip muscles and extend their knees to snap their body forward bending at the waist. This total body movement seems to help the upper arm and forearm move with greater speed towards the ball. In the final

Figure 4-5 *Extended Arm.* Players should be taught to make contact at the highest point possible. (Richard Mackson) ▶

a.   b.

Figure 4-6 *Body Snap.* The Cuban woman and Ohio State man both exhibit a powerful follow-through after spiking. (Richard Mackson (*a*); Department of Photography and Cinema, Ohio State University (*b*))

analysis, the greater the speed of the arm swing and wrist snap, the faster the spiked ball will travel.

SPIKING DEEP SETS

The trajectory of a spiked ball must arc when it is contacted farther away from the net. With deeper sets, the ball must be hit in an arc to land in the opponents' court. Effective spikers can hit the ball with full power at distances of 20 to 30 ft. from the net and impart enough of a topspin to drive the ball into the opponents' court. To accomplish this, a spiker hits the ball directly above or behind the attacking shoulder and makes contact below the ball's midline with the heel of his hand; he wraps his palm and fingers up and over the ball, producing a maximum topspin with a vigorous wrist snap.

The height of the spiker's jump loses some of its significance when he can no longer hit the ball at an angle but must rely on a maximum topspin to put the ball away. A deep set can be contacted below the level of the net and still be hit into the oppo-

a.   b.

Figure 4-7 *Arm and Hand Positions for the Spike.* This varies according to the distance from which the ball is set at the net. When spiking deep sets (*a*), the ball should be contacted over the attacking shoulder. When spiking a close set (*b*), the ball can be contacted up to 2 ft. in front of the attacking shoulder by spikers with a superior jump and reach. (The Ealing Corp.)

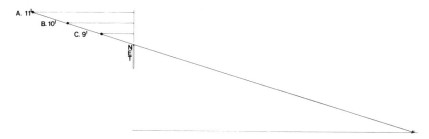

Diagram 4-4 Maximum Distance for Direct Angle Spikes. *The number of feet refers to the point at which the ball is contacted. A = 3 ft. above the net at a position 10 ft. away from net; B = 2 ft. above net at a position 7 ft. away from net; and C = 1 ft. above net at a position 3 ft. away from net. The average player will have to use a lot of topspin and a forceful armswing when spiking the ball more than 8 to 9 ft. from the net.*

nents' court with full power if the ball has enough topspin.

Diagram 4-4 illustrates the maximum distance which spikers can hit the ball without imparting a topspin, which causes the ball to drop or travel in an arc. For example, if a player were spiking the ball 10 ft. from the net, he would have to contact the ball 3 ft. above the net to hit a direct angle spike into his opponents' court.

SEEING THE BLOCK

Experienced hitters with good peripheral vision can see *the hands of the defenders* forming the block while leaping high in the air to spike the ball. Regardless of their approach to the set, they are capable of spiking the ball crosscourt or down the line by rotating their wrist and forearm inward or outward.

a.   b.

Figure 4-8 *Placing the Spike.* Capable spikers can use the same approach and armswing to place the spike anywhere on the court with a last-moment turn of the wrist. Outward wrist rotation sends a spike crosscourt (*a*). Inward wrist rotation sends a spike down the line (*b*). (The Ealing Corp.)

This ability to see the block generally takes two to three years of varsity competition, but it can be developed sooner by instructing blockers to move their hands either to the left or right just *prior* to the spiker's contact with the ball. The spiker will become aware of the blockers and learn to direct his spikes with greater accuracy.

A coach standing behind the spiker can easily signal the blockers to pull their hands left or right or to leave a hole in the middle of the block. If the spiker can successfully direct the ball through a hole in the block, it will seldom be fielded or "dug," since defensive alignments are built around the premise that the front row defenders will present a solid wall of hands to the spiker.

Figure 4-10 *Soft Wipe-Off Shot.* Slowing the armswing and contacting the ball with a lateral motion, and then hitting the blocker's outside hand as he is descending, usually prevents the blocker from maintaining the necessary height to keep his hand between the ball and the sideline. (Stan Troutman)

Figure 4-9 *Spiking Between the Blockers.* The end blocker has not placed his inside hand at the point where the ball crosses the net and middle blocker has not moved fast enough to close the hole. Spikers who have the ability to see the block can take advantage of this situation. (Dr. Leonard Stallcup)

WIPE-OFF SHOT

Spikers should learn to use the blocker's hands to their advantage, particularly on balls set close to the net. Spikers who have the ability to see the blocker's hands can hit or "wipe" the ball off the block into the out-of-bounds area where it cannot be fielded.

There are three types of wipe-off shots: 1) the soft; 2) the hard; and 3) the vertical.

On a close set near the sidelines the slow lateral swing is the most effective. Spikers

Figure 4-11 *Hard Wipe-Off Shot.* The spiker has sent the ball into the blocker's fingers after taking a full swing. (Dept. of Photography & Cinema The Ohio State University)

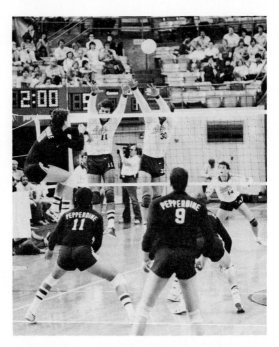

Figure 4-12 *Vertical Wipe-Off Shot.* The ball has been spiked off the blocker's fingertips with the intention of causing it to travel far off the court. (Dept. of Photography & Cinema The Ohio State University)

who use this tactic should delay their armswing until well after the apex of their jump so the blockers hands start to move away from the net as they are descending. The spiker then pushes or slowly hits the ball into the outside hand of the end blocker in a lateral motion (Figure 4-10). Advanced spikers may use their fingertips to impart an "English" or lateral spin on the ball. By swinging slowly it allows the officials to clearly see the blocker contact the ball and if the end blocker manages to block the ball back into the spiker's court, it can easily be picked up by his teammates. The hard wipe-off shot can be used when the end blocker reaches high above the net and presents a target that can be easily seen. The ball should be spiked into the outside

half of the outside hand of the end blocker with great force (Figure 4-11). This shot is risky because referees often do not see a glancing contact of the blocker's hand and if the spiker hits the inside portion of the hand, he may be blocked. In Figure 4-12, the spiker has hit a vertical wipe-off shot with the intention of driving the ball out of bounds after it has rebounded off the blocker's fingertips. This technique is used when the spiker feels he may be stuffed by the block.

In both the lateral and vertical wipe-off shots, the spiker runs the risk of having the referee miss the blocker's touch of the ball, awarding his opponent a point or side out if the ball lands out of bounds. For this reason, a spiker must attempt to hit a good "piece" of the block, particularly if you are at an away match playing in front of a noisy audience.

ROUND-HOUSE SPIKE

The round-house spike is a valuable weapon in the spiker's attack. It is used most effectively on a good set to confuse the opponent's block. It is usually used when the spiker has run in front of the set or when the spiker is unable to get in position for a normal spike. Few people in this country have mastered the correct technique, and it is rarely attempted by poor jumpers since the arm action requires more time off the floor than their jumping height normally allows.

To perform the round-house spike, the spiker takes a normal approach and jumps with his left arm extended in the usual manner. When his right arm reaches head height, he rotates it downward and backward in a windmill motion while extended.

Upon contact, the arm is fully extended over the shoulder. The ball is hit with the heel, with the palm and fingers tightly cupped. Since the arm action takes longer than the usual technique, the spiker always contacts the ball after he has reached the height of his jump. Opposing players are usually confused by this maneuver and are not in an optimum blocking position when the ball is hit.

OFF-SPEED SPIKE

The off-speed spike is effective only when the defense is braced for a hard kill. If the spiker is off-balance or does not use a normal approach, the defense will expect the spiker to hit the ball with less force. The

Figure 4-13 *Off-Speed Spike.* With a turn of his wrist, player No. 8 directs an off-speed spike through a hole in the block. (Dr. Leonard Stallcup)

speed of the striking arm is reduced just prior to contact to confuse the defense. If the spiker uses his normal approach and a slower armswing, the blockers will lose their timing and the backcourt defenders will find the ball losing momentum and landing in front of them. The off-speed spike is most effective when used infrequently and when directed toward a definite weakness in the defense—whether it be an individual or an open area of the court.

THE DINK

The dink is a soft shot that is used to catch the defense off-guard. It is used most effectively on a good set when the defense is expecting a hard-driven spike. The attacker should cock his spiking arm in the normal manner and swing at a reduced speed to contact the ball with his fingers (Figure 4-14).

Even if the opposition picks up the dink shot, it will open up the defense for hard-

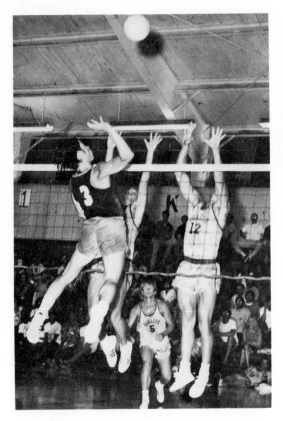

a.

Figure 4-14 *Arm Action.* Arm action of the one-hand dink closely resembles the spike. Most players make the mistake of "telegraphing" their intentions to the defense by straightening their arm too soon. Toshi Toyoda demonstrates the spiking action that he uses when delivering the dink shot. (Dr. Leonard Stallcup)

driven spikes later in the game. Spikers must use the dink to keep the defense off balance. There are two distinct types of contact for the dink: the lob style and the tip style.

In the lob style shown in Figure 4-15, the ball is contacted with the fingers and palms with the elbow bent so the ball can be lobbed over the block or to an open area of the court.

b.

Figure 4-15 *Lob Dink.* The arm is flexed at the elbow and contact is made with the fingers and palm. (Richard Mackson)

a.   b.

Figure 4-16 *Tip Dink.* The arm is extended and contact is made with the fingertips. (Richard Mackson)

In the tip style shown in Figure 4-16, the ball is contacted with the fingertips. The elbow is extended so contact can be made as high as possible. The ball is tipped over the block or slapped down to the floor very quickly if there is a weakness in the block. Setters often attack off the pass using the tip dink.

SPIKING THE ONE-SET

A well-executed spike of a fast vertical set, requiring split-second timing between spiker and setter, is one of the most exciting of-fensive plays in volleyball. The fast vertical set, or one-set, is extremely important to the success of the combination offense.

Spiking the one-set was popularized by athletes and spectators in the United States by the touring Japanese National Men's and Women's teams shortly after the 1964 Olympic Games. It was perfected by the Japanese to make the small spiker effective and to create one-on-one blocking situations for their outside spikers.

Spiking the fast vertical set is performed in this manner: The spiker approaches to within a few feet of the setter as the setter moves into position to receive the pass. If he intends to spike the ball as it is still rising above the net, he gathers momentum to jump and is in the air before the setter touches the ball. His spiking arm is cocked with little body torque or shoulder rotation, ready and waiting for the setter to deliver the ball in front of his attacking arm. The spiker should be at the apex of his jump just as the ball is clearing the tape at the top of the net. He contacts the ball with a quick armswing.

There is little opportunity for the beginning spiker to consciously direct his spike using this technique. The emphasis is on quickly hitting the ball to the floor with a sharp downward flight—not on power. If the ball is contacted before it crosses his attacking shoulder, he usually hits it to his right. If the set is contacted in front of or past his attacking shoulder, the spiker generally hits the ball straight ahead or to the left. Better spikers can direct the ball to any area of the court using several different armswings.

When a spiker hits a high one-set, the opposing blocker must jump with the attacker to block successfully. Defending against a high vertical set requires the middle blocker to jump with the middle attacker before the ball is set. The play has developed to force the middle blocker to commit himself in this manner so that the other two spikers would have the opportunity to receive a normal set against one blocker. The proficient setter must watch the ball, and the approaching spikers while deciding where to deliver the ball. Some outstanding setters also watch the blocker on a close pass.

In a three-hitter attack, this places the other two spikers in a one-on-one situation with the end blockers. Since the middle blocker is usually the most proficient, this technique takes on added significance when

a weak spiker is able to take the opposition's best blocker out of the play with a feigned attack. When the middle attacker constantly forces the middle blocker to jump with him, the best percentage play is usually a wide set to the on-hand spiker. The middle blocker thereby cannot recover fast enough to join the end blocker if he has left the floor, and the on-hand spiker is given the opportunity to attack from his power side against one blocker.

Figure 4-17 *Hitting the One-Set.* The spiker has jumped when the setter contacted the ball and has beaten the middle blocker. (Norm Schindler)

Spikers with quick reflexes and good co-ordination can hit the ball inches out of the setter's hands when the setter jumps to deliver a pass that is high and close to the net.

The one-set is usually attempted from the on-hand side so that the setter does not have to push the ball across the attacker's body in front of his attacking arm.

The back one-set is more difficult because the setter can only watch the ball and the opposing blocker. The spiker's timing must be very good because the setter will only hear his footsteps and can rarely compensate for a poor approach (Figure 4-18).

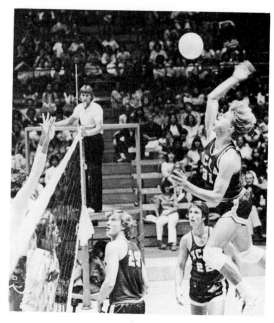

Figure 4-19 *Hitting the Two-Set.* The spiker has crossed in front of the setter to hit a two or X set from his right side hitting position. Only the middle blocker has had time to get his hands over the net. (Richard Mackson)

SPIKING THE TWO-SET

Many players prefer to jump after the ball is released and hit a slightly higher set, generally called a two-set.

The spiker contacts the two-set at the top of its flight; consequently, he has enough time to use a normal armswing and body torque to spike the ball in any direction. The set should be low enough to prevent more than one blocker to get in good position and high enough to allow the spiker to place the ball accurately.

SPIKING THE THREE-SET

A low fast set is used to split the end and middle blockers. It requires the same split-

Figure 4-18 *Back One-Set.* This requires excellent timing on the part of the spiker as the setter is concentrating on the ball and does not watch the spiker. (Stan Troutman)

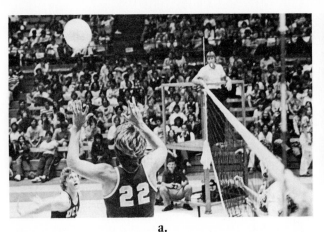

a.   b.

Figure 4-20 *Hitting the Three-Set.* This set is designed to split the block. It is delivered 10 ft. from the left sideline and is usually hit away from the middle blocker. (Norm Schindler)

second timing as the one-set and is generally called a three-set.

Ideally, the ball is passed to the setter at a point 2 ft. from the net and about 10 ft. from the right side line. The spiker quickly moves to a point about 10 ft. from the left side line between the end and middle blockers. The spiker should time his approach so that he jumps as the ball is being released from the setter.

Figure 4-21 *Hitting the Four-Set.* The spiker has just hit crosscourt against the end blocker. The middle blocker has been beaten and has dropped off the net to get a block deflection or dink shot. (Stan Troutman)

SPIKING THE FOUR-SET

The four-set or shoot-set is delivered low and fast to create one-on-one blocking situations. It is usually placed a few feet from the side line and contacted at a height of 1 to 3 ft. above the net, depending on the vertical jump of the spiker. The set is extremely difficult for the middle blocker to cover when the ball travels a distance of 10 ft. or more from setter to spiker. This is the best method of creating a one-on-one spiking situation in the two-hitter attack. The spiker should start his approach closer to the net and slightly outside the side line. Normal takeoff and spiking technique should be used.

SPIKING THE FIVE-SET

The five-set is a back lob to the sideline that is designed to defeat the middle blocker. When the serve is passed accurately, a good setter creates a one-on-one situation with

Figure 4-22 *Hitting the Five-Set.* This photo was taken in 1965 when the USA defeated the Japanese men's team for the first time. At that time, the Japanese middle blockers were small and quick. Today they are tall and quick. (Stan Troutman)

this popular set. In Figure 4-22, the Japanese middle blocker has just left the floor after the spiker has contacted the ball. If the middle blocker is late the ball is usually spiked crosscourt. The set should be wide enough so that the spiker can use the line shot if the end blocker closes toward a late middle blocker.

SPIKING THE HIGH SET

More practice time should be devoted to hitting the high set than any other set. A

team who runs a fast side out attack may not call the high set as one of their attack patterns but the setter will usually be forced to set high if the pass is more than 10 ft. from the net.

The rule we use at UCLA is the further the pass is from the net, the higher the setter is to deliver the ball. The middle blocker has more time to react when the ball is passed deep because the threat of a one-set or two-set is minimized and the ball must travel farther to reach the outside hitter. Therefore, if the setter delivers a normal four-set or five-set to the outside attacker, he will still have two blockers in front of him. A high set coming from off the net gives the spiker a better view of the blockers and thus a better opportunity to defeat them. At UCLA we vary the height of the set according to the jumping ability, quickness, and preference of the spiker.

In Figure 4-23 a high set is descending as a six foot eight inch spiker is ascending to meet the ball at the apex of his jump. As a general rule, quicker players prefer lower sets and slower players require higher sets on deep passes.

All players should be able to hit a high set so that the setter can take advantage of a small blocker. Generally, a small blocker will switch to defend against the smallest hitter or (if the hitters are equal) the blocker will switch to his left side so the setter will have to backset to his position. It is good strategy for the setter to watch the small blocker to see which position he is switching to and deliver a high set over his position. Since small blockers rarely block middle, spikers must learn to hit a high set over a small end blocker (Figure 4-24).

The high set should be the staple of the side out offense at the high school level. When the serving team digs a spike the high set is used to score the majority of the time

Figure 4-24 *Hitting Over a Small Blocker.* Even smaller spikers can learn to hit a high flat shot over or into the end blocker's fingertips. (Stan Abraham)

Figure 4-23 *A High Set.* The height of the set depends on the capability of the setter and the preference of the hitter. (Norm Schindler)

at all levels of play. At the international level, the East German men trained tall spikers to hit the high set with a fully extended arm and almost had total reliance on this type of set in the mid-sixties. They won the 1970 World Volleyball Championships in Sofia with twenty three of the best teams in the world competing against them. Their offense consisted of hitting over the block to weak areas in the defense. They did not hit the ball as powerfully as their opposition because they extended their arm and wrist relatively early and snapped the wrist against the ball during contact. This method gave them added height to hit over the block. The large block of the Russians and the changing backcourt defenses of the Japanese caught up with the method after 1970. The Russians block deflected the spikes to their backcourt teammates and even though they hit over some of the Japanese blockers, their backcourt managed to come up with the slightly slower spikes of the East Germans. In 1971, Burt De Groot and Harlan Cohen trained the Santa Monica YMCA team in this method of hitting. This disciplined team relied entirely on high outside sets and defeated a group of USA team members that were using a multiple offense in the finals of the 1971 USVBA Championships. Since 1971 major championships above the high school level have been won by teams who have mastered the high set and have mixed up their offense with the various play sets already discussed.

SPIKING DRILLS

Most of the following spiking drills can also be used to improve dink shots, off-speed shots, and round-house spikes. To increase the difficulty add blockers or an entire defensive alignment.

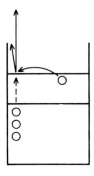

Spikers line up near the left side line, about 12 ft. from the net. Work on long and short line spikes. Repeat the drill from the right side line.

Diagram 4-5

Use a straight approach and spike the ball crosscourt. Place a towel on the floor for the spiker to use as a target.

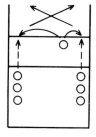

Diagram 4-6

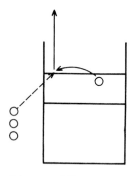

Using an angle approach from the on-hand side, spike the ball down the side line.

Diagram 4-7

Figure 4-25 *Crosscourt Spike.* Using a straight approach, the spiker has held the blocker on the line and contacted the ball before it passed in front of his shoulder to drive it crosscourt. (Richard Mackson)

Figure 4-26 *Line Spike Using a Crosscourt Approach.* The spiker has turned his body at a ninety degree angle to the net and the blocker has positioned himself to take the crosscourt spike. Notice that the spiker's head is looking crosscourt. He had allowed the set to travel in front of his shoulder before contact. (Richard Mackson)

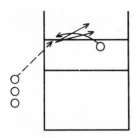

Using an angle approach from the on-hand side, spike the ball crosscourt.

Diagram 4-8

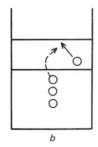

b

Diagram 4-12

The coach passes the ball to the setter at various locations inside the 10-ft. line. The spiker must adjust his approach to the pass to get in a favorable position to hit a one-set.

Using two lines of spikers and one setter, set either side. The spiker should not rotate until he hits.

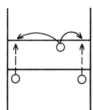

Diagram 4-9

Spikers hit a shoot set from the left side.

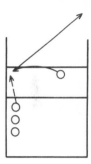

Diagram 4-13

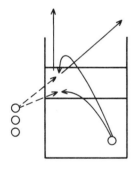

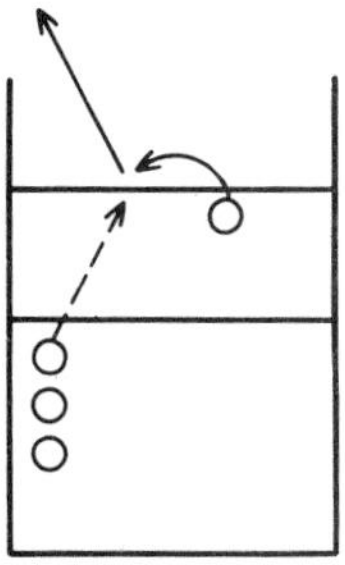

Spike a backcourt set crosscourt and down the line. Vary height and placement of the set.

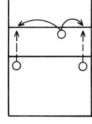

Diagram 4-14

End spikers hit a three-set 10 ft. from the left side line.

Spikers hit a one-set. The setter stations himself 10 ft. from the right side line, a foot from the net.

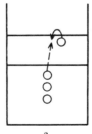

a

Diagram 4-11

Middle spikers hit a three-set 10 ft. from the left side line.

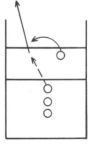

Diagram 4-15

Diagram 4-10

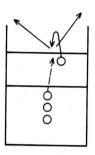

Diagram 4-16

Middle spikers hit a front two-set.

Spikers practice hitting the ball off the end blocker's hand into the out-of-bounds area.

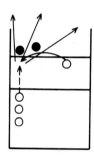

Diagram 4-20

Off-hand spikers hit a back two-set.

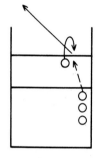

Diagram 4-17

When the ball is in the air, the blockers leave a vulnerable spot in the block. The spiker must hit the open area.

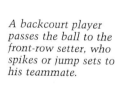

Diagram 4-21

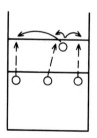

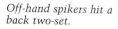

Diagram 4-18

Three spikers work with one setter.

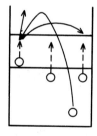

Diagram 4-22

A backcourt player passes the ball to the front-row setter, who spikes or jump sets to his teammate.

Spikers practice hitting the ball over the blocker's hands. Blockers can stand on a bench to regulate their height.

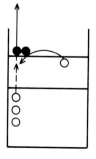

Diagram 4-19

Recover a blocked spike and set the ball to a front-row player. Pass the ball to the setter if he does not field the blocked spike.

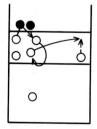

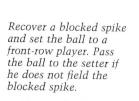

Diagram 4-23

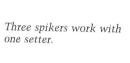

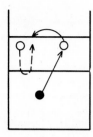

Diagram 4-24

The coach throws balls over the net for players in blocking positions to hit sharply downward or to set.

The player simulates a block and, as he is returning to the floor, the coach throws the ball to a teammate who sets him.

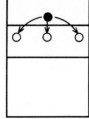

Diagram 4-25

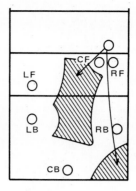

Diagram 4-28

The end spiker attacks weak areas of the man back defense by dinking and hitting off-speed shots into the center of the court and driving long spikes over or off the fingertips of the end blockers.

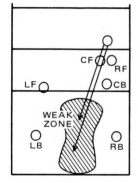

Diagram 4-26

The end spiker attacks weak areas of the man in defense by using dinks, off-speed shots, and spikes.

The middle spiker attacks weak areas of the man back defense by dinking and using off-speed shots to the front corners and deep spikes to the back corners.

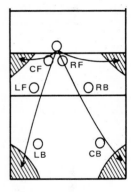

Diagram 4-29

The middle spiker attacks weak areas of the man in defense by dinking and using off-speed shots to the front corners and hitting the ball over or off the blocker's fingertips to the deep corners.

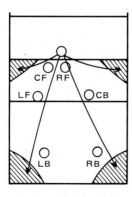

Diagram 4-27

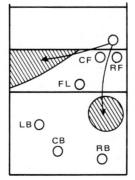

Diagram 4-30

The end spiker attacks weak areas of the off-blocker defense by hitting a sharp angle by the middle blocker or dinking and hitting off-speed spikes down the line.

5

Blocking

Blocking is a play by one or more players who attempt to intercept the ball over or near the net. Any or all of the players in the front line are permitted to block. Blockers are allowed to reach as far over the net as possible, as long as they do not touch the ball before the offense attacks. The most common type of block is a two-man block. At the collegiate level a one-man block occurs about 25 percent of the time. Some coaches try to use three persons blocking whenever possible.

When one or more players participate in the block and make only one attempt to intercept the ball, they may make successive contacts with the ball. A player participating in the block may participate in the next play which counts as the first of the three hits allowed to the team. A team fielding a ball that is blocked may have three additional contacts with the ball before the ball must cross into the opponents' court.

The most effective way to demoralize a team is to prevent the star spiker from hitting the ball over the net. Good spikers find it increasingly difficult to put the ball away because the opposition realizes the importance of aligning its best blockers against them.

During the last few years, it has become popular to block the serve. This is not very difficult for tall middle blockers who start close to the net and can at least get both elbows over the top of the net with an approach. Currently, serve blocking is not quite as popular with the women, because they usually do not reach as high above their net as the men and thus have a lesser range.

At the high school level most males can at least get their elbows to the top of the net when blocking; their female counterparts can reach the top of the net with their forearms. Besides blocking the serve, the

a.   b.   c.

Figure 5-1 *The Block.* The block is a defensive play in which any or all front-court players place one or two hands above their heads while in a position close to the net. One blocker is shown in *a,* two blockers are shown in *b,* and three blockers are in *c.* (Richard Mackson, *a,b*; Ohio State University, *c*)

most effective way to demoralize the opponents is to *attack block* or to intercept the ball before it crosses the net and stuff the ball back into the spiker or to the floor. An aggressive men's block at the top collegiate level will directly score four points in a fifteen point game. At a recent NCAA Men's Championships match, 34 of the 125 points scored were stuff blocks. This is slightly lower for women because the men penetrate further over the net and block at a sharper downward angle. A ball hit by a male spiker at the top level of competition travels one third faster and, thus, the ball rebounds off the block harder and faster and is harder to recover.

Women at a recent Olympics averaged three points directly scored with the block in a fifteen point game. The intimidating effect of the block causes numerous spiking errors and block deflections enable spikers to score up to another one-third of their team's points in a match.

SWITCHING POSITIONS

Blockers must be ready to switch to their assigned blocking positions as soon as their server contacts the ball. The blockers should not look at their server contact the ball, but should scrutinize the opposing setter while he is giving the signals to the hitters. Many blockers will know what plays the opposition will be running by concentrating on the opponents while they are giving signals. As soon as the blockers hear the ball being contacted by the server, they switch to their blocking assignments. In Figure 5-2, number 34 is switching from area four to area two while watching the route of the opposing area four hitter who is running in the middle after the ball is dug. Number 22 is an outside hitter and hits and blocks in area four about 90 percent of the time. In some instances, the setter will be hitting from area four in a side out attempt and will not have time to switch blocking po-

Figure 5-2 *Switching.* Number 34 is a setter and is switching to area two where he will block and be in excellent position to make a transition from blocking to setting. (Norm Schindler)

sitions with the outside hitter in area two during a quick rally. By loudly yelling, "Stay," the other outside blocker will know the switch is off during that particular play. Number 22 is moving to his left to line up in front of Number 6, the Japanese setter. The middle blocker is already raising his arms to prepare to block an attack of the second ball by the Japanese front court setter or defend against a quick hitter coming into his area of responsibility. The middle blocker is also a quick hitter and always blocks in area three and hits a "one-set."

STARTING POSITIONS

In the preliminary position, the right blocker should start about eight feet from the sideline, and the left end blocker about ten feet from the other sideline, with the middle blocker in the center of the court. After the pass, they move in front of the spiker in their area of responsibility. Figure 5-3 shows the blocker starting an arms length away from the net to be in position to spike a ball passed over the net. Many players have difficulty spiking an overpass because their chest is too close to the net.

Figure 5-3 *Starting Positions.* The blockers stand with their knees bent watching the flight of the pass ready to move in front of the attacker. (The Ealing Corp.)

To increase the height of their jump, shorter players and blockers with poor jumping ability may need to take a short approach of one or two steps. This approach should be used only if the blocker cannot achieve the necessary height with a standing jump. If blockers start their approach farther from the net, they increase the risk of netting when they attempt to transfer their forward momentum into a vertical jump. Taller players or good jumpers should rarely start their approach more than one arm's length from the net.

A few years ago, blockers in international competition were able to stop opponents by jumping as high as eye level to the top of the tape. Now some blockers in international competition can get their

Figure 5-4 *Armpits Over the Net.* Japan aligned its tallest blocker against Poland's area four hitter. In many instances the tallest blocker is not quick enough to block the middle. (Richard Mackson)

armpits over the net to stop high-hitting spikers. An example of this is seen in Figure 5-4, where the Japanese blocker has his hands on the top half of the ball.

FOOTWORK

Footwork varies according to the reach and jump of the blocker. The *slide step* is used by blockers who do not have to travel great distances quickly. End blockers use the slide step most of the time. Middle blockers who are quick and jump well also use the slide step.

The slide step involves moving the lead foot laterally and closing the trailing foot to within 6 in. of the forward foot. When arriving at the blocking area, the front foot hits the floor first and points slightly inward as the trailing foot closes approximately to shoulder-width.

The step close is used by end blockers who are poor jumpers and must start a few feet from the net. The step close requires greater timing, coordination, and practice than the slide step. The first step uses the inside foot and the last step uses the outside foot. It is particularly important for the end blocker to turn the outside foot toward the center of the court during the last step so the block will not drift toward the sideline. This is a natural movement for most blockers on the left side because the majority of players take the last step with the left foot when spiking. If blockers cannot learn to take the last step with the outside foot on the right side, they will drift toward the sideline while jumping and leave a hole between themselves and the middle blocker. End blockers should lean towards the center of the court when they jump.

The popular blocking approach for middle blockers is the *crossover step,* which is faster than the slide step and allows the blocker to gain additional inches during the vertical jump. The first step is with the lead foot; then the trailing foot takes a long crossover step and pivots toward the net so that the blocker's shoulders are parallel to the net as the third step is completed. The foot should be planted slightly inward on the third step to enable the blocker to jump straight up rather than laterally.

The crossover step allows the blocker to use an approach and armswing similar to the one used for the spike, which gives extra lift on the vertical jump. This step is fundamentally sound because it allows the blocker to point the feet toward the net so the arms can be raised above the shoulders. If a middle blocker cannot cover at least 12 ft. in three steps or starts in the wrong direction, additional steps must be taken to reach sets by the antenna. The important point is to plant the feet at a 90° angle to the net before jumping so the body faces the net when the jump is completed.

Occasionally end blockers also use the crossover step for additional height on the block. I recommend the crossover step over the step close for blockers who cannot jump high enough using the slide step. In Figure 5-5 Numbers 2 and 6 are both using a crossover step to put them in position to block an outside set.

A few outstanding middle blockers use a more complicated technique. They take the first step by crossing over with the inside foot, which positions the body at a 90° angle to the net; the second step is long and taken parallel to the net. The third step places the blocker in position for the step-close takeoff used in the spike. At the completion of the second step, the knees should be flexed and the arms extended backward at almost shoulder level. The arms drive downward, pointing toward the floor as the

Figure 5-5 *Crossover Step.* Short end blockers also use the crossover step when they need additional height on the jump. (Norm Schindler)

player completes the third step; the arms are then moved forward and up as the player leaves the floor. Then the blocker must turn in mid-air and square the shoulders to the net. In other words, the blocker uses a crossover step with a step-close takeoff and a half turn in mid-air. This is the fastest method for the middle blocker and allows for the highest vertical jump. It also requires excellent coordination and timing. Most blockers fail in this technique because they cannot transfer their forward momentum into a vertical jump. Instead, they move laterally and collide with the end blocker.

Jumping height will increase as the player uses an approach and armswing. Because better control is achieved without a full armswing, the coach should determine if an approach and armswing are necessary. The average end blocker starts at an arm's length from the net when blocking smaller players and teams that use quick, low sets. When opposing taller players, a step-close or crossover step may be necessary.

Some end blockers may have to use an approach on every block, while good jumpers and taller players should be able to use a standing takeoff with no armswing.

TAKEOFF FOR THE JUMP

The most important point to make about the takeoff is that the player should bend at the knees, not at the waist. The player who bends at the waist tends to swing and bat at the ball, resulting in ineffective blocking. The position of the blocker's feet is also critical: the feet should point slightly inward in a pigeon-toed stance aimed at the attacker. This stance squares the body toward the net and helps the blocker to press his hand toward the center of the opponents' court.

In order to determine what degree of leg flexion gives the greatest vertical jumping height, blockers should experiment with the angle of the squat, or gather, used to prepare for the jump. Small players may use a full squat, but most taller blockers may be more effective squatting one-third to halfway down. Normally, players do not squat low enough to produce maximum jumping height until instructed to do so. Most volleyball players in high school have played more basketball than volleyball and consequently have not been trained to use a low squat for added height.

Rebounding does not give a player the training necessary to prepare for the maximum jump used to block the spike of a high, wide set. The coach can point this out rather dramatically after he instructs

the player to increase his block jump by squatting lower; this starting position brings the stronger quadriceps and *gluteus maximus* muscles into play to aid the muscles of the calf.

At takeoff most blocker's ankles should be bent at an angle of 80° to 90°, the knees at 100° to 110°, and the hips at 90°.

Good end blockers should use a standing takeoff without armswing. By eliminating excessive body movements, the blocker is able to wait for the spiker to commit himself and he can use better body control to counter his opponent's attack.

The correct arm and hand position for the blockers are shown in Figure 5-6; the hands are above and in front of the shoulders. The arms will not fully extend until the blocker takes off. If the ball is set within two feet from the net, then the blocker jumps shortly after the spiker leaves the floor.

Figure 5-6 *Arm and Hand Position.* This is the starting or so-called "Mickey Mouse" position for the blocker's hands. (Stan Troutman)

  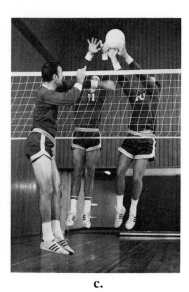

a.   b.   c.

Figure 5-7 *Blocking a Spiker with a Late Armswing.* Spikers with a slow or late armswing usually contact the ball several inches below the apex of their jump. For correct timing, blockers should jump well after the spiker has left the floor. (The Ealing Corp.)

Because spikers use a longer approach, they are able to jump higher and remain in the air longer than blockers. If blockers jump with the spiker on a normal set, they will be returning to the floor when the spiker contacts the ball. Blockers must wait even longer when the ball is set deep into their opponents' court. Some spikers create the illusion of hanging in the air by spiking the ball on the way down from the apex of their jump.

Blockers must constantly remind themselves to hesitate when facing an opponent who uses a late armswing and spikes the ball well after the apex of his jump. Figure 5-7 shows how to block a spiker with late armswing. Blockers must discipline themselves to stay on the floor until the spiker nears the apex of his jump. Blockers should time their movement so that they are at the height of their jump as the late-swinging spiker is contacting the ball on his re-

turn to the floor. Better spikers can defeat this blocking tactic by switching to a quick armswing and hitting over the blocker's hands.

A short blocker must have superior timing to block the middle position because his hands cannot remain above the net as long as his taller teammates'. A taller player can jump too soon and still block the spike, but the short blocker must time his jump perfectly.

Short blockers should normally jump after their taller teammates, particularly when facing a very tall spiker. The blocker who has his toes on the floor in Figure 5-8a is 5 ft. 11 in. tall; his opponent spiker, who uses a late armswing, is 6 ft. 7 in. tall. The late-jumping blocker leaves the floor just prior to the hit and attempts to contact the spike at the height of his jump.

When the setter delivers a quick set to a spiker who jumps before the ball is out

a.   b.

Figure 5-8 *Late Takeoff by Short Middle Blockers.* A late takeoff allows short middle blockers to coordinate their jump with taller teammates as the spike approaches the net. The short blocker is above the net for a comparatively brief period and must time the jump precisely for a coordinated block. (Bob Van Wagner)

of the setter's hand, the blocker must jump with the spiker (Figure 5-9). In this situation, jumping ability is not as important as quickness.

Figure 5-9 *Defending Against a Quick Middle Set.* The middle blocker has jumped with the spiker before the ball has left the setter's hand. This is the only way for a short middle blocker to defend against the one-set. (Andy Banachowski) ▶

AFTER THE TAKEOFF

As the player jumps, the arms are raised with the elbows out in front of the shoulders until the arms are fully extended. The player should be sure to reach forward from the shoulders; he should not swing or bat at the ball. The back is slightly hunched and, although the head may appear to tilt slightly downward, the eyes are on the spiker—not on the ball. The fingers are spread wide apart to cover as much of the ball as possible. The arms seal the net as the wrists force the ball back into the opponent's court.

The two blockers in Figure 5-10 have their eyes on the spiker as he makes contact with the ball. They are blocking as much space as good form will allow with the distance between the hands and the portions of the arms extended above the

Figure 5-11 *Deltoids Touching Ears.* This technique can be used for zone blocking when the players are protecting an area of the court and not reading the spiker. (Richard Mackson)

Figure 5-10 *Eyes On the Spiker.* During blocking drills, the coach should stand behind the spikers to make sure the blockers' eyes are open as shown above. (Stan Abraham)

head leaving a space approximately the circumference of the ball.

In Figure 5-11, we see that the blockers' heads are down with the chins on the chest. It appears that the deltoid muscles of the shoulders are touching the ears. Number 5 is the end blocker, and he has turned his hands toward the center of the opponent's court. Both blockers have sealed the net with their head and triceps. Number 8 has spread his fingers to take up more area (with the exception of his right thumb which is taped to the palm of his hand to prevent further injury). Both blockers appear to have their

Figure 5-12 *Spiking Through a Blocker.* A slight closing of the blocker's (No. 15) arms and hands would have blocked the spike. (Bob Van Wagner)

eyes closed. Closing the eyes are a common mistake when the head is down. I prefer blockers to keep their head level because it is easier for them to watch the spiker. Some coaches with advanced teams teach their blockers to keep the head down, because this helps emphasize the action of penetrating or sealing the net with the triceps and forearms. When the head is back, the body and arms usually pull away from the net and the ball can bounce between the blocker and his side of the net (see Figure 5-12). A basic rule is that the distance between the hands and the portions of the arms extended above the net at the moment of the spiker's contact normally should

be less than the circumference of the ball. An exception to this occurs when a ball is set outside the court; in this instance the blocker may widen the space between his hands due to the angle of flight the ball must travel to legally pass the antenna on the net.

As the blocker descends, his arms and hands draw away from the net and down the sides of his body. The shock of landing is absorbed by the toes, soles, and heels of both feet and then by the legs. If the ball does not rebound into the opponents' court, the blocker turns his head in the direction of the spike as he descends so that he will be ready for the next play.

A popular technique that could cause chronic knee problems calls for the blocker to land on one foot and pivot towards the ball as he lands. This was introduced by the Japanese several years ago and is currently practiced by top players all over the world because it is tactically superior.

ATTACK BLOCK

The attack block is an attempt to intercept the ball before it crosses the net. Blockers may reach across the net, but they may not contact the ball until their opponent has attempted to hit the ball across the net.

Blockers should extend their arms above the net and move them downward from the shoulders as they jump. Upon contacting the ball their wrists tilt forward while keeping their hands and fingers rigid.

Ideally, contact with the ball should be made with the heels of the hand just as the body is descending. In competition, spikes are also blocked with forearms, palms, fingers, and occasionally the face.

The capable blocker will always attack block when in a good position. If the spiker receives a low set close to the net, the blocker should form a "roof" around the ball with the hands, trapping the ball and the spiker (see Figure 5-13).

SOFT BLOCK

Blockers should also master the technique of soft blocking. The soft block is usually used when the ball is set away from the net. It is called a soft block because the blocked ball rebounds back into the opponents' court at a lesser angle or is deflected to the blocker's side of the court. The forearms are held parallel to the net, and hands

Figure 5-13 *The Roof.* When the blocker gets her hands on top of the ball, it is commonly known as "putting the roof on." (Richard Mackson)

are held either tilted backward or parallel to the net (see Figure 5-14).

Smaller blockers must use the soft block a majority of the time so that they can reach high above the net to prevent spikers from hitting the ball over their hands. There are many occasions that call for the blocker to attempt to slow up the spike and to deflect the ball to a teammate. A blocker can cover a much greater area above the net by attempting to deflect a spike than he can by reaching over the net (see Figure 5-15).

When the middle blocker must swing his arms toward the end blocker to shut off the path of the oncoming spike, he often finds himself too far away from the net. To prevent the ball from striking his hands and falling between himself and the net, he should stay close to the net and tilt his hands backward to soft block. Number 12 in Figure 5-16 is using this technique.

Figure 5-14 *Soft Block.* It is a good tactic to soft block when the opponent is spiking a deep set. (Norm Schindler)

Figure 5-15 *Blocking a Tall Spiker.* Soft blocking allows the players to cover more vertical area above the net. (Stan Troutman)

Figure 5-16 *Closing the Seam.* Middle blocker, Jon Roberts, closes the seam with a soft block. (Bob Van Wagner)

Blockers should normally use the soft block to intercept deep spikes. They must jump after the spiker does when the spiker is hitting a ball that is not set close to the net. If blockers jump with the spiker, they will not have the necessary height to block effectively by the time the ball approaches the net. The soft block gives the blocker a greater margin of time to assess the direction and speed of a deep spike.

In Figure 5-16, the middle blocker tries to close the hole between the blockers; he must move his arms laterally and is prevented from reaching over the net if he is late in arriving at the point of attack.

ONE BLOCKER

Against teams that can pass and run a sophisticated offense at least 25 percent of the blocks will be one-on-one situations. In today's defense, the end blocker does not stay 2 feet or 6 feet or 10 feet from the sideline, but plays head-on-head with the opponent coming into his area of responsibility. If the opponent runs a lot of Xs, the left blocker may start 13 feet from the sideline. Number 15 and Number 3 are in good position in Figure 5-17, because they were directly in front of the attacker in their area. By the position of the setter, we can

Figure 5-17 *One-on-One.* On a perfect pass, the blockers have to move directly in front of their assigned hitters. (Norm Schindler)

see the serve was received accurately, and that the offense will get a one-on-one situation.

The reason that there are so many one-on-one situations is that teams are passing better and middle hitters are jumping before the ball is set. Thus on a good pass, the middle blocker has to move over in front of the approaching hitter and jump with the set as it comes out of the setter's hands—like Steve Salmons did in Figure 5-18.

If the ball is not set to the middle and the middle blocker was up, he usually cannot recover in time to form a two-man block. In one-on-one situations, the outside blocker can usually count on the spiker hitting crosscourt and should make a cross

Figure 5-19 *Defending Crosscourt.* The average area four hitter will hit crosscourt at least 80 percent of the time when faced with one blocker. (Richard Mackson)

Figure 5-18 *Stopping the Quick Set.* Blockers have to anticipate to block one-on-one to defeat fast combination offenses. (Ohio State University)

court penetration with her arms as the Cuban blocker does in Figure 5-19.

When spiking a fast four-set, the attacker will usually hit a low hard shot crosscourt. The alert end blocker in Figure 5-20 has successfully defended against this play by dropping the inside arm to stuff the spike. During the last few years, many middle blockers have decided to take both angles of a quick hit and leave the middle open. In Figure 5-21a, the Korean blocker stuffs a quick spike against Poland using this technique. It is not necessary to jump

Figure 5-20 *Dropping the Arm.* It does not take much penetration to stuff the low hard spike. (Norm Schindler)

high, but it is necessary to jump quickly and penetrate the net when stopping the quick set. Of course, if the blocker is going to take both angles and leave the middle open, the face will become vulnerable to attack (see Figure 21b).

When blocking one-on-one, the blocker should line up in front of the spiker and take away his best shot. At lower levels of play, this might be the spikers only shot, but experienced spikers can still come up with innovative ways to get out of trouble as Steve Salmons demonstrates in Figure 5-22 with a round-house spike of a quick set.

a.

b.

Figure 5-21 *The V Block.* This type of block should only be tried as an occasional tactic or an intelligent spiker will give the middle blocker a constant facial massage. (Richard Mackson, *a;* Norm Schindler, *b*)

a.   b.

Figure 5-22 *Take the Spiker's Best Shot.* The blocker lines up in front of the spiker's attacking arm, but gets fooled by the roundhouse. If contacted too slowly, this spike resembles a slam dunk and will be ruled a throw by the referee. (Norm Schindler)

TWO BLOCKERS

The goal of the defense is to have two blockers up against the attacker on every play. The end blocker sets the position of the block on outside sets and should penetrate with her hands pressing into the center of the court. The middle blocker should have her hands facing the opponent's back line (see Figure 5-23).

When the blocker contacts the ball, his outside hand should be between the ball and the sideline. This prevents the ball from being "wiped off" the blocker's hands into the out-of-bounds area where the backcourt men cannot reach it (see Figure 5-24).

When a blocker senses that the spiker may deliberately hit the ball toward the out-of-bounds area in an attempt to contact his

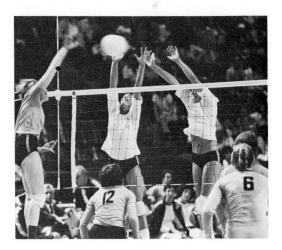

Figure 5-23 *Two Blockers.* These blockers have sealed the net and are keeping their arms shoulder width apart in good form. (Richard Mackson)

Figure 5-24 *Turning the Spike In.* The blocker reaches over the net with his outside hand between the boundary line and the ball in order to prevent a wipe-off shot. (Richard Mackson)

Figure 5-26 *Reading the Spiker.* When the blockers watch the approach and body alignment, they can "read" the direction of the spike and block the shot. (Norm Schindler)

Figure 5-25 *Drop Hands.* The Polish blocker has pulled his arms down and ducked his head to allow the Russian to hit the ball out of bounds. (Richard Mackson)

hand, he should quickly drop his hand below the level of the net to allow the spike to travel out of bounds (see Figure 5-25).

The end blocker's primary responsibility is to position the block on wide sets and align himself to block the ball on the inside hand.

Notice how the two blockers in Figure 5-26 have both made an effort to close the hole in the center of the block while still keeping their arms shoulder width apart to protect a large area above the net. The primary responsibility of the middle blocker on outside sets is to get to the point of attack as quickly as possible, and then to protect against the crosscourt spike. In Figure 5-27, Steve Salmons is making a penetrating crosscourt move to stuff the spike.

Figure 5-28 *Three Blockers.* The Russians are known for their power at the net and use three blockers when the opportunity exists. (Richard Mackson)

Figure 5-27 *Cross Court Move.* The middle blocker who can learn to make this move just prior to the spiker contacting the ball will be a most valuable player. (Norm Schindler)

BLOCKING STRATEGY

To win at advanced levels of play, a team must control the center of the net. Those teams that dominate the net with big middle blockers usually win. Six or seven years ago, teams could still dominate at the college level with small, quick, intelligent middle blockers. Now the middle blockers should be tall enough to cover a one-set and jump quick enough to recover and move outside to form a two-man block. The small middle blocker has to jump too high on the quick set and, if he is fooled, cannot recover in time to participate in a two-man block on a wide set. The big blocker can

THREE BLOCKERS

Because of the increased attacking ability of men's and women's teams, it is now desirable to use three blockers whenever possible. In Figure 5-28, the three Russians are soft-blocking because the Cuban is dinking. The two end blockers are turning their outside hands in towards the center of the court. The other four hands should be held parallel to the net.

often tiptoe block the quick set or just jump a few inches to protect against that play and still recover to get outside. The best middle blockers need to have quickness, power, endurance, size, and the intelligence to recognize the rotations and to remember the tendencies of the opposition. Unfortunately, these athletes are not available to every team; when they are, a team should build their tactics around that type of athlete. The middle blocker's responsibilities are to stop the opposition's middle attack and still get outside for the wide sets. Normally, the tall quick blocker switches to the center, the next strongest blocker to area two and the third blocker to area four.

The middle position allows a mobile blocker to participate in almost all of the blocks against a two-hitter attack, as well as in the majority of the blocks against a three-hitter attack. Since most teams set their area four spiker more often than their area two spiker, the next best blocker usually switches to his right. This generally leaves the remaining blocker to cover fewer spikes. Through the course of the season, the attacks made by many teams become predictable as they try to set the ball to a particular spiker in a certain rotation. A simple rotation chart kept on the opposition will tell the coach how to position his blockers in each rotation (see Chapter 13).

The coach can instruct his blockers to go after the ball or to protect a given area of the net. For example, the blockers may protect the line and force the spiker to hit crosscourt. The obvious advantage of this tactic is that the backcourt defenders can position themselves in the open area of the court. The disadvantage is that the blocker becomes less aggressive and does not directly score as many points. A good middle blocker should not be instructed to zone

Figure 5-29 *Overlapping Block Coverage.* This situation should be avoided because it causes net errors and decreases the area of coverage. (Dr. Leonard Stallcup)

block when playing next to a small or inefficient blocker. Since opposing spikers will attempt to hit over the smaller blocker, the middle blocker must have the freedom to key on the ball.

When blockers are instructed to go aggressively after the ball, the backcourt players must constantly adapt to the changing patterns of the block. Unless backcourt players are capable of reacting very quickly, they will not dig as many balls. An additional hazard is that blockers begin to overreact to the ball to such an extent that they begin to interfere with each other (see Figure 5-29). To prevent this the coach can tell the end blocker to move into the seam and the middle blocker to concentrate on crosscourt spikes.

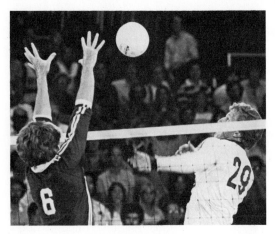

Figure 5-30 *Line Up in Front of the Quick Hitter.* The middle blocker has good body position, but he should take one of the angle shots as the spiker now has both angles open. (Norm Schindler)

Blocking the Quick Offense

The middle blocker starts about an arm's length from the net with his hands at shoulder level. The weight should be on the balls of the feet with the knees slightly bent. The middle blocker should watch the pass and then the route of the approaching quick hitter before switching complete attention to the setter. If the pass is close enough to the net to allow a one-set or three-set, the arms should now be extended. By watching the setter, the quick hitter will come into view. Position the head directly in front of the quick hitter's attacking arm (see Figure 5-30). Do not jump until the setter releases the ball; jump quickly and penetrate using a shoulder width arm spread. The one-set is delivered close to the net and most hitters will contact the ball low and spike a severe angle towards either sideline. Some outstanding players advo-

Figure 5-31 *Blocking Both Angles.* This is what happens to the infamous V block when the spiker has observed the blocker leaving the middle of the court open. (Norm Schindler)

cate spreading the arms in a V and attempting to block both angles and then closing the block if possible when they determine the direction of the spike. Of course, this leaves the middle open as shown in Figure 5-31.

Blocking the X play where the middle attacker hits a one-set and the area two spiker crosses behind for a two-set presents real problems for the middle blocker. In 1979 (31-0) and 1981 (32-3), UCLA won the NCAA Championships with a four play offense running Xs approximately 40 percent of the time. There are three ways teams in our league defensed our well-scouted X play. The least effective is called the *stack* and has the left blocker lining up behind the middle blocker and following our right side or X hitter. The middle blocker keys on our quick hitter, thus creating a one-on-one blocking situation. The stack was popularized in the professional league, where two big middle blockers could be together in the front row. In college play, a line blocker was coming to the middle following the X hitter and then trying to form a two-man block when we set a four outside. The second method has been called the *slide,* and uses the end blocker to key on the quick hitter. The slide still creates one-on-one situations and usually matches up a smaller end blocker against a tall quick hitter who cuts the spike back into the center of the

court as shown in Figure 5-32. We will call the third method *reaction blocking;* it is used by many of our better college teams. This method of blocking requires tall blockers who can jump quickly once the ball has been set. The area four blocker calls "X" alerting the other two blockers and slide steps in front of the quick hitter. The middle blocker gets his hands up and is ready to block any of the three attackers. The right blocker is ready to help on the X hitter and moves toward the center of the court. Often reaction blocking will allow two blockers to go up with the quick hitter and takes both angles as shown in Figure 5-33b. If the right hitter fakes an X and comes back, the left blocker yells, "Fake," and the blockers still react to the set.

Figure 5-32 *End Blocker On Quick Hitter.* This usually creates a mismatch in favor of the attacker. (Richard Mackson)

Blocking the Outside Set

The blockers start an arms length from the net so they can spike balls passed over the net. They look at the setter and spiker in front of them to pick up any signals as to what play is going to be run. If the coach gives serving signals, they should know what area the ball will cross the net and thus be in position to block the block of the serve. Blockers do not look at the server or they will miss the spiker's routes to the point of attack. They watch the approaching spiker or spikers in their area, talk to each other as they watch the flight of the pass, and then pick up the setter. As the setter releases the ball, the blockers immediately look at the approaching spiker. End blockers move to the point of attack and set the block with the outside hand between the ball and the sideline. Middle blockers close to within a foot or two of the end blocker and both players move their

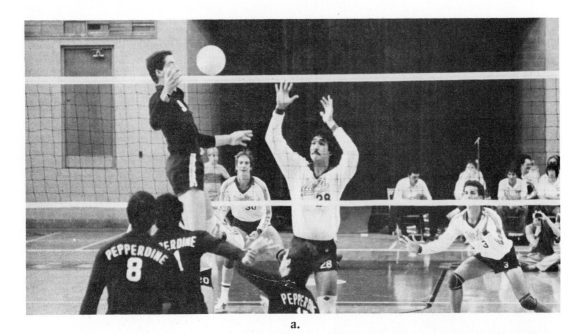

a.

b.

Figure 5-33 *Reaction Blocking.* The blockers wait until the ball is set before leaving their feet to block. This tactic requires tall players. (Ohio State University)

Figure 5-34 *Blockers Move Together.* After playing next to the same person for a season, it is easier to anticipate each other's moves and form a solid block. (Ohio State University)

arms together in the direction of the spike, as shown in Figure 5-34.

READING THE SPIKER

Spikers usually attempt to avoid the block by hitting the ball crosscourt or down the line. A better blocker knows whether the average spiker plans to hit inside or outside the block. He can judge this by analyzing or "reading" the spiker's approach to the set, his body alignment and, most important, his armswing. All spikers give some indication of where they plan to hit the ball,

although better spikers try to conceal their intentions until the last split second or until the blockers are in mid-air. The blocker should watch the spiker's approach, upper body and armswing.

The following hints will help the blocker to "read" or analyze certain types of spikers and situations.

1. The spiker with a right angle or straight approach to the net is in a good position to hit a line shot.
2. A right-handed spiker usually can hit the line shot with accuracy and power from area four.
3. Short spikers usually have developed a good line shot.
4. When the ball is set close to the sideline, it is easy for the spiker to hit the ball down the line.
5. Right-handed spikers who begin their approach off the court usually have a weak line shot from area two.
6. The spiker almost always hits the ball crosscourt on a low, quick set.
7. Almost all spikers hit significantly more crosscourt angle shots than line shots from both the strong and weak sides of the court.
8. As balls are set farther away from the net, the tendency to hit crosscourt is increased.
9. When blocking a taller player or a spiker with a slow or late armswing, the blocker should jump later than he normally does.
10. If the spiker runs under the ball, the blocker should expect a low spike or an off-speed shot.
11. A slow approach or a lack of height on the jump usually indicates an off-speed spike.
12. Tired or off-balance spikers tend to dink or hit off the blocker's hands.

13. Prior to the serve, signals are often exchanged between the spiker and the setter. Close observation of verbal or hand signals often tells the blocker what type of play to expect.

14. A closer starting position prior to the spiker's approach indicates that there will be a play.

15. If the set travels inside the spiker's attacking shoulder, he will hit the ball across his body.

16. An average spiker on a poor set should not be blocked.

17. Every opposing spiker has favorite shots. *Learn them.*

Figure 5-35 *Reaching Backward.* If the spiker hits a tape shot at the middle blocker's arms, the ball will bounce down the body on the blocker's side of the net. (Bob Van Wagner)

COMMON ERRORS

There are several common errors that players make while attempting to block.

Touching the Net

Caused by jumping forward or bending at the waist. Blockers should jump straight up without bending their waist.

Caused by throwing arms at the ball instead of sliding them over the net in one motion.

Caused by reaching too far over the net. Blockers must learn their safe range of attack blocking.

Ball Bounces Down the Front of the Body on Blockers' Side of the Net

Caused by jumping too far from the net.

Caused by extending the hands behind the shoulders (see Figure 5-35).

Caused by leaving too large a space between hands and forearms (see Figure 5-36).

Constantly Missing the Spike

Caused by closing the eyes. Blockers should see every ball that goes past the block. The blocker must keep the eyes on the ball after the spiker attacks.

Caused by watching the ball instead of the spiker. Primary attention should be focused on the approaching spiker because the ball comes into view as it nears the spiking arm.

Caused by blockers not squaring the shoulders to the net and thereby creating a hole in the middle of the block (see Figure 5-37).

The Ball Ricochets Off the Hands and Goes Out of Bounds

Caused by presenting a flat surface of the outside hand instead of keeping it between

Figure 5-36 *Hitting the Seam.* The low seam between the blockers can be protected by moving the bodies closer together. (Norm Schindler)

the ball and the side line (see Figure 5-38). Caused by the end blocker reaching to the sideline for a dink or offspeed shot. The end blocker should not have his outside hand wider than his shoulder (see Figure 5-39).

TEACHING PROGRESSION

Blocking takes longer to teach and is more difficult to perfect than any other fundamental of volleyball.

During the first or second workout, the coach should instruct his players on block-

ing techniques and include blocking drills in every practice session thereafter. Almost all players should learn the techniques of the end and middle blocking positions to give the coach or captain the necessary flexibility to change blocking tactics during the course of a game. Constant individual attention during blocking drills is necessary because players are rarely aware of their mistakes while blocking.

When teaching the block, train the players in the important individual aspects before attempting to perfect the technique as a team effort. The following are some skills

Figure 5-37 *Right Shoulder Off the Net.* The middle blocker has opened a hole because she did not square her right shoulder up to the net. (Andy Banachowski).

Figure 5-38 *Tooling the Block.* The outside arm has to penetrate between the ball and the sideline to prevent wipe-off shots. (Dr. Leonard Stallcup)

and drills for the coach to use in teaching blocking:

1. Demonstrate and then have players practice the following:
   Slide step and jump
   Step close approach used to block taller opponents
   Crossover step and jump (Note: Alternate to the right and left)
2. Lower the net 2 ft. Then explain and demonstrate the arm and hand position used to attack block, soft block, turn the ball in, and close a hole between players to ensure a tight block. Line up players along the lowered net and have them practice sliding the hands over the net with the elbows in front of the body rather than on the side. Players should hunch the back to lock the shoulders and keep the eyes focused on the area above the net.

Figure 5-39 *Jumping On a Bad Set.* The player at the bottom right of the photo has just tooled the block. The blockers should drop their hands when the spiker contacts the ball below the net. (Stan Troutman)

3. Have two players face each other on opposite sides of a regulation net. One player simulates a spiking motion while the blocker reaches over the net and attempts to touch the spiker's fingertips.

4. Place a spiker on a 2-ft high bench. He tosses the ball up and spikes it at the blocker. The blocker practices the attack block, soft block, and turning the ball in. Add a middle blocker and coordinate a tight block.

5. Have two players face each other on opposite sides of the net about 3 ft. apart. The spiker tosses the ball to himself and jumps straight up to hit it over the net. The blocker uses a slide step to intercept the spike.

6. Pair players of approximate height in two lines on each side of the net. Partners jump and touch hands above the net on the end, middle, and other end of the net. Emphasize a fast slide step and maximum jump. Change the drill by having one player swing his spiking arm as he jumps. His partner must move his arms and hands to intercept the mock spike. Repeat the drill, using the crossover step.

7. Place two benches close to the net, about 3 ft. from the sideline and place a third bench near the center of the net. A spiker stands on each bench, tosses the ball up, and spikes it in rotation as the blocker moves from spiker to spiker using the slide or crossover step. To increase the difficulty of this drill, take away the benches and substitute three lines of spikers who hit in rotation to the single blocker.

GAME SITUATION DRILLS

After the blocker develops a blocking technique that suits his jump and reach, drills simulating game situations should be initiated.

A good athlete requires about three years to be able to read the intentions of opposing spikers in top competition. Some players in open competition are still learning after they have passed the peak of their physical ability.

The following drills can be used to practice situations encountered in competition:

1. The spiker passes the ball to a setter who delivers a high, wide set. The blocker attempts to cut off his strongest shot or block the ball. One-on-one blocking situations are becoming more common each year as more teams switch to combination offenses to set up a one-on-one play. Better spikers can usually beat a one-man block. Emphasize taking away the spiker's favorite angle or the best percentage shot for the particular set and approach used by the spiker.

2. Three blockers defend against two hitters. Station the spikers on the end of the net with the setter in the middle. Emphasize a tight, two-man block, with the off-blocker dropping back to the 10-ft. line to dig a spike driven inside the middle blocker.

3. Three blockers *v.* three attackers. Emphasize that the middle blocker stay close to the net if he is late and that individual blockers take cross-court spiking angles in one-on-one situations.

4. Three blockers *v.* three attackers. The center spiker hits a one-set close to the net, and the outside spikers hit a normal set. Emphasize that the primary responsibility of the middle blocker is the center spiker. Instruct the middle blocker to jump with the set and if fooled to recover and at-

tempt to soft block the end spiker if he is fast enough. If he is out of position to soft block, he should remain close to the net to field a block rebound.

5. Two end attackers *v.* three blockers. The middle blocker deliberately moves in the wrong direction and attempts to recover and join the end blocker. Emphasize that the middle blocker should keep his hands close to the net and soft block when late in contacting the ball. The end blocker must take more of a crosscourt angle and attempt to help close the hole between blockers.

6. After the blocker returns to the floor, throw a ball behind him to set to another spiker.

7. Station two players on opposite sides of the net. Toss a ball about 15 ft. high within a foot of either side of the net. Players must decide to spike or block the ball. Emphasize aggressive attack blocking and the formation of a roof around the ball with the hands. Toss 50 percent of the balls so that they fall directly on top of the net. Emphasize blocking the ball with the heels of the hand when part of the ball splits the net.

8. Instruct the setter to deliver sets outside the court so that the spiker must hit the ball crosscourt. Emphasize soft blocking by the end blocker so that he can turn the ball into the court. Instruct the middle spiker to leave a wide space between his hands so that he can cover more area above the net. Show him that the ball cannot go through his hands (unless he leaves an extremely wide space) because of the angle of the ball's flight.

9. Construct blocking drills patterned to stop the attack of the chief opponent. Instruct the second team to simulate the opposition's attack to familiarize blockers with their patterns.

6

Individual Defensive Techniques

THE DIG

The fundamental digger's stance is illustrated in Figure 6-1. In the digger's stance, the feet are spread farther apart than shoulder-width, and one foot is placed ahead of the other. The digger's weight is on the inside balls of the feet with the heels off the floor. The knees and hips are bent at approximately 90°. The elbows are held in front of the knees which are in front of the toes. The hands are extended frontally about waist high; the weight is forward.

Most players who do not have good forward or lateral movements squat too low to the ground or spread their feet farther than shoulder-width apart. These players cannot move quickly in any direction.

The forearm pass should be used whenever possible because this technique provides the best possible control of a hard-driven spike under current rule interpretations (Figure 6-2). A hard spike received by an overhand pass is almost always called

a "throw" by the official and is a poor percentage play.

Slow-moving balls require the digger to move the arms toward the intended target area in order to provide the necessary momentum for the ball to travel the required distance. Diggers can attain greater accuracy with slow-moving balls if they use the elbow lock pass to provide prolonged contact with the ball (Figure 6-3). When digging a hard spike, the arms do not move, although the rest of the body is in motion. If the arms move toward the ball, the dig will rebound a great distance and will not have a controlled flight.

The digger often "cushions" hard-driven spikes so that they do not rebound back over the net. This is accomplished when the digger moves his hips forward and pulls his shoulders back. Players who use this technique move toward the oncoming ball and contact it while their legs move up from a low squatting position. To enable the dig to travel high in the air on the digger's side

103

Figure 6-1 *Digger's Stance.* This stance is the same for all defenses. The body is in a semi-crouched position, with the feet spread slightly more than shoulder-width apart. The weight is forward on the balls of the feet, and the hands are held waist-high. (Stan Troutman)

of the net, the arms should be held almost parallel to the floor, whenever the flight of the ball permits. Since the dig travels upward rather than forward, the dig rarely is passed back over the net.

MOVING TO THE BALL

Rather than merely reach for it with their arms, players should always strive to use

Figure 6-2 *Forearm Pass.* The Russian captain uses an interlocking finger grip and passes the ball on the forearms below her wrists. (Richard Mackson)

their legs to position themselves in front of the oncoming ball. Figure 6-5 shows the low squatting position used to make a dig. American players are somewhat unaccustomed to the low squatting position and require hours of repetitive drills in the low position until movement becomes automatic. A common error is to keep the legs extended and to bend from the waist.

The side step used in volleyball points the outside foot in the direction of movement as the body squats over the lead leg and leans toward the ball as shown in Figure 6-6.

Many times during a match the player must turn and run to recover an errant dig as shown in Figure 6-7. Players must be drilled to hit the ball over the net from any position on the gym floor.

a.   b.   c.

Figure 6-3 *Digging Off-Speed Shots.* Olympian Barbara Perry contacts the ball after being forced to move into an off-balance position to get behind it. (Dr. Leonard Stallcup)

Figure 6-4 *Cushioning the Dig.* The player does not follow-through but contacts the ball with the hips thrust forward and the arms almost parallel to the floor. (Richard Mackson)

Figure 6-5 *Low-Body Position.* Olympic captain Jane Ward demonstrates good balance with the center of her body above her back foot. (Dr. Leonard Stallcup)

a.   b.

Figure 6-6 *The Side Step.* The one-arm dig should only be used when the player does not think she can get two hands on the ball (*a*). The forearm pass is always preferable (*b*). (Richard Mackson)

ONE-ARM DIG

The one-arm dig is quite common and is used to increase the range of the defender. It should be used only when the ball is out of effective range for the forearm pass to be feasible. The ball can be effectively contacted anywhere from the hand to the elbow joint. Beginning players should be instructed to contact the ball in the middle

Figure 6-7 *Turn and Run.* Number 7 uses the backwards pass to retrieve an errant dig. (Richard Mackson) ◀

a.

b.

▲
Figure 6-8 *Fist Contact for One-Arm Dig.* Fist contact is used when the ball is hard to reach or when the player wishes to pass the ball a greater distance. (The Ealing Corp.) ▶

c.

of the forearm. If they misjudge the ball and contact it higher on the forearm or lower on the hand, they will not misdirect the pass altogether.

The heel of the hand and the knuckles provide a good rebounding surface for hard-to-reach balls that require full arm extension as demonstrated by former All-American Toshi Toyoda. This technique is often used to backup the spiker when passing block rebounds. The back of the hand is also a popular digging surface as this method allows the player to retrieve very low balls and helps break the fall in the same motion. The player in Figure 6-9 has just sprawled forward to pop the ball up with the back of his hand.

Figure 6-9 *Back-of-the-Hand Contact.* This method is well-suited for the sprawl as the contacting hand and arm also breaks the fall. (Norm Schindler)

OVERHAND DIG

Current rule interpretations discourage using the overhand pass to dig a hard-driven spike. Most officials are in the habit of calling every overhand pass of a hard-driven spike a thrown ball (Figure 6-10). Since the overhand dig is a poor percentage play, coaches usually design their defenses so that balls spiked above their player's waist may travel out of bounds. This means that diggers can keep their weight forward to dive or sprawl for balls in front of them and keep their hands below their waist to use the forearm pass or one-arm dig to field spikes.

Off-speed spikes and dinks can be fielded in the overhand position behind the ball

Figure 6-10 *Overhand Dig.* Former Olympian, Ernie Suwara demonstrates an open-handed dig of a hard-driven spike. This was an acceptable technique in his era, but now the officials constantly interpret this maneuver to be a thrown ball. (Dr. Leonard Stallcup) ▶

Figure 6-11 *Double Hit.* Another play that will draw a quick whistle is attempting to use the heels of the hands to dig the ball. (Dr. Leonard Stallcup)

THE SPRAWL

The sprawl or the slide has been seen since the mid-seventies. It was very much in evidence in the women's competition during the 1976 Olympics, and is currently popular with men and women. The sprawl does not cover as much distance as the dive because one of the player's feet usually remain in contact with the floor. At UCLA, our men started using this technique when we moved the starting positions of our defensive players in area one and five 12 feet from the net to dig our opponent's quick attack. They already were so close to the net that they no longer had to dive for the dinks and block deflections, but merely stepped forward with their outside foot as they lowered the chest to the outside knee and pushed off the forward leg in the direction of the ball. In Figure 6-12, Karch Kiraly has just sprawled forward and dug the ball with the back of his right hand, while the left hand cushions the fall as Karch's body is twisting to his right side. Karch completes the sprawl by sliding forward as he

and intended target area. Fingers should be spread and cupped, wrists tilted back so the passer can see the ball above the back of his hands. The ball should be contacted above the forehead; knees and arms should extend simultaneously as the wrists straighten. The best way to dig a hard-driven spike in the overhand position is to clasp the hands together and not attempt to use the fingers. When players are not quick enough to join their hands together as in Figure 6-11, the referee will usually call a double hit.

Figure 6-12 *Right-Side Sprawl.* This technique is often seen by the area one defender to retrieve dink shots and block deflections. (Norm Schindler)

Figure 6-13 *Left-Side Sprawl.* The Cuban girl pivots into the court to hit the ball back to her teammates. (Richard Mackson)

Figure 6-14 *Front Sprawl.* Notice how alert the Korean girls are as they watch their teammate sprawl forward. (Richard Mackson)

contacts the floor with his right leg, hip, and side. We provide baseball sliding pads for our players to use in practice and matches if they desire. Some sort of padding around the hip would be helpful when using this technique. When using the sprawl from area four and five, the player pushes off with her left foot. Notice how her front foot is pivoting towards the center of the court to enable her to dig the ball back to her teammates (Figure 6-13). Because she is pivoting, she will land on her side. Defenders in area six usually have ample opportunity to use a front sprawl as illustrated by the Korean girl in Figure 6-14. She has just collapsed to both knees and contacted the ball with the back of her left hand; now she is about to slide forward on her chest and stomach as her right forearm breaks her fall.

THE ROLL

The player should learn to roll to the floor when his body is placed in an off-balance lateral position. This technique allows the force of the fall to be absorbed by a large area of the body rather than allowing the wrist or knee joint to absorb the shock.

Figure 6-15 shows sequence shots of the side step and side roll. The digger takes a side step with her right leg as her left leg extends in an attempt to position her body behind the ball (a). Upon contact, she is already low to the ground (b). After the ball is hit (c), her buttocks, back, and left shoulder contact the ground as knees bend (d). The player's body continues to roll over her left shoulder as the legs remain bent (e). As her toes contact the ground, she pushes her body to an upright position with her hands (f,g).

The full roll is rarely seen in men's volleyball as men prefer to dive when placed

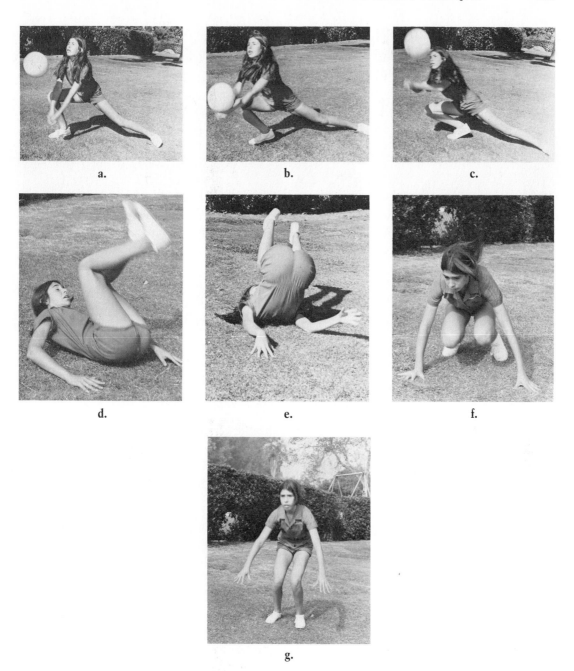

a.

b.

c.

d.

e.

f.

g.

Figure 6-15 *Side Step and Roll.* The digger positions herself in an off-balance position to contact the ball and then rolls to a standing position. (Gary Adams)

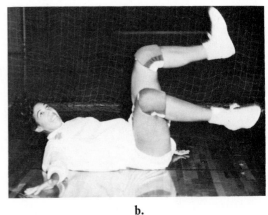

a.   b.

Figure 6-16 *Half Roll.* After digging the ball, the player keeps her head to her chest and rolls to her back while bringing her legs up and then forward to regain her feet. (Dr. Leonard Stallcup)

in an off-balance position. Women use the dive, sprawl, and half roll. The full roll was popularized by the 1964 Japanese Women's Gold Medalist Team and reached its peak of popularity in the late 1960s and early 1970s. The half roll is demonstrated by Bobby Perry in Figure 6-16 and is an easy way to return to the standing position after contacting the ball.

DIVING

Diving is a common defense technique used to reach balls that cannot be passed accurately from a standing position. It is also an emergency play for recovering otherwise out-of-reach balls. Men use the dive more than women because of their greater arm and shoulder strength which is utilized to catch the body when contacting the floor after a medium or high dive. Once a player is a teenager or older, diving becomes a little more difficult to learn because of the increased fear and realization of risk involved by the performer. Elementary school children and lighter teenagers

usually learn to dive quickly as the ratio of arm and shoulder strength to body weight is an important factor. The most common problem with beginners is that they are looking for a place to land rather than concentrating on digging the ball. The defensive player first moves to the ball, and if necessary dives to retrieve it; only then should he think about landing. First, we will look at the side view of Toshi Toyoda performing the dive in Figure 6-17. Toshi has started the dive by moving his entire body close to the floor and has leaned forward ready to push off his front foot (a). He has kept his eyes on the ball and is preparing to contact the ball with his hands and forearms creating a flat surface (b). He has to hit the ball straight up in a high trajectory so a teammate can play it (c). Of course, this is the entire reason for the dive and a fact that most beginners have difficulty in remembering. All players should try and dig the ball as high as they can when diving. Toshi has moved his arms apart after the dig and extended them to the floor in front of his body (d). Next, Toshi is absorbing the shock of landing by bending his arms as his

Figure 6-17 *Side View of the Dive.* Light, strong players like Toshi are usually better defenders than their bigger teammates. (The Ealing Corp.)

Figure 6-18 *Front Dive.* Due to a powerful takeoff, Toshi uses the forearm pass (*c*), and still has time to put his hands on the floor to absorb the shock of landing (*f*). (The Ealing Corp.)

chest lowers to the ground. Notice that his back is arched and his knees are still high in a protected position (e). Heavy athletes or those who do not have sufficient arm and shoulder strength should not keep their knees so high, because they will have difficulty catching themselves with their arms and will probably hit their chin on the floor. In Figure 6-18, a classic front view of the dive is demonstrated. Toshi Toyoda crouches before taking the last step. His arms are in front while his forward foot pushes vigorously off the floor (a). His thrusting leg moves forward horizontally as he keeps his eyes on the ball (b). He contacts the ball with a forearm pass (c), then rotates his palms toward the floor in preparation for the landing (e). As he descends, his legs and feet are higher than his waist, his back is arched, and his head is up. Both arms are extended in order to contact the floor with both hands (f). To prevent violent contact with the floor, his body is arched correctly with his knees above his waist. His chest, stomach and, finally, legs must now contact the floor; his body will spend the momentum by sliding along the floor.

Most people can learn the low dive because the horizontal momentum of the body will allow most of the shock of landing to be absorbed by a sliding action across the floor. For some reason, many players at the college level have only mastered a dive at a certain height and use that dive in attempting to retrieve low balls or high balls. Typically these players start from a standing position and are not in the starting position for the dive which utilizes a crouch. In Figure 6-19, the explosive quickness for most successful low dives is illustrated.

A special problem arises when diving parallel to the net. The player has to try and hit the ball back into the center of the

Figure 6-19 *Low Dive.* Byron Shewman dives close to the ground and snaps the wrist into extension hitting the ball with the back of the hand. This technique enables the player to keep the palms of the hand toward the floor for a quick landing. (Richard Mackson)

Figure 6-20 *Sacrifice.* Sacrifice is one of the major tenets of Japanese volleyball. When diving parallel to the standards or referee's stand, use a one-hand pass so the other hand is free for recovery. (Richard Mackson)

Figure 6-21 *High Lateral Dive.* Only advanced players can safely perform an all-out high diving save. (Richard Mackson)

court and avoid going under the net and hitting the standards. In tight situations, such as Figure 6-20, the one-arm pass is recommended.

In Figure 6-21, the late Dodge Parker makes one of his patented all-out saving digs. Only advanced players should attempt this type of high lateral dive, because the higher the body is in the air, the harder it falls to the ground. In landing, it is important to try to absorb the shock with as much body surface as possible. The momentum should not be stopped by the arms; rather, it should be absorbed by the arms, chest, and stomach in that order. Since the movement is usually downward rather than forward, there is little opportunity to slide. Players with poor arm strength will absorb the fall in a jolting bounce.

LEARNING THE DIVE

Players should not attempt the dive until they develop adequate arm strength. Many people do not have adequate arm strength to slow their landing and, consequently, they hit the floor with their chin. Push-ups and tricep presses develop the necessary arm strength to slow the body's fall to the floor. The correct technique of diving can be learned in several steps. First, the player lies face down on a mat and arches his body so that his knees and feet are higher than his waist. Next, his partner holds his feet while he extends his arms and lowers his body to the mat. Then the player kneels and falls forward, pushing against the mat as his arms flex. The action is then attempted from a standing position: The player moves off the mat to the floor, falls forward from a standing position, and slides forward with his chest touching the floor. He returns to the mat and dives forward from a squatting position. Next he tries a two-step approach and dives forward. Finally, the partner lobs a ball to the player who executes a diving save.

When a player learns the correct technique of diving without the ball, he is ready to progress to the backhand dig on the mat. Initially, the coach or partner should lob the ball in a controlled manner and then gradually increase the distance and speed as progress is made.

A pepper drill can be used to practice the dig. A coach or partner stands at distances of 10 to 30 ft. and alternates hard-driven spikes with off-speed shots and dinks directed at the digger just out of his reach. The digger dives, rolls, and makes whatever movements are called for according to the height, direction, and speed of the ball.

When the player is learning correct techniques, the coach should frequently stop

a.

b.

▲
Figure 6-22 *Dive to the Left.* When diving to the left, the digger jumps off his left foot and should contact the ball with just one arm. (Stan Troutman) ▶

c.

a.

◀ **Figure 6-23** *Digging Slow Balls.* Slow moving balls require the digger to swing his arm across his body to gain the necessary height on the dig. (Stan Troutman)
▼

b.

c.

a.

b.

Figure 6-24 *Lateral Dive Recovery.* The digger protects himself by arching his body and keeping his chin and knees high while catching himself with his hands. (The Ealing Corp.)

the drill and comment on his execution. After the dive is mastered, emphasis should be on many repetitions involving diving and rolling saves. When a player automatically goes sprawling to the floor to dig the ball without any hesitation, the necessary conditioned reflex for competition has been formed.

Players should also receive plenty of instruction at each defensive court position they will be required to play. The coach can stand on a table and attack from various positions along the net to simulate game conditions.

Other players can retrieve balls and form a supply line to the coach so that the drill never has to slow down for lack of a ball. This concentrated digging drill can send the player to the floor numerous times within a short period. If repeated often enough, diving, sprawling and rolling saves will become conditioned reflexes.

The players should try and dig the ball with both arms except on lateral dives. If they can move to dig the ball without going to the floor let them do so. They can probably make a better dig and lessen the chance of injury.

When individual defense techniques have been covered, players must learn their team defensive responsibilities. The coach can use the table spike drill against three backcourt players and an off-blocker. Once defensive responsibilities are learned, two blockers can be added to field a full defensive team. Finally, the defensive team should practice against a live offense.

II

TEAM PLAY

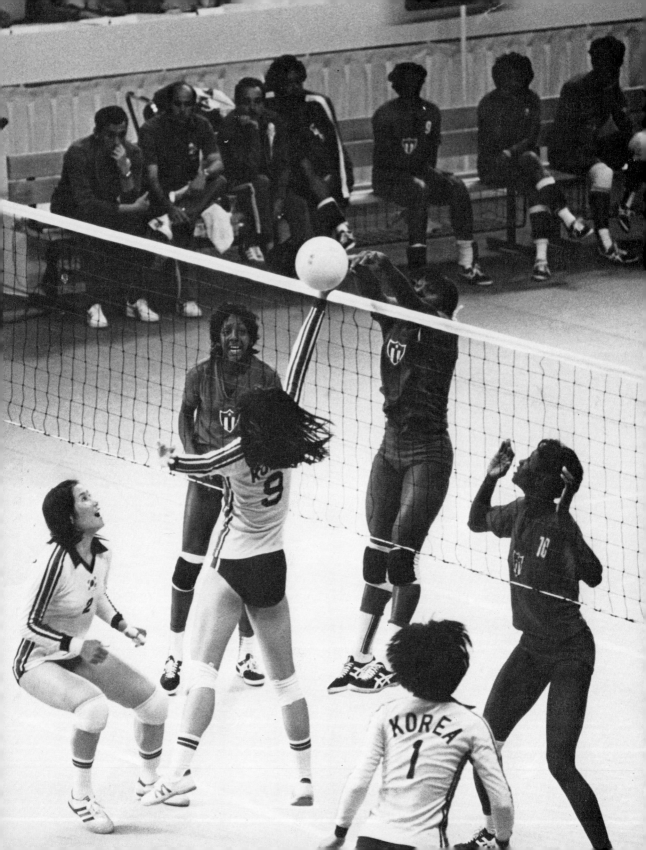

7

Offense

One of the most important decisions a coach has to make is the selection of a team offense. The offense attempts to hit the ball over the net so that the defense cannot return it. All offensive patterns call for the ball to be passed to a setter close to the net; the setter then delivers the ball to a spiker to hit into the opponents' court. The decision to use a simple or advanced attack should depend on the limitations and strengths of the team. The simplest offense is called the four spiker, two setter, or *four-two* and is the system to use with an inexperienced coach or players. A simple four-two system, with a few options, is still the best offense for a majority of high school teams.

Teams that do not pass accurately should use the four-two since one setter will always be in the front row and the other setter will be available to run down errant passes in the backcourt. In the late sixties and early seventies, most college and better open teams began using a six spiker offense

with two of the spikers setting when they rotated to the backcourt. This is known as the *six-two* offense and requires accurate passing and two setters who are good hitters. In the late seventies and eighties, the five spiker, one setter, or *five-one* offense became popular, because most teams could not find two tall mobile players who could set, spike, and block. One player who sets all the time usually becomes more proficient at setting than players who have to practice setting and spiking, and that is the main reason the five-one system is the most popular international offense. Both the six-two and five-one offenses can be simple or very complex depending on the plays the coach selects. Most teams in the USA that use the five-one and six-two systems often attempt advanced plays and options which lead to excessive errors. It is far better to run a few plays well than to be fairly good at a wide variety of plays. Complex plays are successful only if the players have the ability and practice time necessary to pass accurately. Regardless of which system is used, the play sets described in the next section can be incorporated into any front court or backcourt setter offense.

PLAY SETS

A team that passes accurately and has a good setter or setters should use play sets, which normally create situations in which only one blocker defends against the spiker. Setters should be given the freedom to call their own sets or plays. If the coach tells the setter to use only certain sets and plays in particular situations, the opposition will soon be able to predict the offensive strategy. Setters may call for a play at any time during the course of a game, before or after the serve. If the setter is not selecting the plays in an intelligent manner, a time out should be called or he should be substituted out of the game to enable the coach to confer with him about the play selection before he returns to the game.

Signals from the setter to the spiker can be given verbally or by hand signs. Some setters signal by showing a number of fingers that represent a certain play to the spiker. Some coaches prefer to speed up the procedure by using pre-arranged verbal signals. For example, a setter may say "A" to indicate a specific attack pattern to the spiker. It is really not necessary for the setter to be secretive when signaling for the play because the setter has the option of delivering the ball to another spiker when the defense stacks its block on one player.

Play sets are automatically called off if the primary setter cannot reach the pass; otherwise, the spiker or spikers are totally committed to the play. Many coaches stipulate that the setter must always signal one

spiker to expect a regular set in the event that the pass is not accurate enough to deliver the play set. When a back-up setter must step in to deliver the set, a regular set is used. In all other situations, the setter makes the final decision of to whom to deliver the ball. This stipulation motivates each spiker to put forth maximum effort in the approach because each spiker can expect to receive the set.

Six play sets and two variations on these sets enable any team to create an imaginative offense: the one-set, two-set, three-set, four-set, five-set, and regular set are standard procedure in most five-one and six-two systems. The slow-one and slow-three sets may be added if desired. Two-hitter attacks can also use all of the above sets in their offense.

The most exciting and important play in the three-hitter attack is the well-executed spike of a fast one-set delivered above the setter's head as seen in Figure 7-1.

The only way the defender can block this spike is to jump with the spiker before the ball is set, thus placing the entire offense on a one-on-one situation.

The One-Set

Spiking the one-set is a mandatory play in a successful three-hitter attack. The Japanese perfected this play to defeat the block of taller opponents by using split-second timing between setter and spiker.

To hit the one-set, the spiker moves to within a few feet of the setter as the setter is moving into position to receive the pass. The setter must gauge the spiker's approach while watching the pass. If the spiker is late, the setter may drop to a squatting position before contacting the ball in order to give the spiker time to jump (see Figure 7-2).

Figure 7-1 *The One-Set.* To run a quick offense, the spiker must jump before the setter releases the ball. (Norm Schindler)

Figure 7-2 *Setter Waiting For the Spiker.* David Olbright drops to one knee while waiting for the pass to allow Singin Smith to take off for the one-set. (Ohio State University)

a.   b.

Figure 7-3 *Elbow Leads the Way.* When hitting one-, or quick-sets, the elbow should be held high and the ball hit with a quick wrist snap and minimum arm and shoulder movement. (Andy Banachowski, *a*; Norm Schindler, *b*)

If the spiker is early, the setter must extend his arms or jump-set the ball as quickly as possible. The spiker should jump as the ball touches the setter's hands in order to be at the apex of his jump, with his spiking arm cocked as the ball is rising above the tape (see Figure 7-3a,b).

The spiker's approach and takeoff depends on how close the ball is passed to the net. When the ball is passed close to the net after serve reception, the spiker runs directly towards the setter. As long as the setter is within the court boundaries, the spiker runs to the setter and tries to get in front of him to receive the ball. Ideally the

one or quick hitter should use a three-step approach. Most players will use a left, right, left approach. After blocking in the middle, the quick hitter often uses a two-step approach because there is usually not enough time for more steps. Many coaches do not bother to teach their quick hitters which approach to use; those that do have the spiker take the last step with the left foot which serves to brake the forward momentum. When the spiker's last step hits the floor on a *close pass*, he tries to jump straight up to receive the set as shown in Figure 7-4a,b. This is the easiest ball for the setter to deliver, because even beginning setters

a.   b.

Figure 7-4 *Close Pass.* Dave Olbright is waiting for the pass with his hands held high and his fingers spread as Steve Salmons prepares to take off (*a*). Steve jumps straight up close to the setter and the net and turns his body towards the setter to hit a one-set (*b*). (Norm Schindler)

a.   b.

Figure 7-5 *Medium Pass.* The setter is preparing to release the ball as the spiker broadjumps by him towards the net (*a*). Notice that the setter is in excellent position to deliver the ball to any spiker and does not turn towards the quick hitter until after he releases the ball (*b*). (Norm Schindler)

can see the approaching attacker and the ball. Ideally the setter has moved quickly to the pass and his feet are stationary as he sets the ball. Setters can deliver the ball close to the net against small blockers and farther back when faced with tall blockers.

On a *medium pass,* when the ball is set about five feet from the net, the spiker takes off alongside the setter as he prepares to deliver the set (Figure 7-5a). The spiker broad jumps by the setter and spikes the set on its upward flight (Figure 7-5b). The setter must deliver the ball laterally, above and in front of the spiker's attacking arm. If the pass is *deep* or near the ten foot line, the spiker must take off well in front of the setter and angle his approach so that he can watch the setter release the ball and

still be in position to see the blocker (Figure 6a).

As in all quick plays, it is important for the spiker to yell as he takes off to help the setter know where he is. Many setters have trouble seeing the quick attacker on a deep pass and rely on sound to locate the spiker. The deeper the pass, the quicker the set should travel. This rule keeps the timing between the spiker's takeoff and the setter's release relatively the same. On a deep pass, the set should have enough force and height to cross the net without being touched by the spiker. A lot of side outs and points are scored on broken plays because the setter put enough force behind the "one shoot" to have the set drop to the court behind the blockers.

a.

b.

Figure 7-6 *Deep Pass.* Even though Steve Suttich is about ten feet from the net, he does not give away the play because he has kept his feet pointed at the sideline as he releases the ball in front of the quick hitter. (Norm Schindler)

The spiker has to determine when the ball is going to be passed and then use the correct approach for the close, medium, or deep pass. As he takes his last step on the takeoff, he should yell to let the setter know where he is. He should use a maximum jump to attain the greatest height possible. The height will be greater on a close pass because he will not have to broad jump. Once the spiker leaves the floor, he must have his arm cocked ready to snap quickly at the set. The quick set does not give the spiker time to wind up or use body torque; he must rely on a quick arm.

The setter must gauge the spiker's approach while watching the pass. If the spiker is late, the setter may drop to a squatting position before contacting the ball in order to give the spiker time to jump. If the spiker is early, the setter must extend his arms or jump-set the ball as quickly as possible. The setter must not turn toward the spiker before he receives the pass. This is probably the most common mistake and tips off an alert middle blocker. The setter can face the passer during serve reception and then rotate the torso so the shoulders are perpendicular to the net when the set is released as shown in Figure 7-7a,b. The setter should put enough force on the ball to make the attacker extend high above the net so he can hit sharp angles that drop in front of the backcourt defenders. Most importantly, the setter must deliver the ball in front of the spiker's attacking arm.

If the blocker jumps with the spiker, the setter may set to another player; if the blocker does not jump, the spiker should easily put the ball on the floor. When a spiker becomes very proficient at hitting

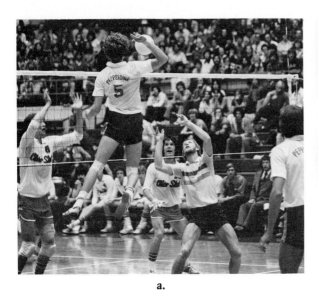

a.   b.

Figure 7-7 *Back to the Net.* Rod Wilde ignores the blockers and keeps his back to the net when delivering the ball (*a*). This is an advanced technique and is common at the international level (*b*). (Ohio State University, *a*; Richard Mackson, *b*)

one-sets, the setter may choose to deliver the ball to him even though one defender will always block against him.

At UCLA, we try and keep the set away from the middle blocker by running close to the setter, or even by the setter to keep our spiker in the seam of the block. We are successful at this because we have setters who can be taught to deliver the ball laterally and keep the set in front of the spiker's attacking arm. Our opponent's quick hitter rarely goes past an imaginary line between the setter's feet and the net, which is an easier style to learn; in our opinion, it is also easier to read and block. Most teams should use the basic approach shown in

Diagram 7-1 because their setters will have difficulty delivering the ball laterally.

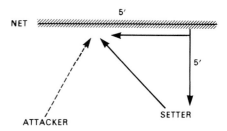

Diagram 7-1 *Basic Approach for a Quick Hit.* When the setter is 5 ft. away from the net, the spiker should angle the approach so that he arrives 5 ft. away from the setter who then delivers the ball to the spiker at a 45° angle.

Figure 7-8 *Back One-Set.* The back one-set usually gives the spiker a chance to hit crosscourt against an outside blocker. (Richard Mackson)

The slow one-set is used by players who do not have a quick armswing, and by players who can beat the middle blocker in a one-on-one situation. The spiker attacks the ball after it reaches its peak, about 2 ft. above the net. If the spiker hits the ball after it reaches its peak, he has a better opportunity to direct the spike. The ball is therefore set almost straight up to give the spiker the best opportunity to defeat the middle blocker. There is a disadvantage to the offense on a wide set, because the middle blocker does not have to commit himself until after the ball is set, and thus has a better opportunity to reach the outside spiker.

The *back one-set* shown in Figure 7-8 has become a very popular call for the area two hitter. It should only be attempted on a good pass, since the setter cannot see the spiker. Once the back one-set has been established, the middle spiker can cross behind the area two spiker in what is called a reverse X pattern.

The Two-Set

The ball in the two-set usually travels from 3 to 5 ft. above the net depending on the coach's preference. The set should be low enough to prevent a two-man block and high enough to allow the spiker to place the ball accurately. The two-set play does not require the same split-second timing as the one-set and can be hit by any good spiker. Because of the extra height on the set, the spiker usually encounters at least one blocker defending against the play. Although the approach is almost completed before the setter touches the ball, the spiker does not jump until after the setter contacts the ball. The spiker hits the ball on its downward flight; consequently, he has enough time to use a normal armswing and

body torque to spike the ball in any direction. The placement of the players along the net is determined by the placement of the pass because the spiker runs to the setter for the play. The two-set can be set forward or backward and to any one of the three attackers in combination plays such as the right cross, fake cross, and tandem.

The right cross is shown in Figure 7-9a,b. Number 4 came from the right sideline and

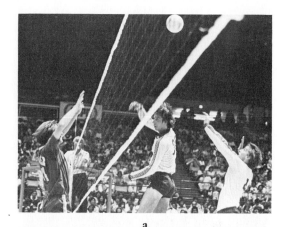

a.

b.

Figure 7-9 *The Right X.* The right cross is an excellent play to use after the offense has established the quick one-set. (Norm Schindler)

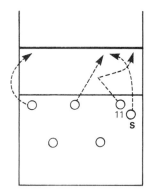

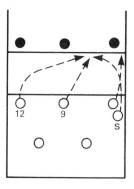

Diagram 7-2 *The Fake X.* The Cuban quick-hitter has taken the Russian middle blocker into the air to give No. 11 a one-on-one situation.

Diagram 7-3 *Tandem.* The Koreans must use the quick offense to defeat the stronger, taller, slower Russian women. Number 9 comes for the quick set, while No. 12 follows from the left sideline for a two-set.

crossed behind Number 30 who jumped for a one-set. The setter (No. 11) delivered a two or X set to the second man through on this combination play. Number 4 came from area two and used a four-step approach. All area two hitters should use a right, left, right, left four-step approach if their team runs combination plays like the right X. As the setter contacts the ball, the area two spiker should be on his left foot or second step of the four-step approach directly behind the setter. This approach allows the spiker to come in late and fast to keep the block guessing until the last split second as to his pattern; it also enables the spiker to broad jump into the set which gives him a better range and relieves the pressure on the setter to make a perfect set.

The fake X shown in Diagram 7-2 and Figure 7-10 uses a back two-set. The area two spiker pivots off his left foot during his second step six to eight feet from the net directly behind the setter. The setter should be contacting the ball as the attacker pivots and then steps right, left, and takes off for the spike. In Diagram 7-3 and Figure 7-11, the Koreans are running a tandem play against the Russians. Number 9 is in the

Figure 7-10 *The Fake X.* The Cuban quick-hitter has taken the Russian middle blocker into the air to give No. 11 a one-on-one situation. (Richard Mackson)

Figure 7-11 *Tandem.* The Koreans must use the quick offense to defeat the stronger, taller, slower Russian women. Number 9 comes for the quick set, while No. 12 follows from the left sideline for a two-set. (Richard Mackson)

air for a quick set while the area four spiker (No. 12) has come from the left sideline to hit a two-set directly behind her. The two-set can have the same height and trajectory for the tandem, X or fake X. Of course national teams with the ideal practice situations have several variations of the tandem, X, and fake X sets. To keep it simple and accurate at the high school and college level, using one type of two-set for all three plays is recommended. Figures 7-12 and 7-13 show variations of two-sets delivered by a professional setter in the defunct International Volleyball Association.

The tandem X utilizes a two-set to the right side hitter (No. 13), who takes off just as the quick hitter (No. 4) is landing in Fig-

a.   b.   c.

Figure 7-12 *Tandem X.* The two-set is delivered a few feet from the net directly behind the quick hitter to enable the spiker to hit over the middle blocker as he returns to the floor. (Tom Leja)

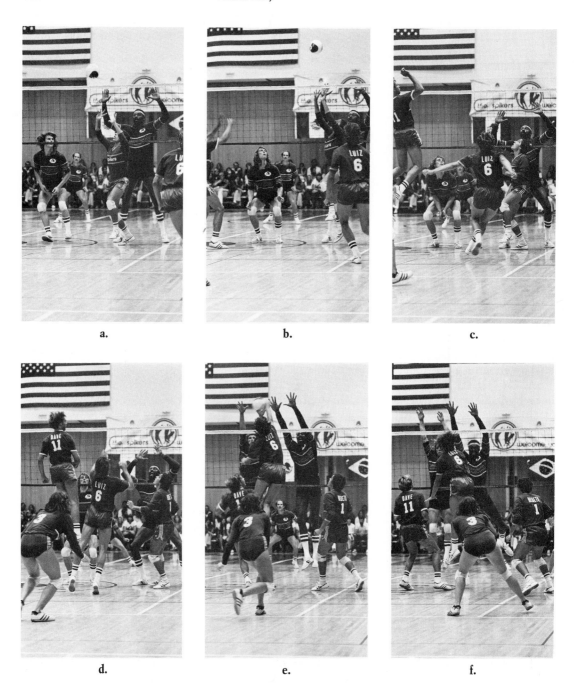

Figure 7-13 *Inside Tandem.* The tactic is for the quick hitter (No. 11) to draw the middle blocker into the air. The middle blocker was not fooled because No. 11 was late and still on the floor when the setter released the ball enabling the defense to form a two-man block. (Tom Leja)

ure 7-12b. Notice how Number 13 stays near the sideline in Figure 7-12a, so the middle blocker will concentrate on the quick hitter. The success of this play depends on a late, fast approach and takeoff by Number 13, and the placement of the two-set about two feet from the net behind the quick hitter. If the spiker takes off as the quick hitter is returning to the floor, the middle blocker (Figure 7-12c) should also be on the floor when he jumps with the quick hitter. Another play utilizing the two-set is the *inside* tandem. This entire play is shown in Figure 7-13a,b,c,d,e,f. In 7-13a, Number 6 takes the first step of his four-step approach with the right foot directly at the net as the ball is descending a few feet from the setter's hand. The second step with the left foot is taken eight feet from the net behind the setter at the same time the setter is releasing the ball. Up to this point, the footwork for the area two or playset hitter is exactly the same as for the right X, fake X, and tandem X. On the third step, shown in Figure 7-13c, the hitter takes a long step (right) to position himself close to the setter. As the left foot touches the floor, the spiker takes off and attacks the

ball. The blockers, Roberts and Chamberlain, read this play well and did not jump with the quick hitter, but were able to form a two-man block as shown in Figure 7-13d,e.

The Three-Set

The three-set is delivered 10 ft. from the left sideline as quickly as the players' capabilities will allow. The height of the set depends on the height the hitter can attain above the net. The setter should jump-set every ball that is passed close to the net; the jump-set is particularly effective in speeding up the three-set and giving the middle blocker less time to react as shown in Figure 7-14a,b,c. The spiker jumps as the setter is contacting the ball. The setter delivers the ball as fast and as high as the attacker can spike the ball. The ball, in Figure 7-14b, is between two and three feet above the net. Since the middle blocker is usually late, the best place to spike the three-set is into area one (see Figure 7-14c). When a team uses the three-set in its offense, the easiest position for the quick or middle hitter to start at is ten feet from the left sideline at the three meter line. Then

a.   **b.**   **c.**

Figure 7-14 *Jump-Set.* At the collegiate level, many coaches are insisting that their setter jump-set every ball that is passed close to the net to give the blockers less time to react. (Stan Troutman)

Figure 7-15 *Watching the Pass.* All players should look at the pass so they can step in and set if it is going off target. (Stan Troutman)

the quick hitter runs straight ahead for a three-set and at the setter for a one-set. The UCLA men first began using this set in 1969 and have put it in the yearly offense about 50 percent of the time since then. We usually have our quick hitter start fifteen feet from the sideline for serve reception purposes and then run the one or three approach from that position. Regardless of where the quick hitter starts, he should look over his left shoulder when the ball is served to his left as shown in Figure 7-15.

When the ball is passed to the quick hitter's left in area six, he should pivot on the right foot towards the passer with the left foot back and use a three-step approach to get to the set. The great majority of players

naturally take their last step with the left foot so the normal procedure is for the quick hitter to step left, right, left. When the ball is served to the middle hitter's right side, he can look over his right shoulder to area one or pivot on his left foot to watch a pass from area six. If the attacker pivots, the right foot will be back and the player rocks off this foot and steps left, right, left. The two-step approach is usually seen in the transition from blocking to attacking to save time. Some attackers only need a two-step approach from the three meter line during serve reception. In Figure 7-16a, Steve Salmons takes his first step with his left foot; in Figure 7-16b, he takes his second and last step. In a quick transition the mid-

Figure 7-16 *Broadjump Takeoff.* Better quick hitters can use a two, three, or even four-step approaches when they have a long route to the point of attack. The spiker above uses a two-step approach and a broadjump to get to the three-set. (Norm Schindler)

Figure 7-17 *Vertical Takeoff.* When the pass is close to the net, the spiker takes off a few feet from the center line and tries to jump straight up to hit the three-set. (Stan Troutman)

dle blocker must get to the point of attack
starting on either foot. Because the ball has
been passed about eight feet from the net,
Steve is going to broad jump into the set
following the same rules explained earlier
in the chapter for the one-set. Notice that
the feet are together and pointing toward
the net in Figure 7-16b, as Steve is preparing to take off. The right foot should always be behind the left so the body can
easily turn toward the setter and the feet
should be close together to jump forward
and upward when the pass is medium or
deep. When the pass is close to the net on
the three-set or one-set, the hitter (No. 9 in
Figure 7-17a) blocks his forward momentum by pointing his feet at the setter and
putting his left foot ahead of his center of
gravity. Some quick hitters take their last
step with their right leg; but as mentioned
earlier, the overwhelming majority of players take the last step with the left leg. This
is convenient since the area two or combination spiker has to use a four-step approach with the last step with the left foot
to successfully execute the fake X attack.
Therefore, players that take the last step
with the right leg in area three and four
will have to also learn to take the last step
with the left leg in area two if using Xs and
fake X plays. This has not been a problem
for experienced players, but using two different approaches would probably thoroughly confuse beginners. When taking off
to hit the three-set, the right foot has to be
back to allow the spiker to rotate his body
to the right and to put him in better spiking
position, as shown in Figure 7-18. The slow
three-set can be used by the left attacker
when the middle spiker is approaching for
a one-set. The set is lobbed 10 ft. from the
left sideline. It is only effective when the
middle attacker can "freeze" the middle
blocker to allow the left spiker to hit the
ball crosscourt. The height of the set de-

Figure 7-18 *Face the Setter.* The quick hitter
turns and faces the setter to give him a greater
range when hitting the one-set or three-set. The
setter delivers the ball very quickly to prevent
a two-man block from forming. (Norm Schindler)

Figure 7-19 *Four-Set to a Left Hander.* The ball
should be set high and wide to give the spiker
the option of hitting down the line or crosscourt. (Bud Fields)

pends on the jumping ability of the attacker.

The Four-Set

The four-set is placed close to the sideline in area four. The height and speed of the set depend on the jumping ability and quickness of the attacker. When setting left-handed spikers, as shown in Figure 7-19, the ball should be delivered high and wide so the spiker can force the blocker to stay on the line and open up the crosscourt attack.

When the attacker is quick, often a very low fast "shoot set" is used. This is a particular favorite of the Japanese women and is shown in Figure 7-20.

In Figure 7-21, the Russian blocker takes the crosscourt spike as the Polish player hits the four-set down the line.

Figure 7-21 *Tactical Maneuvering.* On one-on-one situations better end blockers will make a crosscourt move because the great majority of the four-sets are spiked in that direction. The spiker above faces crosscourt and then deceptively allows the set to cross his body and spikes down the line. (Richard Mackson)

The Five-Set

The five-set is a back lob set to the spiker on the right sideline. It is designed to create a one-on-one situation for the off-hand spiker. On a perfect pass, the five-set travels about 10 ft. before the spiker contacts the ball. If the pass is made away from the net, the ball must be set higher to give the attacker time to see the block and the ball from a more difficult approach.

The High Set

This is usually delivered to the outside attacker in area two or four. The one, two, three, four, and five sets are used to get one-on-one situations for the attacker; the high set should be used to take advantage

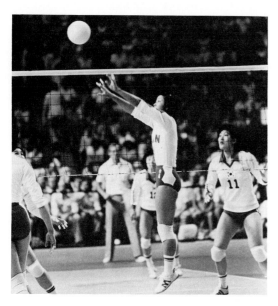

Figure 7-20 *The "Shoot" Four.* This ball is delivered as fast as the setter can release it to prevent the middle blocker from participating in the block. (Richard Mackson)

Figure 7-22 *The Five-Set.* The setter releases this back set with an arched back as his hands extend over his head. (Stan Troutman)

Figure 7-23 *The Mismatch.* The only time the high set is used following a good pass in the UCLA offense is when a tall spiker is opposed by a small blocker. In this situation, it does not matter if a two-man block is up, as the spiker will attempt to hit over the small blocker. (Norm Schindler)

of tall spikers being opposed by a small blocker. In Figure 7-23, Number 5 is a 6 ft. blocker opposing a 6 ft. 7 in. attacker who will try and spike over his position. When the ball is passed inaccurately, the best set to use is a high set to the outside attacker. When the spiker contacts the ball with full arm extension high above the net and hits a flat shot, as shown in Figure 7-24, the defenders will find it very difficult to block

Figure 7-24 *High Flat Shot.* The spiker who can contact the ball high above the net will rarely be blocked for a point when he hits for the opponents' back line. The high flat shot should be hit over the end blocker in the middle-back defense. (Norm Schindler) ▶

Figure 7-25 *Face Line—Spike Crosscourt.* The spiker reaches out and contacts the set before it crosses her shoulder. By facing the line, she keeps the middle blocker's arms in a vertical position and opens up the court. (Richard Mackson)

Figure 7-27 *Off-Speed Spike.* When the defense is expecting a hard spike, the blockers will often net and the other defenders will be too "dug in" to field a soft spike looped over the block. (Norm Schindler)

Figure 7-26 *Face Crosscourt—Hit Line.* By facing crosscourt and then hitting across the body, the attacker keeps the middle blocker thinking about protecting the middle and may open up the line or a seam between the blockers. (Norm Schindler)

for a point. When spiking against a two-man block, it is also important to disguise the direction of the attack to confuse the block. In Figure 7-25, the Cuban spiker faces the line and very deceptively spikes away from her body. In Figure 7-26, Singin Smith turns his body towards the setter and faces crosscourt before hitting across his body to defeat the Japanese blockers.

Besides varying the direction of the spike, it is also important to vary the force as illustrated by Peter Ehrman in Figure 7-27 as he contacts the ball under the midline to loop it over the block to an open spot on the court. Very often the block is confused on this type of shot and commits a net violation.

Experienced spikers will also use dinks (Figure 7-28) and wipe-off shots (Figure 7-29) when attacking high sets against a two-man block. Most great spikers diversify their attack trying to direct the ball to points in the court where the defense is not expecting it. Putting the ball away against a single

Figure 7-28 *The Dink.* Hard spikers like David Saunders should occasionally dink the ball on a good set to discourage the defense from always staying deep where they have a better chance of digging the spike. (Norm Schindler)

Figure 7-29 *The Wipe-Off.* The best tactic to utilize on a close set is to push the ball off the end blockers' arm so it rebounds out-of-bounds or into the antenna. (Norm Schindler)

Figure 7-30 *Backcourt Spiker.* Teams that are fortunate enough to have a strong hitter who can spike from the backcourt should set him in all rotations. (Norm Schindler)

block is not that difficult; the outstanding outside spikers can put the high sets away by varying tactical maneuvers to meet the varying defensive situations.

Setting Backcourt Spikers

When a team is using a front court setter, the ball can be set to a backcourt spiker about six to seven feet from the net. The attacker takes off from behind the three meter line and broad jumps to the set. When the two front court spikers are involved in combination plays and the pass is bad, a backcourt spiker can be used to spike a high set. A strong spiker can be set in any position on the court and, in fact, should be in a five-one attack. In Figure 7-30, the ball

is set about seven feet off the net at the proper depth for a backcourt spiker.

FOUR-TWO

The basic offensive alignment is the *four-two*. The four-two uses four players (spikers or hitters) who are responsible for hitting the ball over the net and two players (setters) who are responsible for setting the ball to the spiker. This is the basic formation for teams that cannot pass well and for beginning coaches and players. This offense has not won a major men's or women's national collegiate championship since the 1960s and probably never will. However, it

Figure 7-31 *M-Formation.* A high pass is dropping into the center of the court within two to four feet of the net. The setter is in a good position to receive the pass. (Los Angeles City Unified School District)

is the system that most high school teams in the country should be using.

M-Formation

The M-formation—the first formation that beginning players should learn—positions the setter at the middle-front of the court. Many teachers require each player to set when rotating to the middle-front position in order to give every player an opportunity to develop setting skills. In competition, however, coaches only allow the best setters to set.

In Figure 7-31, the setter is in the middle-front position, ready to receive a pass. The five remaining players are lined up in a receiving formation that resembles the letter "M." The set should travel in an arc at a height of 6 to 10 ft. above the net and drop about 2 ft. from the net at the outside right- or left-front corner of the net (see Figure 7-32).

Setter Switch

When the front row setter rotates to an outside position, he must switch to the center after the serve so that he is in position to receive the pass. The switch starts as soon as the ball is served; the setter can remain in this position until the ball is dead. Before the next serve, the setter must return to his original position.

In Figure 7-33, the setter is in the right-front position. He should start about 5 ft.

Figure 7-32 *Set.* The setter has placed the ball high in the air for the spiker in the right-front position. (Los Angeles City Unified School District)

Figure 7-33 *M-Formation: Setter in the Right-Front Court.* The team's two best ball-handlers are setters who stand diagonally opposite one another so that one setter is always in the front row. (Stan Troutman)

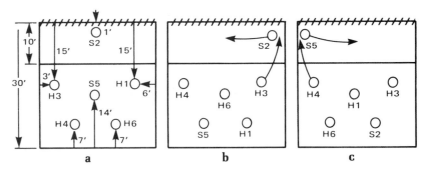

Diagram 7-4 *Setter Switch.* The setter (No. 5) is in the middle (*a*); on the right (*b*); and on the left (*c*).

from the sideline to allow the spiker on the right to maintain a normal serve receiving position, as in Diagram 7-4. The rest of the players line up in an M-formation as they did when the setter was in the middle.

When the front-row setter rotates to an outside position (Digram 7-4b,c), a switch to the center of the court should be made to put the setter in a better position to set to either spiker (Diagram 7-4b,c). The "switch" is started as soon as the ball is contacted for the serve. The setter must return to the original position in the rotation before the next serve.

The two setters line up diagonally opposite each other, as do the two best spikers, so that one will always be in the front row. As basic fundamentals are learned and as skill and experience increase, the strongest spikers become apparent.

As the setter switches into the middle of the line up from the outside, one of the spikers must switch with the setter. If the best spikers are lined up so that they precede a setter in the service order, they should switch so that they hit twice from their on-hand, or left-front, side; of course, this applies to a right-handed spiker. A left-handed spiker should line up so that he hits twice

from his on-hand, or right, side. In Diagram 7-4b, hitter No. 4, who is in the left-front position, spikes from the on-hand side as setter No. 2 switches onto the center. In Diagram 7-4c, after rotation of setter No. 2 to the back row, the other setter (No. 5) comes to the net. Hitter No. 4 now switches with the setter next to him and hits for the second time from the left-front position.

There is no need to switch when the setters rotate to the middle of the court. The front spikers pull back off the net to about center court, with the left-front player very near the left sideline and the right-front player crowding toward the center of the court, slightly toward the side from which the opponents are serving. The center-back player is in the center of the court, even with or slightly behind the front-row spikers, in order to cover the area vacated by the setter who is at the net. The left- and right-back players stand between the front-row players, about 7 ft. from the backline.

Facing the Stronger Hitter

If one of the two spikers is significantly stronger than the other, the setter in the

Figure 7-34 *Facing the Strongest Hitter.* By moving as far to the side of the court as possible without overlapping the off-hand spiker's position, the setter (left foreground) can deliver a larger percentage of sets to his on-hand spiker (far right). (Stan Troutman)

middle-front rotation may move to the opposite side of the court and face the stronger player. Since forward sets are usually delivered with greater accuracy than over-the-head or back sets, this tactic allows the setter to make a better percentage play. Since the setter is still in the middle-front position, he may not overlap the right-front spiker.

Backing Up the Passer

When the ball is served, at least one player should back up the passer. If the ball is served to the middle-back, as in Figure 7-35, the player behind him moves directly

in line with the serve in the event the frontcourt player decides to let the ball go by him. Spikers do not begin their approach until they see that the pass will reach the setter. In the event of a bad pass, all five players must be ready to step in and set the ball to one of the players at the front corners.

Front row receivers should not take balls above waist height and should step away from serves that are too high and "open the lanes" for backcourt passers. The player who wants to receive the serve should call, "Mine!" If the serve is in, the player should say nothing; if the serve is out, they should call, "Out!"

Figure 7-35 *Backing Up the Passer.* The right-back player is shown backing up the middle-back passer in the four-two formation. (Stan Troutman)

Backing Up the Spiker

After the set, all players back up the spiker to handle *block rebounds.* This means covering the spiker in case the ball rebounds off the blocker's hands back into their court.

If the ball is set to the left-front spiker, the setter and other players move quickly in unison to a designated area. The left back comes in behind the spiker down the line from about 2 to 5 ft. behind the spiker—depending on how close the set is to the net and the abilities of the opposing blockers. The center-back player stations himself behind the spiker at the same distance as the left back, but between the left back and the setter. The setter completes the half-circle that surrounds the spiker by positioning himself about 2 to 3 ft. from the net. The right-front player pulls back off the net toward the rear of the court, and the right back moves toward the center of the court to the left side near the base line; both are then ready for a ball hit off the block.

If the set is to the right-front player, the coverage is exactly the same on the opposite side of the court. If the ball is set within 18 in. of the net against aggressive blockers, the back-up players should crowd very close to the spiker in anticipation of the ball being blocked straight down. This tactic is not necessary against a small or poor block.[1]

[1]Allen E. Scates and Jane Ward, *Volleyball* (Boston: Allyn and Bacon, 1975), p. 46.

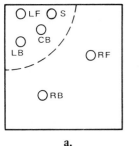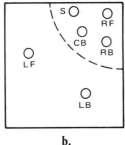

Diagram 7-5 *Four-Two Spiker Coverage.* Covering the spiker should be stressed constantly during practice. Sets to the left front (*a*); and right front (*b*) are shown.

Once the players reach their assigned positions, they should squat close to the floor, with their arms outstretched and weight forward. Even All-American performers sometimes lose their concentration and watch the play. The key to backing up the spiker is for the closest three players to stay low to give them more time and distance to react to the block; the other two players are in a medium defensive position to enable them to run down deep block defections.

FIVE-ONE

Teams that win with the five spiker, one setter attack have an outstanding setter. Of the eight major national collegiate men's and women's championships won by five-one offenses since 1970, they all have had a great setter who could convert bad passes into perfect sets. Two of the setters who have come out of the programs at USC have become world class performers and set for the USA Men's and Women's National Team. Debbie Green and Dusty Dvorak can convert deep passes into one's, two's, and three-sets from the three-meter line and

Table 7-1 *Major National College Champions Using a 5-1 Since 1970*

	Men		Women
1975	UCLA	1976	USC
1977	USC	1977	USC
1978	PEPPERDINE	1980	USC
1980	USC	1981	USC

deeper passes into excellent outside sets. These five-one teams also had one or two primary hitters to carry the spiking load particularly when in the two-hitter rotations.

In 1980, USC won the NCAA Men's Championships with a spiker named Pat Powers, who received 48 of the team's 159 sets. Even though USC did not let Powers receive a single serve and he probably did not dig more than a few balls, he was their key player. When things got tough, they set him in the backcourt, and he put the ball away. His spiking percentage was .333 compared to the USC team average of .214, and he had 23 of USC's 61 kills. The typical six-two offense distributes the sets rather evenly as verified by the 1981 NCAA Volleyball Box Score. UCLA ran a six-two offense and the first six players listed started and hit between 33 and 47 sets. USC ran a five-one offense and their starters had a range of 10 to 81 sets. Tim Hovland and John Hedlund accounted for 160 of their team's 247 sets. The five-one offense usually designs combination plays to set up the key spikers. The problem is that if the setter or key spiker is having an off day, there has to be a substitute available to take his place or the team will lose against a competitive opponent. Teams that do not have a lot of talent can do quite well with this offense providing they have a fine setter, two very good spikers, and they can

Table 7-2 *NCAA Volleyball Box Score.*

UCLA	NO	ATTACK K	E	TA	PCT.
Peter Ehrman	2	16	5	33	.333
Ricci Luyties	11	21	10	47	.234
Rick Amon	23	15	9	37	.162
Steve Salmons	29	24	6	38	.474
Steve Gulnac	30	18	4	35	.400
Karch Kiraly	31	16	9	40	.175
Dave Saunders	4	4	4	9	.000
Doug Partie	20	0	0	1	.000
Team Total		114	47	240	.279
Game 1		22	9	44	.295
Game 2		18	5	34	.382
Game 3		29	13	59	.271
Game 4		14	10	39	.103
Game 5		31	5	61	.426

USC	NO	K	E	TA	PCT.
Fulvio Danilas	3	11	2	18	.500
Bill Stetson	5	6	3	12	.250
Steve Timmons	6	16	3	38	.342
Tim Hovland	10	31	10	71	.296
John Hedlund	11	33	15	89	.202
Robert Chavez	15	2	1	10	.100
John Morrow	2	0	0	1	.000
Todd Miller	4	0	1	2	(.500)
Steve Rottman	8	0	0	2	.000
Greg Irvin	12	2	0	4	.500
Team Total		101	35	247	.267
Game 1		24	6	47	.383
Game 2		16	13	45	.067
Game 3		14	5	47	.191
Game 4		14	3	36	.305
Game 5		32	8	66	.364

FINALS	1	2	3	4	5
UCLA	11	15	15	8	15
USC	15	7	11	15	13

CODES: NOTES:
K—Kill   TA—Total Attack   UCLA Takes Title
E—Error   PCT—Percent   USC Takes 2nd

REFEREE: Davenport
UMPIRE: Ricketts

avoid injuries. Currently on the international level the best teams use a five-one offense.

When the setter rotates to the front row, he can spike a good pass or jump-set to another spiker. The setter must be enough of an offensive threat to delay one blocker. Ideally, the setter should be tall and left-handed to be able to block on the right side and have options of spiking the pass or of jump-setting to the other two front-court players. When the blocker does not jump with the front court setter, he can attack the ball. In Figure 7-36, setter Karch Kiraly is hitting the ball to area four with a left-hand round-house spike.

Figure 7-36 *Front-Court Setter.* When the setter is in the front court, he should have the capability to spike or dink with either hand from a setting position. (Norm Schindler)

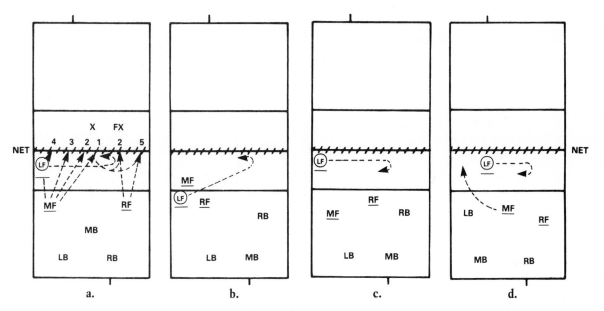

Diagram 7-6 *Setter in the Left Front.* The two hitters can spike all of the sets described earlier in the chapter from any of the starting positions shown in *a, b, c,* or *d.* In 7-4*a,* some of the possible routes of the spikers are diagrammed. The left spiker (MF) can easily hit a four, three, two, or one, and the right spiker (RF) can hit an X, back two, or fake X, and a five-set. The left spiker could also run to the right sideline to hit a back-two or five-set, if the ball was passed accurately.

Two-Hitter Formations

There are many different ways that teams can line up to receive the serve. A few rules must be remembered to prevent violations. Firstly, there can be no side-to-side overlapping between the front-row players, and no side-to-side overlapping between the back row players. The exception is the server, who is excluded from the overlap rule. This means that at the time the ball is served, the middle-front player cannot be as close to the right sideline as the right front, nor as close to the left sideline as the left front. In the back row, the middle back cannot be as close to the right sideline as the right back, nor as close to the left sideline as the left back. The second point to remember is no back-row player can be as close to the net as the corresponding front-row player.

Although the left-back player cannot be in front of the left front, he could be in front of the middle front and right-front player. The formation in Diagram 7-6a is the standard way most teams line-up that do not use combination plays. This is ideal for setting fours and fives. The middle-front (MF) spiker can also hit threes, twos, and ones, while the right front can also hit Xs or fake Xs. The formations shown in Diagram 7-6b,c are excellent for hiding a poor passer (RB) and giving him the easy area two serve receiving responsibility. If a team has a strong front court player who can attack from behind the three-meter line, he should be placed opposite the setter; then he will never have to receive a serve in the backcourt and will always be available to take off from behind the three-meter line and spike the ball when the two-hitter offense bogs down. In Diagram 7-6b, the three front-court players are stacked on the left sideline, while the right-back player is nestled close to the right sideline where the server will have to lob the ball to make him receive it. The setter can talk to both hitters in this position and alternate quick hitting and playset hitting assignments, while keeping the right-back player available for a high set six to seven feet from the net in area one. A back-row player must clearly take off from behind the attack line, and after contacting the ball may land in front of the attack line. A spiker with a good jump can be set several feet in front of the attack line. If a five-man receiving formation is desired, the right-front player can be moved to area three (see Diagram 7-6c). If the left-back player is a weak passer, the formation used in Diagram 7-6d can be used to protect him. The middle-front player can still hit fours from this position. The backcourt players in all of the formations can run routes to confuse the blockers as if they were eligible spikers; the backcourt player, who lines up to receive near the front court, can do the most convincing job. The frontcourt setter can further confuse the blockers by moving into the backcourt as if he was in the back row and penetratng to the net from behind the three-meter line. When the setter is in the middle front, the basic formation is the W as diagrammed in Diagram 7-7a. In Diagram 7-7b, the middle-front setter lines up behind the middle-back player and then moves in front of him just prior to the server contacting the ball. If the middle-back player is a poor passer this relieves him from receiving hard serves, and he can hold the middle blocker by approaching for quick sets as a decoy; then the setter can deliver play sets to one of the legal spikers. Of course,

if the middle back is capable of putting the ball away when taking off behind the attack line, the coach may not want to use him as a decoy. In Diagram 7-7c, all the front-court players are in a stack formation in area four; this allows the setter to talk directly to them to set up plays. The stack is a good formation for varying the attack when both hitters can hit quick sets and playsets. The setter looks like he is in the backcourt in Diagram 7-7d, and the right-back player can run decoy patterns to hold the end and middle blockers. The right-front player is at the net to block short serves and still recover to hit quick sets when he misses the serve. He can also start on the attack line where he has more range to loop outside to area two and four. In Diagram 7-7e, the left back moves to the front row and can run decoy patterns. This formation is very confusing to blockers as it looks exactly like three hitters in the front row. The setter can exploit this situation by hitting a close pass without the defenders blocking. When the setter is in the right front, the basic W formation is as shown in Diagram 7-8a. By moving the middle-front spiker up towards the attack line in area two, the middle-back player may move up to the front row and try to convince the middle blocker he is a quick hitter (Diagram 7-8b). In Diagram 7-8c, the formation hides the player opposite the setter (LB) and relieves him of all serve receiving responsibility; he is also in an excellent position for a back-row attacker. When the right-front setter lines up behind the right-back spiker (Diagram 7-8d), he must be sure to move in front of the spiker before the ball is contacted by the server or he will be out of rotation. This formation will confuse many umpires, who will mistakenly call a side out for overlapping, because the setter is moving before the ball is served. In Dia-

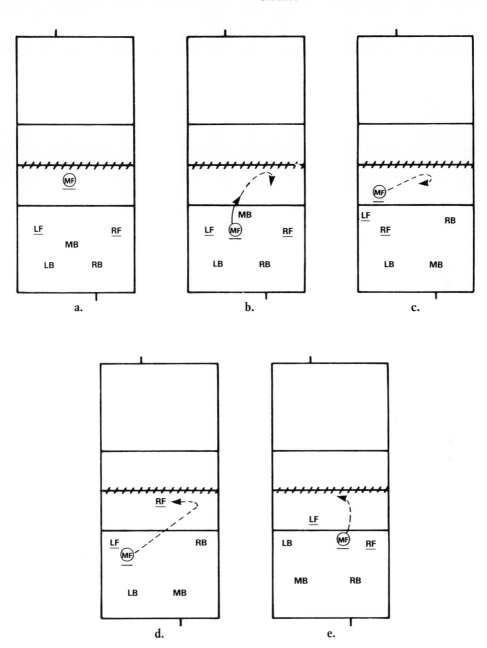

Diagram 7-7 *Setter in the Middle Front.* Teams should practice more than one formation to take advantage of tactical situations that may arise. For example, if the ace spiker is in the left front (LF), and a weak blocker is opposing the area-two spiker, the formation in Diagram 7-6a should be used. The right front (RF) could run a back-one route to draw the blocker in and the left front could hit a five-set.

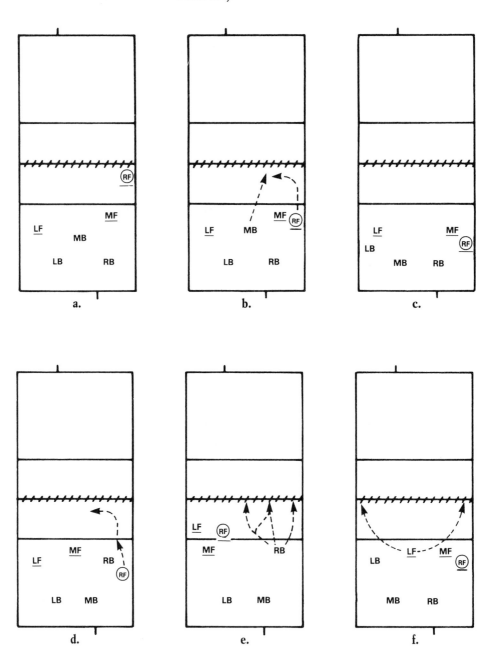

Diagram 7-8 *Setter in the Right Front.* This rotation is the favorite starting position of five-one teams at the beginning of a game. It is easy to disguise as a three-hitter attack as diagrammed in *b, c, d,* and *f,* and gives the setter a chance to attack a close pass.

gram 7-8e, we have the stack offense that puts both spikers on the sideline and uses the right-back player as a spiking decoy. When the left-front spiker can hit equally well from all areas, it is advantageous to start him in the center of the court and send him to the weakest end blocker, as shown in Diagram 7-8f.

SIX-TWO

In the three-hitter attack, all six players can spike. Two spikers are designated as setter-hitters because of their superior ball-handling ability. The three players at the net spike and one back row player sets. This formation offers skilled players an opportunity for multiple offensive plays.

Coaches find that most players prefer the three-hitter attack over the two-hitter attack because it usually divides the sets on an equal basis and does not depend on one or two players to carry the spiking load. If the offense is executed correctly, spikers have an opportunity to hit the ball against one or no blockers.

The Pass

The attack usually functions in direct relationship to the accuracy of the first pass. Longer practices and concentrated individual and team passing drills are needed to perfect passing techniques.

Since a poor pass in this system destroys the offensive patterns by forcing the weaker ball-handlers to set and the weaker spikers to hit, it is not beneficial to use this offense unless players can pass accurately. If a team is continually forced into the four-two system by bad passes, it is better to play a straight four-two on the serve reception and allow the best ball-handlers to set the best

Figure 7-37 *The Pass.* The pass is the most important offensive technique in a combination attack. (Norm Schindler)

hitters. A poor ball control team may elect to use the three-hitter attack only on the "free ball," when it can be passed accurately.

On-Hand Spiking

If the ball is passed within 5 ft. of the net and approximately 8 to 12 ft. from the right sideline, the setter can easily deliver a front set to either the left- or center-front spikers, who will approach the set from their advantageous on-hand side.

Right-handed spikers have an excellent opportunity to boost their spiking efficiency because they approach the set from their strongest side in two out of three rotations. The off-hand spiker, who approaches from behind the setter in the right front, is often relatively ignored by the blockers who tend to concentrate on the quick hitter.

Back-Row Setter

In the three-hitter attack, the setter always comes from the back row. They are placed diagonally opposite each other and a setter is assigned to each of the three back row positions. When a slow setter is in the left-back position, it is difficult for him to run across the court to the right of center, turn, face the two on-hand hitters, and set the ball.

A few teams revert to a four-two play set when their setter is in the left-back position. Most teams use a four-man receiving pattern when the setter is in the left-back position and move both the setter and left-front spiker up to the net. This gives the setter a shorter distance to run to the predetermined passing area and enables the spiker preceding the setter to hit the quick set in the middle when in the left-front and middle-front positions. This type of offensive specialization increases the effectiveness of spikers and setters.

Six-Two Serve Reception

In lining up to receive the serve, the three front players move away from the net to about midcourt. The left-front player plays a few feet off the left sideline and the right-front player moves in a direct line between the server and the right-back corner of the court. The middle-front player stands between these players. The left- and right-back players play about 6 ft. behind and between the front-row players. Players must assume their positions as quickly as possible so they will not be surprised by a quick serve. Every player must anticipate receiving the serve. The front-row players should let balls go that are above the waist. Backcourt players should call "Mine!" when they want to receive the serve. If the ball is above the

Figure 7-38 *Two On-Hand Hitters.* The setter should run to his assigned position ten feet from the right sideline, close to the net, to await the pass and face area four to deliver the set. This usually enables him to deliver the easier front set to two of his attackers. (Norm Schindler)

backcourt players' shoulders, it will be called out. The player closest to the receiver should yell "Out!" on long or wide serves and say nothing on good serves.

Receivers should watch the server even before he has the ball. Most servers stand near the sideline when serving crosscourt and 7 to 10 ft. from the sideline when serving down the line. Other servers move up

Figure 7-39 *Watching the Pass.* All players should watch the pass closely, so they can set the ball if the primary setter has trouble reaching it. (Norm Schindler)

to the endline to serve short to a front-row player. Almost all servers point their front foot toward the area to which they intend to serve. A few good teams learn to take advantage of a clue like this by adjusting their position a half step or so toward the area to which the serve is aimed.

Players should move directly in front of the ball whenever possible and should avoid receiving the serve while backing up. When balls are served in the seam of two positions, the player moving toward the target area is in the best tactical position to receive the serve. When one receiver is superior to another, the coach may designate the seam to be up to two-thirds of the area toward the inferior receiver, rather than the mid-line between the players. The traditional method for the passer is to use a slide step to move toward the ball and point the outside foot to the target area before contact. Many coaches now teach the passer to put the same foot forward regardless of where the serve is received. When the re-

ceiver contacts the ball, all five players turn and watch the passer in case they must set an inaccurately passed ball (Figure 7-39).

In any system, the jump-set is used effectively by the front-row player, who reacts with split-second timing to the opposing block. If the blocker does not jump with the setter, the setter delivers a one-set; if the blocker does jump, he sets the ball to an end spiker and creates a one-on-one blocking situation. The jump-set is used by backcourt setters to confuse the block.

Backing Up the Spiker

When backing up the hitter, the two spikers who do not receive the set and the setter from the back row must move quickly to form a semicircle around the hitter.

The depth at which the three front players supporting the spiker play depends on the closeness of the set, the ability of the opposing blockers, and the spiking habits of the attacker. Attackers who hit low tend

Figure 7-40 *Jump One-Set.* The jump one-set forces the blocker to jump with the quick hitter instead of waiting to see where the ball will be delivered. If the blocker guesses incorrectly, he will be out of the play. (Norm Schindler)

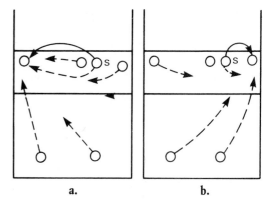

Diagram 7-9 *Covering the Outside Set.* The set may be to the left front (*a*); or to the right front (*b*).

to be blocked straight down and require supporting players to move close to the net in low positions. Small blockers tend to soft block the ball deep into the attackers' court so supporting players should stay deeper in the court.

The two players providing secondary coverage fill the gaps in between the front-line players and cover the ball that rebounds deep in the court. The setter is the key player who moves into the area where most of the blocked rebounds fall. Setters must be reminded to follow their set, particularly when setting over their heads.

In Diagram 7-9a, the ball is set to the left-front spiker; the center front has approached and jumped for the one-set. The center front must now move quickly to assume the "back-up" position about 2 to 3 ft. from the net. The setter, in turn, must go around the center-front spiker to get into position behind the spiker and between the left back and center front. The remaining

players back up the spiker as they would in the four-two system.

In Diagram 7-10a, the center spiker receives the set. The outside spikers must move in quickly to back up the hitter while the setter moves to get behind the hitter and between the two outside spikers. The

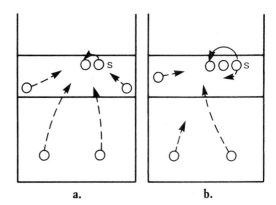

Diagram 7-10 *Covering Play Sets.* Supporting players must get close to the spiker when opposed by strong blockers (*a*). The right-cross play uses a two-set to the right-front spiker, who crosses behind the middle spiker (*b*).

two back-row players are deep between the setter and the outside spikers.

In Diagram 7-10b, the middle attacker is still in the air feigning a one-play when the ball is hit; he is obviously out of the play. The setter steps toward the attacker as the left-front and right-back players form the rest of the semicircle. The left-back player covers deep rebounds off the block.

Player Specialization

Offensive plays should be based on the physical strengths and qualifications of team members. Until the coach knows who the best six players are, it is impossible to refine the three-hitter attack. Players should be trained to take advantage of their physical capacities in order to perform specific assignments on the offense.

From 1970 to 1983, UCLA won ten NCAA Volleyball Championships using a slightly different three-hitter attack with each team. Beginning with the 1974 season, UCLA concentrated on three positions: the quick spiker, the power spiker,

and the setter. The quick spiker hits the one-set from all front-court positions (as well as other sets in area two) and plays the middle blocker position. After the quick spiker blocks the middle, he hits a one-set during any scoring opportunity. The power spiker hits in the left front in his left and middle rotations (see Diagram 7-11b,c) and blocks on the left side. This player hits from the left during any scoring opportunity. The setter hits left, middle, and right and blocks the right side. During a scoring opportunity, the setter is a right-side specialist. Substitutes are designated for the three positions as quick, power, and setter and pick up the same offensive assignments as the first team when they enter the game. When the UCLA team is on defense, the players are always stationed in their specialty areas, ready for the transition to offense.

Advanced Patterns and Plays

Many different serve-reception patterns and plays are used in the six-two attack, depending upon the personnel, playing rota-

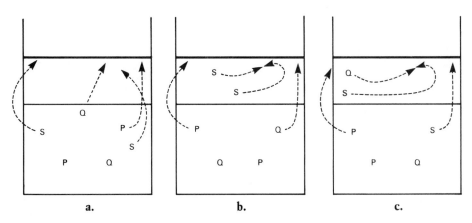

a.   **b.**   **c.**

Diagram 7-11 *The UCLA System.* S = Setter, Q = Quick spiker, and P = Power spiker. In *a,* the setter is in the right-back position; in *b,* in the middle-back position; and in *c,* the left-back position.

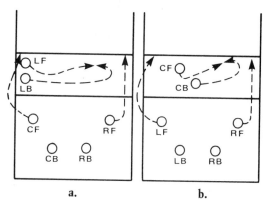

a.   **b.**

Diagram 7-12 *Four-Man Receiving Pattern.* It is not necessary for the setter to run very far when this pattern is used (*a*). If the center-front player is a poor passer, he should move under the net so he is taken out of the receiving pattern and can concentrate on the attack (*b*).

tion, and the opponents' strength. If the middle-front spiker is a good passer, but not quite fast enough to hit the one-set from a normal position, he can start from the spiking line that is 10 ft. from the net. When the middle-front player is not a valuable passer, the four-man receiving pattern shown in Diagram 7-12 can be used.

Many outstanding teams use a four-man receiving formation to receive the serve. It is a very efficient method if four superior passers receive the serve because the player approaching for the one-set is divested of serve-receiving responsibilities and can concentrate on the attack.

It may be desirable to use the four-man receiving pattern when the setter is in the right-back position if the left-front spiker wants to switch attack positions with the center-front spiker.

Coaches may elect to change attack assignments only when the middle-front player receives the serve in the regular formation. Many middle spikers have great difficulty in passing the ball accurately and

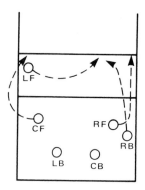

Diagram 7-13 *Changing Attack Positions.* This is easily accomplished by assuming the four-man receiving pattern.

in recovering to arrive at the point of attack in time for a quick one-set. By switching outside for a normal high set, they have time to concentrate fully on the accurate placement of their pass (see Diagram 7-14).

There are many other variations that can be used when the first pass is perfected. The cross, tandem, and fake X plays are particularly effective when the opposition begins to block the "one-play." These plays require a great deal of practice before timing is perfected.

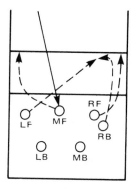

Diagram 7-14 *Pass and Switch.* Upon receiving the serve, the middle-front player changes assignments with the left-front spiker.

a.

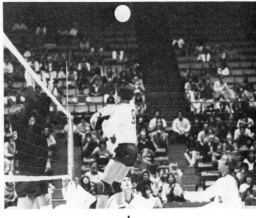

b.

c.

Figure 7-41 *Right X.* The setter delivers the X set as Number 30 takes off for the hit (*a*). Number 30 is the right-side hitter and is completely unopposed as both blockers jumped with the quick hitter (*b*). (Norm Schindler)

If the blocker jumps with the first attacker, the setter has the option of delivering the ball to the right-front spiker who crosses behind the middle attacker and jumps immediately after the first spiker jumps. The second spiker receives a two-set and approaches behind the first spiker's heels or from the middle of the court (see Figure 7-41). The fake cross should be used after the right cross has been perfected. The right-front player fakes a right cross and returns behind the setter to hit a two-set. The outside blocker usually jumps with the quick attacker because the middle blocker is assigned to the right-front player during the right cross. The right-front player should contact the ball as the opposing blocker is returning to the floor after defending against the quick attacker.

The thirty-one is particularly effective when the right spiker is left-handed and can open his attacking shoulder to the setter

Figure 7-42 *Fake X.* Number 30 takes the middle blocker out of the play leaving the right side hitter with one blocker to contend with. (Norm Schindler)

Figure 7-43 *The Thirty-One.* Toshi Toyoda drops to his knee and shoots a fast back one-set to Kirk Kilgour which catches the blockers on the floor. This occurred in 1969, and blockers were not yet familiar with fast offenses. (Bob Van Wagner)

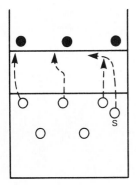

Diagram 7-15 *The Thirty-One.* Toshi Toyoda drops to his knee and shoots a fast back one-set to Kirk Kilgour which catches the blockers on the floor.

Figure 7-44 *Tandem.* Joe Mica (No. 32) runs in from the left sideline to hit a two-set over a blocker on the floor as the other blocker (No. 4) is too wide to touch the ball. (Norm Schindler)

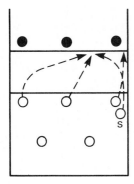

Diagram 7-16 *Tandem.* Joe Mica (No. 32) runs in from the left sideline to hit a two-set over a blocker on the floor as the other blocker (No. 4) is too wide to touch the ball.

who delivers a one-set. The middle spiker runs in for a three-set to draw the middle blocker (No. 6, Figure 7-43) in his direction as the right spiker approaches and jumps for the quick back set.

In Figure 7-44, No. 32 runs from the left sideline to hit a two-set behind the quick attacker (No. 29). The left-front attacker should approach straight ahead for a step or two to freeze the end blocker before running to the setter to complete the play.

8

Defense

The two basic defensive alignments used in volleyball are the *middle back* and *middle in.* In both defenses, each player is assigned an area of the court that varies according to the pass, approach of the potential attackers, the set, and the block. The success of any defense depends on the quick and accurate response of the defenders to those factors

MIDDLE-BACK DEFENSE

The middle-back defense is known as the white defense or six-back defense. The USA team used to use three defenses; the red or middle in, the white and the blue, or off-blocker defense. The six back refers to area six or middle back on the court. The middle-back defense that will be presented here has incorporated the best aspects of the blue defense and red defenses. This defense is effective against any type of offense, but is particularly effective (in comparison to other

defenses) against teams that use combination plays and attack from the middle of the court.

Starting Position

The individual's backcourt position is the same in all defenses. The body is in a semi-crouch position, with the feet spread about shoulder-width apart. The player's weight is forward and his hands are held about waist high. The team starting position depends on the offensive capabilities of the opposition. In better competition, teams usually have to defend against the quick hit in the middle. In men's competition the area one and five defenders start on the three-meter line about 3 ft. from the sideline. In women's competition the quick hitters usually hit deeper in the court so the area one and five defenders usually start 15 ft. from the net. When the area one defender is serving, bring the middle-back player in about 10 ft. from the endline in the center

165

Figure 8-1 *Defensive Starting Positions.* The left-front blocker starts close to the center of the court when playing a team using combination attacks. Corner diggers start from 15 to 10 ft. off the net to stop the quick hit and then move back for the high outside set. (Ohio State University)

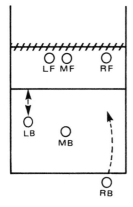

Diagram 8-1 *Defensive Starting Positions.* The left-front blocker starts close to the center of the court when playing a team using combination attacks. Corner diggers start from 15 to 10 ft. off the net to stop the quick hit and then move back for the high outside set.

of the court in case the ball is passed over the net. The area four blocker starts 8 to 10 ft. from the sideline at the net; the middle blocker in the center of the court. The area two blocker starts 3 to 8 ft. from the right sideline. Women usually start the area one and five diggers 15 ft. from the net. In good men's competition they start at the three-meter line because there is not time to move to this position and dig a quick hit that has not been deflected by the blocker. In order to dig the quick hit, the player has to be in position before the ball is spiked. Even when the player is in perfect position, this is a difficult spike to dig unless the player has attempted to dig hundreds of hard 10 to 15 ft. spikes during practice and competition. In Figure 8-1, Number 22 has just

Figure 8-2 *Reading the Play.* The blockers did not leave the floor with the quick hitter and will be ready for the high wide set. (Ohio State University)

served and is moving in to defend area one. All of the defenders are watching the pass.

Versus a Wide Set

In Figure 8-2, the middle blocker is already pushing off on his inside foot to move outside. Since the pass was about 8 ft. from the net, the area one digger did not penetrate to the three-meter line to defend against the quick hitter and is already in position to dig an outside set.

The defense for the left-side attack is shown in Figure 8-3. Number 22 in area one is expecting a spike and has stayed deep. Since the end blocker appears to have covered the line, the average player should have run in to cover the dink shot. However, Number 22 is Singin Smith who is one of the quicker players in the country and will

Figure 8-3 *Defense for the Left-Side Spike.* The four diggers have read spike and are in excellent position behind the two-man block. (Ohio State University)

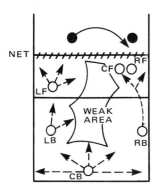

Diagram 8-2 *Defense for the Left-Side Spike.*
The four diggers have read spike and are in excellent position behind the two-man block.

stay deep unless he reads a dink—then he takes one step and dives to cover it.

Off-Blocker Variation

When playing against a team that hits high flat shots down the line, it is desirable to keep the area one player deep and use the off-blocker to cover the dink shot. This player should also cover the dink anytime the middle blocker takes the crosscourt spike away from the spiker. Frontcourt setters blocking on the left can make a quick transition to area two from this position. In Figure 8-4, the off-blocker from area four is moving into the center of the court, while the area one defender stays a few feet from

Figure 8-4 *Off-Blocker Takes Dink.* The left-front blocker starts close to the center of the court to help stop teams that set the middle hitter. It is easy for him to cover dinks from this starting position. (Norm Schindler)

Figure 8-5 *Off-Blocker Defense.* Since the off-blocker is in the center of the court, the left-back digger comes closer to the three-meter line to compensate. (Norm Schindler)

the back line. As the spiker contacts the ball, the off-blocker is about 7 ft. off the net in the center of the court, and the area five digger has moved close to the three-meter line to dig the sharp crosscourt spike. The area six defender plays near the end line in the seam of the block and the area one defender stays deep (Figure 8-5). This variation can be built into the middle-back defense by having the off-blocker share the dink shot whenever the middle blocker takes away the crosscourt spike. When the off-blocker has sole responsibility for the dink shot, the area behind the area two blocker is particularly vulnerable, and the area one defender should share dink responsibility if the end blocker in front of him puts his hands between the ball and the sideline.

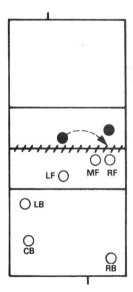

Diagram 8-3 *Off-Blocker Defense.* Since the off-blocker is in the center of the court, the left-back digger comes closer to the three-meter line to compensate.

a.   **b.**

Figure 8-6 *End Blocker.* In 8(*a*), the end blocker correctly protects the line on a close set. In (*b*), the end blocker should have set up head-on-head with the attacker, who is in the process of pounding the ball straight down in front of the line digger. (Dr. Leonart Stallcup, *a*; Norm Schindler, *b*)

Figure 8-7 *Good Defense Versus Crosscourt Spikes.* Two to three diggers can have chance to field a crosscourt spike in the middle-back defense. (Norm Schindler)

End Blocker

On a good set the end blocker should line up even with the spiker and keep his outside hand between the ball and the sideline to block the line shot and to encourage the spiker to hit crosscourt. On a good set the average backcourt defender, positioned on the sideline directly in front of the attacking spiker, must move to within 15 ft. of the net when the ball is attacked in order to field balls dinked over the block. When this defender rushes in to field the dink and the spiker drives a ball down the line, it is rarely dug. For this reason, it is often good strategy for the end blocker in the middle-back defense to block the line and to try to force the spiker to hit crosscourt (Figure 8-6). The middle-back defense is particularly strong against crosscourt spikes because two or three defenders are in position to dig the crosscourt spike (Figure 8-7).

When the ball is set deep the end blocker should move towards the center of the court and leave the line open. The spiker will make errors trying to hit the line on a deep set and the line digger can stay deep and still recover the dink shot on a deep set.

Off-Blocker

The off-the-net blocker moves about 10 ft. away from the sideline and the net to field the spike that has been driven sharply by the middle blocker. This player is also responsible for dinks and off-speed shots hit into the left side of the frontcourt. The off-blocker must concentrate on moving away from the net quickly and stopping before the spiker contacts the ball. When the spiker contacts the ball, the off-blocker's body weight must be forward or she will not be able to move forward quickly enough to field balls hit off the block or to field soft placement shots.

Figure 8-8 *Off-Blocker.* The off-blocker must react quickly to the direction of the set in order to gain a position deep enough in the court to dig the sharp spike angled by the block. (Richard Mackson)

The off-blocker must react quickly to the direction of the set in order to gain a position deep enough in the court to dig the sharp spike angled by the block. The middle blocker who aggressively blocks over the net will force the setter to deliver the ball about 2 or 3 ft. from the net so that most spikers cannot angle hard-driven crosscourt spikes inside the 10-ft. line. The off-blocker has a tendency to continue running back beyond the 10-ft. spiking line where she might overlap the left-back player who usually has a much better angle on the approaching spike.

Left Back

The left-back defender (No. 30 in Figure 8-9) is stationed in the "power alley" of the

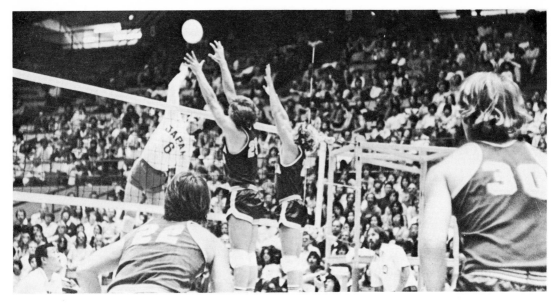

Figure 8-9 *Left Back.* No. 30 is the left-back player and he is responsible for hard hit spikes that go inside of the middle blocker. The middle blocker is going to help him by slowing this spike down. (Norm Schindler)

volleyball court. Some coaches switch their best back court digger to this position because most of the time the area four spiker delivers the ball to this area of the court. This position is the key to backcourt defense because most teams set to the on-hand spiker significantly more often than the other hitters in both two- and three-hitter attacks. No. 30 in Figure 8-9 has lined up off the center blocker's left shoulder so that he can watch the ball and spiker when making contact with the ball.

Middle Back

The middle-back player (No. 10 in Figure 8-10) is responsible for balls hit through, off the top or over the block. Many of the balls he fields are deflected by the block and can be passed to the setter. In the traditional middle-back defense, this player is not responsible for short dink shots.

Figure 8-10 *Middle Back.* Number 10 wisely lines up behind the poor V block of No. 1. Normally, he would line up between the seam on No. 1 and No. 2. (Norm Schindler)

The middle back must be ready to move forward when he sees that the blockers have not closed in fast enough and have left a hole in the block. When stationed behind a good block, the middle back should be in a direct line behind the blockers and attacking spiker.

Right Back

The Japanese girl sprawling on the floor in Figure 8-11 is playing the right-back position. She is responsible for covering balls hit down the line as well as dink shots and soft shots looped over the block. The right-back position requires a player with the ability to "read" the intentions of the opposing spiker. It is extremely difficult for her to recover a soft dink shot that drops at the heels of the blockers when she has ruled out that possibility and has moved close to the floor in preparation for a hard-driven spike. The initial starting position for this player depends on what type of offense the team is facing.

Defending Against the Quick Hitter

When the center spiker in a three-hitter offense receives a one-set, it is difficult to defend the play with more than one blocker. The blocker should normally attempt to stay in front of the spiker's attacking arm and try and take away his best shot.

If time allows, the off-blockers (LF and RF in Figure 8-12) back away from the net to cover dinks and balls deflected by the blocker. The corner-back player (No. 24 in Figure 8-12) lines up outside the blocker's arms so that he can see the spiker contact the ball. The middle-back player stays behind the blocker and reacts to the spike (MB in Diagram 8-4).

Better front-row setters in all offenses are creating new problems for blockers as setter Randy Stoklos demonstrates in Figure 8-13 as he dumps the ball over his right

Figure 8-11 *Right Back*. A slashing sprawl to the hardwood by the Japanese defender. (Richard Mackson)

Figure 8-12 *Stopping the One-Set*. Teams usually go to the quick hitter early in the game and then use him as a decoy and set the second man through in a combination offense. (Ohio State University)

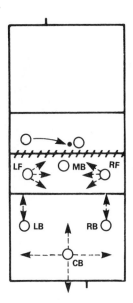

Figure 8-14 *End Blocker.* When balls are passed to the right sideline, the end blocker has the responsibility of stopping the quick hitter. (Norm Schindler)

Diagram 8-4 *Stopping the One-Set.* Teams usually go to the quick hitter early in the game and then use him as a decoy and set the second man through in a combination offense.

Figure 8-13 *Setter Dumping.* Frontcourt setters are jump setting above the net, which puts extra pressure on the blockers who must defend against the setter and quick hitter. (Norm Schindler)

shoulder into area four. The area four blocker is defending against this play, but has missed the ball. An important rule for the area five and one defender is to always play for the dink shot if the blocker in front of you is involved in blocking a quick set, combination play, or dump by the setter. When the ball is passed close to the net by the right sideline, the end blocker should take the responsibility of defending against the quick attack. Notice the middle blocker in the corner of Figure 8-14 waiting for an attacker to come into his area. When the opponents are particularly effective using the middle attacker, the defense should try to stop them with two blockers. The middle blocker for Poland in Figure 8-15 did not take the deceptive cut back of the Japanese middle attacker and the block was defeated. The left-back player (LB in Diagram 8-5) will automatically move forward from the three-meter line when the blocker in front of him defends against the quick set. The end blockers must start close to the

Figure 8-15 *Two Blockers.* Two blockers are defeated by the tricky Japanese spiker who looks at the sideline and cuts the shot crosscourt. (Richard Mackson)

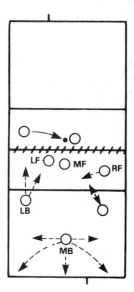

Diagram 8-5 *Two Blockers.* Two blockers are defeated by the tricky Japanese spiker who looks at the sideline and cuts the shot crosscourt. (Richard Mackson)

center of the court when combating a team with a good combination offense. The blockers have to know the tendencies of their opponent through previous scouting and read their attack routes to anticipate what combinations have been called.

Stopping the Right X

In Figure 8-16*a*, the end blocker has moved in front of the setter who is about to set a perfect pass. They have let Reede jump uncontested and are waiting for Jose (*b*). As Reede descends, the middle blocker reads the set and closes on the end blocker who is directly in front of the attacker (*c*). Jose looks at the two-man block and decides to dink to area four (*d*). The blockers had an excellent starting position and read the developing play as they formed a solid two-man block. If the defender in area five remembered to automatically play for the dink when the area four blocker is involved in blocking a playset, the ball may have been dug. A key play in stopping the right X is the area two blocker. In Figure 8-17, Number 7 comes to the center of the court to join his teammates in a three-man block to combat the second or X man in the play. This defense can also be used on a high set to the middle.

Using three blockers against an accomplished spiker who has been hitting well against a two-man block can be most effective. This three-man block is also valuable against players who cannot dink well or use a soft spike.

One way to insure blocker coverage against the right X is to commit to a man-to-man defense. This is not recommended, although some good teams have used this tactic, including the Russian and USA National Teams. If a team has outstanding one-on-one blocking, this would be an effective

a.

b.

c.

d.

Figure 8-16 *Stopping the Right X.* The end blocker should line up on the inside of the setter and try and jump after the set (*a*). The middle blocker reads the play and moves over to form a two-man block (*c*) taking away the main area of the court (*d*). (Tom Leja)

Figure 8-17 *Three Blockers.* A lot of coaches advocate blocking with three players whenever possible. (Norm Schindler)

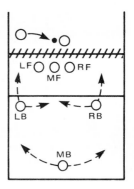

Diagram 8-6 *Three Blockers.* A lot of coaches advocate blocking with three players whenever possible. (Norm Schindler)

Figure 8-18 *One-on-One Blocking.* The only thing the offense likes better is none-on-one. (Ohio State University)

defense. The area four blocker keys on the quick hitter and the center blocker waits for the X man as shown in Figure 8-18.

The Fake X

After a defense has managed to stop the X play a few times, the setter will usually call a fake X. In this play, the area two attacker starts around the setter and flairs back to the sideline for a back two-set. The area four blocker first calls, "X", to warn the middle blocker, then calls, "No", to indicate the area two hitter is not crossing. The middle blocker then has primary responsibility for the quick hitter, and the area four blocker takes the area two hitter. On a good pass, this usually means a one-on-one situation. Number 1 in Figure 8-19 is head-on-head with the attacker who is about to wipe the ball off his outside hand. According to our rules, the area five defender (No. 2) should be moving in for the dink shot or deflection; when number two moves in, number six rotates to area five. The middle blocker, who has been trained to react with the set, will not go up with the

Figure 8-19 *The Fake X.* The blocker (No. 1) is lined up well and is trying to take both angles at once. Number 2 is too deep to recover the wipe-off shot. (Norm Schindler)

quick hitter, but will join the end blocker in defending against this play.

Versus a Fast Outside Set

Many times a fast outside set will beat the middle blocker, and in that situation, he should take the dink responsibility instead of watching the play. The right-back defender moves back for a spike and should put his outside foot forward on the sideline and faces toward the center of the court so the ball will be dug towards his teammates. He can "dig in" because the middle blocker should have all dink responsibility when he is not quick enough to form a two-man block. The middle-back defender moves towards area one to balance the court and put two defenders on each side of the end blocker who makes a crosscourt move to protect the center of the court. The left-back defender moves just inside the middle blocker, and the off-blocker tries to move beyond the three-meter line as shown in Figure 8-20. Since this is a fast set, it is unlikely that these defenders will all make this ideal defensive position, as they must stop when the attacker starts his armswing and be prepared to move in any direction when the ball is contacted.

Figure 8-20 *Versus a Fast Outside Set.* The off-blocker has moved fast and is already straddling the three-meter line. The middle blocker should be covering the dink shot. (Ohio State University)

MIDDLE-BACK DEFENSE TO OFFENSE

Frontcourt Setter

If the digger does not pass the ball accurately when fielding the attack, one of the remaining five players who is closest to the pass should set the ball to one of the front-row spikers.

When the pass or dig can be controlled, the transition from the middle-back defense to the two-hitter offense depends on the location of the setter. Normally, the setter is not the strongest blocker in the front row and is not capable of blocking the middle position effectively. When a team has a tall, mobile setter who is talented enough to block the middle position, its transition to offense is very smooth because there is no setter-spiker switch. Because the attack usually comes from the opposition's on-hand spiker or from the area four attacker, the weak blocking setter usually switches to the left to block the area two attacker. This allows the setter to become the off-blocker, with the responsibility of digging crosscourt spikes (S in Diagram 8-7a). In this situation the setter could move to the center of the court to take dink responsibility to give him a better transition to offense.

When a teammate digs a ball, the setter switches with the center blocker and sets to one of the front-row players. This is the best system for defending against the opponents' attack, but it is most inefficient

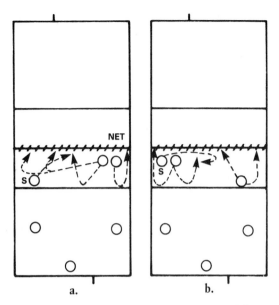

a.   **b.**

Diagram 8-7 *Setter Blocking on the Left.* If there is not enough time for the middle blocker to run to the left side of the court in order to approach from the on-hand side, the approach for the set can be made from the middle of the court (*a*). If the attack is from the opponents' weak side, the middle blocker can easily approach along the sideline from the middle (*b*).

for the middle blocker. The player who blocks the middle position must use a shortened approach if he wants to reach the left-front spiking position in time for the set. He may choose to attack from the middle by verbally signaling the setter while the first pass is in the air. An attack on the middle position has the disadvantage of allowing the opposing blockers to cover 15 ft. of the net instead of 30 ft.; this means they should be able to block successfully with two or three players if they so desire. If the first pass is not high, the setter has his back to the on-hand spiker and is not sure of the location of the approaching spiker.

When the attack is from the weak side of the team, the switch is relatively easy

(S in Diagram 8-7*b*). The former off-blocker may approach for a play set because the setter is facing him. If the setter is a strong end blocker, he should block on his right side. When the attack is from the opponents' strong side, the center blocker can approach from the middle or use a short switch and approach from the right side. If the attack is from the weak side, the middle blocker should attack from the middle so that the set can be approached from the on-hand side.

Most teams that run the five-one offense station their setter on the right side to block, even though their setter is a noticeably weaker blocker than their spikers. Their diggers always pass the ball to the right side of the court to allow the setter to face two on-hand spikers, which allows for greater accuracy in the placement of the set.

When the attack is dug from the opponents' strong side, the middle blocker can approach from the on-hand side in the middle or from the sideline (Diagram 8-8*a*). When the attack is dug from the opponents' weak side, the middle blocker should

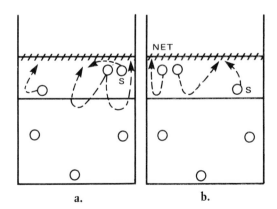

a.   **b.**

Diagram 8-8 *Setter Blocking on the Right.* When the setter is a capable blocker, he should switch to the right side of the court for an easy transition to offense.

approach from the middle of the court (Diagram 8-8*b*).

Backcourt Setter

The transition from the middle-back defense to the three-hitter attack is a bit more complicated. If the defense does not pass the ball accurately when fielding the attack, the backcourt setter probably will not be able to set the ball. When the backcourt setter digs the ball, he should direct it toward the frontcourt setter so the team can use the two-hitter attack. If another player digs the ball, it should be directed about 10 ft. from the right sideline, a few feet from the net. The most convenient place for the backcourt setter to be in order to make a speedy transition to offense is the right-back position (Diagram 8-9). With continued

practice, it is possible for the backcourt setter to move under a good dig from any defensive assignment, turn and face the two on-hand spikers, and set the ball.

Down Block

Teams must be able to make quick adjustments from defense to offense. The serving team must anticipate a good pass, a good set, and then the spike. If the pass is not good and the setter has trouble getting to the ball, or if another player must step in and set the ball, the defense should be ready for a bad set. If the set is good enough to be hit by the spiker at a downward angle, but not sharp enough to block, the blockers yell, "Down!" or "Stay down!" At this call, the blockers drop their arms and the off-blocker and three backcourt players at-

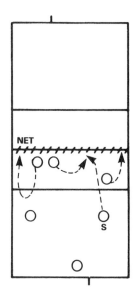

Diagram 8-9 *Setter in Right Back.* This is the only place for back-court setters with average quickness. Some setters are quick enough to play middle back where they can dig more balls and still make the transition to offense.

Figure 8-21 *Down Ball.* At this call, the blockers drop their arms and pull away from the net. (Bud Fields)

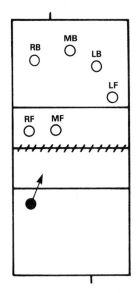

Diagram 8-10 *Down Ball.* At this call, the blockers drop their arms and pull away from the net.

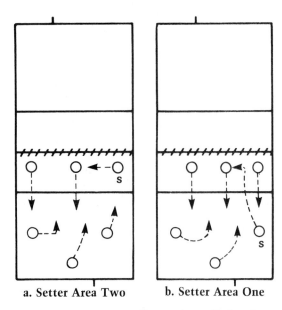

a. Setter Area Two   **b. Setter Area One**

Diagram 8-11 *Free Ball.* On this call the players move to a five-person serve reception formation.

tempt to dig the ball. The two blockers cover half speed shots and dinks. When a backcourt setter digs the ball, it should be directed to the area two player.

Free Ball

When the defense sees that the offense is going to hit the ball over the net with an upward flight or weak spike, it should call, "Free!" Then the blockers drop away from the net to help their backcourt teammates field the ball. An arranged free ball play should be used according to the offensive system in effect. Some teams use a direct set to an attacker who has the option of spiking or setting to another attacker. Other offensive systems call for a low, fast pass to the setter in order to make a quick play before the opponents' defense is set up. When a free ball is converted into a scoring

Figure 8-22 *Passing a Free Ball.* In good competition, there are at least four or five free balls in a game. Free balls should usually be received with the overhand pass because they can be controlled with greater accuracy. (Richard Mackson)

play, the receiving team is given momentum.

MIDDLE-IN DEFENSE

The middle-in defense is strong against dinks, off-speed hits, and high flat spikes. Teams with quick, tall blockers can prevent the opposition from attacking the weak zone located in the center of the court beyond the 10-ft. line. It is a weak defense to use against teams that use a quick attack and combination balls. For that reason, it is being used less every year at the top levels of play. It is still popular at the high school level, because it offers an easy transition to offense for slow backcourt setters who play the middle-in position.

Versus a Wide Set

This is the only type of set this defense can stop with any regularity. As long as the middle blocker can slow down spikes hit into area six so the left-back and right-back players can run them down, this defense will be successful. When the center blocker is late to the outside this defense breaks down because the middle of the court is vulnerable. When faced with a quick offense, the middle blocker will often be late and the middle-back defense will provide an additional digger and, thus, a better defense. If the defense can serve tough and force the opponent to pass badly, this defense will work. The positions will be discussed below in relation to a wide set.

End Blocker

When the ball is set off the net the end blocker should line up about 3 ft. from the sideline and move the block toward the

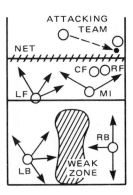

Diagram 8-12 *Versus a Wide Set.* This is a good defense against a team that uses high wide sets and dinks.

center of the court in an attempt to encourage the spiker to hit the ball down the line (Figure 8-23).

If the ball is set near the sideline and close to the net, the end blocker will have

Figure 8-23 *End Blocker Encouraging Spiker to Hit a Line Shot.* The end blocker (No. 7) leaves the line open in the hopes that the spiker will hit to No. 12. Instead, the spiker hits the ball to the open zone in the middle of the court. (Norm Schindler)

to line-up on the ball to prevent a straight-down spike that cannot be dug by the defensive player on the line.

Left Back

The left-back player (No. 12 in Figure 8-23) should be in line with the ball and the armswing of the spiker. He should start about 5 ft. in and adjust to the set and block. When the block is set deep in the court he moves back to the endline. Although his primary responsibility is to dig spikes hit outside the blocker's left hand, the left-back player is also responsible for balls hit through the block. He must have good lateral movement.

Middle-In

Balls looped over the block are covered by the middle-in player who first starts behind the center blocker on the 10-ft. line. The middle-in player is not responsible for hard-driven spikes; instead, he concentrates on retrieving dinks, off-speed shots, and block rebounds. He should be able to dive quickly to retrieve balls, and often becomes the setter when the team uses a three-hitter attack.

Figure 8-24 *Protecting Against the Dink Shot.* The middle-in player starts on the ten-foot line from which he must dive to field well-placed dink shots. (Norm Schindler)

In Figure 8-24, the middle-in player starts on the 10-ft. line behind the blockers and concentrates on the possibility of a dink shot and his chances of retrieving balls rebounding off the block. If the spiker manages to drive a hard spike through the middle of the block, there is little chance that the middle-in player will field a successful dig at such a close distance.

Right Back

The right-back player is responsible for spikes hit into his area and for long balls hit off the block that fall on the right side of the court. The right-back player does not take any responsibility for the short dink shot and can concentrate fully on spikes. If the right back is a good digger, the middle blocker should concentrate on making a tight block and rely on the right back to dig the crosscourt spike inside the block as shown in Figure 8-25.

Off-Blocker

The off-blocker should quickly back off the net to the three-meter line while watching the setter and remaining blockers (Figure 8-26). When the ball is set toward the cen-

Figure 8-25 *Hitting to the Right Back.* Number 12 hits a high flat crosscourt shot that the middle-in defense is designed to stop. (Norm Schindler)

Figure 8-26 *Off-Blocker Lining Up the Spike.* The off-blocker is in a perfect position to dig a spike by No. 12. (Dr. Leonard Stallcup)

the middle blocker usually lowers his hands below the net to allow the player behind the block to pass an easy ball.

In Figure 8-27, the middle blocker should have shouted, "No!" or "Down!" to warn his teammate not to deflect the ball away from the middle-in player.

Defending Against the Quick Hitter

When a blocker finds himself alone in the block and defending himself against the middle spiker, he should cover the center of the court. This is particularly important in the middle-in defense because there are no backcourt players behind the block.

Figure 8-27 *Middle Blocker Allowing the Dink to Go By.* The middle blocker drops his hands to allow the middle-in player to field the dink shot. (Bob Van Wagner)

ter of the court, she should move close to the sideline. When the middle blocker does not jump, the off-blocker should move toward center of the court.

Middle Blocker

The middle blocker is responsible for closing any spaces or holes in the block. Because there is no deep middle backcourt player, the middle blocker must slow up or block spikes hit in the center so that the backcourt players have time to move laterally to field the ball. If the spiker dinks,

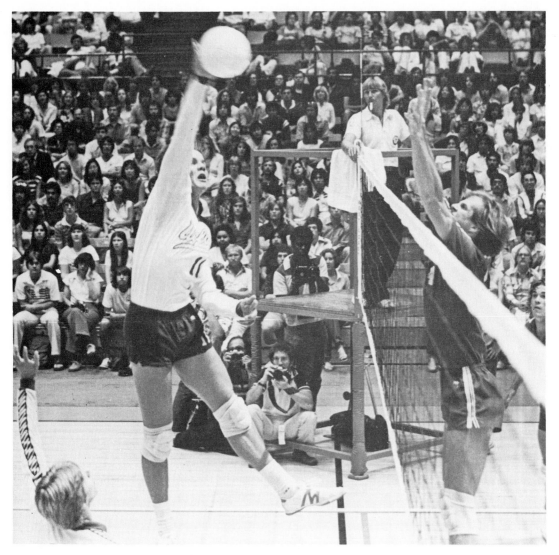

Figure 8-28 *Protecting the Middle.* Normally this would be a bad block since quick hitters rarely hit straight ahead; but in this defense, the middle of the court should be protected. (Norm Schindler)

In Figure 8-28, the blocker has found himself alone on the block and realizes that he must defend the center of the court. He does so by blocking straight ahead. Blockers should remember that there are no backcourt players behind the block in the middle-in defense. In top competition the coach may instruct the blocker to read the spiker and take the angle spike even though the middle of the court will be open. The

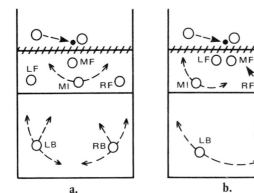
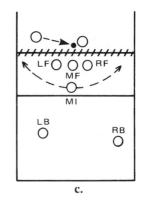

a.   b.   c.

Diagram 8-13 *Center Spiker v. Middle-In Defense.* The middle-in player should stay to the right of a one-player block when the set is coming toward him because most spikers dink away from the direction of the set (*a*). When two players block the middle attacker, the middle-in player must cover the area vacated by the end blocker. In this situation, the off-blocker (RF) must share the responsibility for the dink shot (*b*). When the entire front line blocks, the middle-in player lines up behind the middle blocker and relys on the end blockers to deflect balls dinked toward the sideline.

reason for this tactic is that the middle-in defense starts the area one and five defenders too deep to dig a good quick hitter.

The ideal court coverage for a one-player block is shown in Diagram 8-13*a*. Both off-blockers (LF and RF) drop away from the net to dig a block deflection or off-speed shot hit toward the sideline. The middle-in player lines up off the blocker's right shoulder to cover dink shots. This player "cheats" to the right because most dink shots are placed in the same direction as the set. The backcourt players (LB and RB in Diagram 8-13*a*) line up off the outside shoulder of the blocker in order to see the spiker contact the ball and then react to the attack. On a higher set, two blockers can reach the center spiker (Figure 8-29).

When the end blocker joins the middle blocker to stop the center attack, the middle-in player covers the area vacated by the· end blocker (M1 in Diagram 8-13*b*) rather than charging the 10-ft. line to defend

against a possible "straight-down" spike angled inside the left-front blocker. The right back lines up outside the middle blocker's arms to watch the attacker contact the ball. The left-back lines up behind the blockers (LB in Diagram 8-13*b*) to dig balls deflected by the block.

When all three blockers leave the floor, the three remaining defenders will have to be alert for off-speed spikes looped over the block.

MIDDLE-IN DEFENSE TO OFFENSE

The middle-in defense is ideal for the transition to the three-hitter attack when a setter plays behind the block. When the best setter in the backcourt is also the best digger, the strategy may call for the setter to play in the left-back position, where the greatest number of balls are usually hit.

Figure 8-29 *Defending With Two Blockers.* Rick Amon uses his 41-in. vertical jump to tip the ball directly over the two-man block. (Norm Schindler)

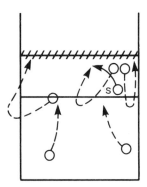

Diagram 8-14 *Changing from the Middle-In Defense to Offense.* This can be accomplished smoothly when the setter plays behind the block.

Normally, the middle-in player will set the ball if this is the case. When there is an obvious free-ball situation, the setter in the left-back position has ample time to run to the net before the ball is passed. When the setter is in the front in the four-two or five-one offense he should block in area two and the least skilled digger should play the middle-in position.

III

SPECIAL GROUPS

9

Coeducational and Doubles Play

COEDUCATIONAL PLAY

Coed playing rules are the same as those for the regulation game, with the following exceptions:

1. There are three males and three females on a team.
2. The serving order alternates males and females.
3. When the ball is contacted by more than one player on a team, one of the contacts must be made by a woman.
4. One male backcourt player may also block when there is only one male player in a frontline position.
5. The height of the net for coed play shall be 2.43 meters (7 ft. 11⅝ in.).

Offense

Coed play should be conducted with an emphasis on equal participation, a high level of sportsmanship, and a spirit of team play. For equal participation and enjoyment, the basic M-formation is recommended because it allows every player to become the setter when he or she reaches the middle-front position. When a woman is in the middle-front row, the pass can be directed to her so that she can set the ball to either end spiker. When there is only one man in the front row, he can approach from the left side (if he is right-handed), and the woman on his left can switch to the center of the frontcourt to be in a position to set (see Diagram 9-1a).

On a high pass, the woman should turn to face the man so that she can deliver a front set to him. The woman playing in the right-front position should approach for a back set. If the male spiker is a good passer, he may choose to remain in the center of the court where he can field a greater percentage of the serves. After the pass, he can

193

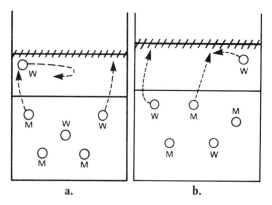

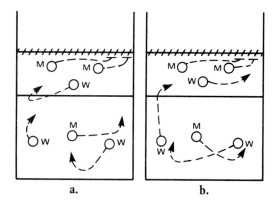

Diagram 9-1 *Offense.* A high ball should be passed near the center front of the court so that the setter (LF) can turn and front set the player approaching down the left sideline (*a*). When the setter is on the right side of the court, the ball should be passed 10 ft. from the right sideline and a few feet from the net to allow the player to approach from the middle of the court and to attack the ball from the on-hand side (*b*).

Diagram 9-2 *One Woman in the Front Line.* The woman plays the off-blocker position in the middle-back defense (*a*) and the middle-in position in the middle-in defense (*b*).

spike from the center of the court (see Diagram 9-1*b*).

Defense

It is possible to include two men on the block during the entire game if the woman in the middle front moves away from the net prior to the serve. In Diagram 9-2, the man in the middle-back position can switch to area one if he is the backcourt setter.

When two women are in the front row, they can block the end with the man blocking the middle, or a man can be brought in from the backcourt to block. When women spikers hit on a man's net, the defense must be ready to call, "Down!" and "Free ball!"

In Diagram 9-3, the backcourt man on the sideline can exchange positions with the frontline women in both the middle-back (*a*) and middle-in defenses (*b*). In the middle-in defense, the remaining back-

court man and women may move toward the center of the court and switch positions to allow the best digger his or her choice of positions.

The USVBA sponsors a National Co Ed Championship. A popular innovation at the Championships is the reverse division which uses a 7 ft. 4¼ in. net with women as blockers and spikers and men setting the ball.

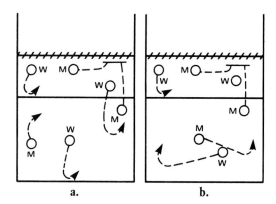

Diagram 9-3 *Two Women in the Front Line.* A special coed rule allows one backcourt player to block if there is only one male player in a frontline position.

DOUBLES PLAY

Playing rules for doubles in the *Official Volleyball Guide* are the same as those for the regulation game, with the following exceptions:

1. Each team's court is 30 ft. by 25 ft.
2. No substitutions are allowed.
3. The serve shall be made from any position behind the end line.
4. The game is 11 points or, if time is a factor, 5 minutes of ball in play—whichever occurs first.

Generally, tournament directors do not use a timer, and the length of the game is increased to 15 points. When doubles are played indoors, the same light, fast regulation ball as that used in the six-man game is in play.

Offense

The server has an advantage when the "short-court" rule is enforced because the serving line is 5 ft. closer to the net. This gives the receiver less time to react, especially on fast, low serves directed along the server's sideline. The serve should not be merely a way of putting the ball into play—it should be an offensive tactic to score points.

In doubles volleyball, most of the serving aces are scored in the short middle (within 10 ft. of the net), on the boundary lines, or in a seam that lies exactly between the two receivers. Almost all the aces scored in doubles are due to hesitation on the part of the passer. The passer may hesitate because the ball looks as if it is going out of bounds, will hit the net, or be in his partner's receiving area. When a player is tired, the ball should be served deep in the court so the passer will have to run from the back line to the net to spike the set.

The ball should rarely be served to the poor setter because balls set over the net or deep in the setter's court are usually converted into a point for the serving team. The ball should be served repeatedly to a receiver standing in the same position only if a definite weakness has become apparent. The placement, speed, breaking action of the ball, and selection of the receiver should vary to prevent the opposition from falling into a groove.

Occasionally, the ball should be served to the stronger player, particularly if he has a tendency to relax or to cover a weaker partner. When the last serve results in a serving error, the next server should take a little power off the serve to make sure that it lands in fair territory.

Passing, setting, and endurance are the keys to attack in doubles. Almost anyone can spike well if the set is placed within a few feet of the net. Excellent spikers who do not have the necessary setting and passing skills do not enjoy great success in doubles volleyball. A poor setter must select an outstanding spiker as a partner to compensate for a lack of precision setting. Spikers must learn to vary their attack and to take advantage of the moving defensive player before the ball is contacted.

Many top players ask their friends for the "book" on their spiking patterns to see if they have become predictable in their attack. More successful players compete with the same player for the entire doubles season to learn where the ball will be passed and set in every situation by that player. There is nothing more satisfying to a spiker than to know that his partner can deliver a set close to the net. Instead of watching the setter and trying to guess where he will place the ball, a spiker who is confident of his partner's setting ability can concentrate on a correct approach and a maximum jump, which are necessary to spike well.

Defense

Defenders find it very difficult to dig a good spiker in doubles when the set is right on the net. Most of the time a poor digger should block when defending against a good set. If the spiker can be blocked a few times, the setter will be reluctant to put the set close to the net and the spiker may begin to "be dug" and to commit spiking errors.

The most successful teams also perform well on defense. Better players keep a mental "book" on their opponents and find that certain players usually hit the ball in the same place when they approach the set in what has become a predictable manner. The defense moves into this area before the ball is spiked and, in effect, dares the spiker to alter the attack or to try a shot he does not have in his offensive arsenal.

BEACH DOUBLES

California coaches generally agree that the long-term national dominance of California men's and women's teams can generally be attributed to the thousands of hours of beach volleyball that their athletes play before they reach the college level. The players struggle and sacrifice to become the best on the beach, and the ones that make it to the top continue to win at the collegiate level. Although beach volleyball is popular in Brazil, France, and in other countries, Southern California has the largest number of participants who play the year round, due to the extensive availability of free public courts, and the popularity of the game.

History

According to beach lore, the doubles game started in the 1940s at Will Rogers State Beach and Hermosa Beach in Southern California. The emphasis was on finesse and defense with all serve reception and digs being taken with the overhand pass whenever possible. The nets at State Beach were kept well above 8 ft. to allow many long rallys. Short quick players, such as 5 ft. 9 in. Bernie Holtzman, were among the dominant players. In 1950, Gene Selznick brought the powerful spike to the beach and teamed up with Holtzman to dominate the sport until 1956. Informal tournaments started in the early 1950s and became very popular by the late 1950s with a standard Saturday and Sunday double elimination format. By 1960, the sport was attracting top athletes who were tall and powerful, and could spike the ball with resounding authority. Mike Bright and Mike O'Hara were two such players, along with football stars Bill Leeka, Lee Grosscup, Randy Carter, and UCLA basketball standouts, Keith Erickson, John Vallely and Greg Lee.

The women finally managed to get a few nets lowered on the beach in the early 1960s and started their own tournaments, as well as competing in mixed doubles. The Santa Monica Recreation Department began classifying players for "A", "AA", and "AAA" tournaments, and publishing the beach tournament schedules which now include open, novice and "B" tournaments.

Among the outstanding beach players who have represented the United States in six-man international competition are: setters—Dusty Dvorak, Jack Henn, Karch Kiraly, Ron Lang, Ricci Luyties, Sy Marlowe, Dan Patterson, Gene Selznick, Singin Smith, and Randy Stoklos; and spikers—Mike Bright, Mike Dodd, Keith Erickson, Tim Hovland, Kirk Kilgour, Butch May, Duncan McFarland, Mike O'Hara, Pat Powers, Larry Rundle, Ernie Suwara, and Rudy Suwara. Some of the great women players include: Kathy Gregory, Mary Joe Peppler, Mary Perry, and Jane Ward.

Until 1976, volleyball players competed on the beach for self-satisfaction, and were presented with a trophy of some sort for their winning efforts (Figure 9-1). By 1981, sponsors donated $20,000 prize money for a tournament that attracts up to 15,000 spectators. This prestigous tournament is called the World Championship of Beach Volleyball. In 1983 an innovative scoring system was introduced where a point was awarded for each ball served. Games were two out of three to 25 in the winner's bracket, and one game to 35 in the loser's.

Official and Unwritten Rules

Many beach doubles' rules vary from those published in the *Official Volleyball Guide*. The following rules and interpretations are in effect for the California Beach Volleyball Association (CBVA)[1] and National Outdoor Volleyball Association (NOVA).[2]

Court size is 30 ft. by 60 ft. as opposed to the 30-ft. by 50-ft. court used in indoor doubles. Instead of lines, ropes are used to outline the courts. A center rope is placed under the net only if six-man volleyball is played. Stepping across the center of the court below the net is legal if players do not interfere with the opposing team. Players may serve from anywhere behind their end line. The net is placed 8 ft. above the sand for men and co-ed matches, and 7 ft. 4¼ in. for women. The ball is in play if it passes between the wooden posts supporting the net.

The ball has an 18-piece cover and is heavy in comparison to the indoor ball. This heavier ball is relatively stable in the wind and is always preferred on the beach. The C.B.V.A. uses the Spaulding 18-patch leather volleyball for tournaments that they sanction. The California Pro-Beach Tour tournaments use the Mikaska Suede Spike, which is also endorsed by the National Outdoor Volleyball Association.

Figure 9-1 Mike Bright and Mike O'Hara were two members of our 1964 Olympic Team who learned the game on the southern California beaches. (Dr. Leonard B. Stallcup)

[1]For specific details regarding beach doubles, rules, and tournaments in California, readers are advised to write the Santa Monica Recreation Department.
[2]For details regarding the NOVA tournament schedule in California, East Coast, Southern Region, Midwest, Oregon, and Rocky Mountain areas, send a stamped self-addressed envelope to: NOVA, 936 Hermosa Ave., Suite 109, Hermosa Beach, CA 90254.

There are no scorers, umpires, timers, and usually no linesman; the referee keeps score, and there are no time limits on the games. The referee usually sits on a platform attached to one of the volleyball posts or stands against one of the supporting posts. A player on a team in the preceding match usually referees the following match except in the money tournaments when professional referees are used. Any player may request a time out when the ball is dead. Each team is allowed two time outs of one minute.

Since no substitutions are allowed, players are also granted uncharged time outs for stretching out leg cramps. Players must keep the same serving order throughout the game, but they can change court positions at any time. Because most players are left- or right-side specialists, they do not change positions except during prolonged rallies. Teams change sides of the court every four points in 11-point games and every five points in 15-point games. This neutralizes the advantage of serving, setting, and spiking into the wind and sun.

Blocking is permitted by any player, but the blocker may not reach over the net. The blocker may play the ball again after blocking, but it counts as second of three hits. Players who contact the net are expected to stop the play immediately and to award the ball to their opponents. It is considered poor form to wait for the referee to call the net foul. For that matter, it is considered a point of honor to call throws or other infractions on yourself if the referee has missed an obvious call.

Players also call the lines except in some professional tournaments where a paid linesman sits on a platform opposite the referee and calls all the lines.

In recreational beach games, it is still considered "bad form" for the setter or dig-

Figure 9-2 *Blocking.* Players are not allowed to block over the net in beach doubles. Former USC football and volleyball star, Steve Obradovich, shows the blocking form that helped him win the 1978 World Championship of Beach Volleyball. (Bruce Hazelton/Event Concepts)

ger to hit the ball over the net before the third contact unless one's partner is definitely out of position. In tournament play, "shooting" the ball over the net with a two-hand set to catch the opponent out of position is uncommon because it is a poor tactic.

In competition mixed doubles, the man is expected to hit the ball over the net after the woman contacts it. Since the net is 8 ft., women do not generally pose much of an offensive threat on the beach.

The ball may be hit by any part of the body, including the foot, whereas the USVBA rules a "dead ball" for contact below the waist. Protests are decided on the spot by the referee; in unique cases, the tournament director handles the protests.

The setter is not allowed the freedom of moving his arms across his body to deliver the set. Even the most accomplished setters must squarely face the direction of the intended set. Almost all of the players bump set the ball to eliminate the chance of the referee calling a thrown ball. Open hand dinks are automatically "called" throws, and most players use a *cobra shot* when they want to hit an off-speed shot. The cobra is hit with the ends of the fingers or with the knuckles and is usually directed to a deep corner in the opponent's court. Overhand passing of the serve is not allowed unless an overhand bump is used. On the other hand, overhand digging is interpreted quite leniently and successive contacts of a hard

Figure 9-3 *Cushioning the Overhand Dig.* The player in the right foreground leans backward to cushion, or give with, the overhand dig of a hard spike in order to keep the ball on his side of the net. (Bob Van Wagner)

Figure 9-4 *Diving Dig.* Former UCLA All-American setter, Jim Menges, digs the ball to former San Diego State All-American and USA setter, Chris Marlowe, on their way to the 1977 World Championship of Beach Volleyball. (Bruce Hazelton/Event Concepts)

driven spiked ball are allowed if they constitute one attempt to play the ball. Therefore, on a good set, the defense may move close to the net and attempt an overhand dig with the open hand as shown in Figure 9-3. This lenient interpretation of the overhand dig promotes long rallys which are exciting to the spectators.

It is much easier to dig a ball on the beach than in the gym, because players cannot jump as high off the sand as they can off the floor, and because they are spiking a heavier ball that is partially inflated, and thus travels slower. Some of the best diggers on the beach, such as Jim Menges and Sy Marlowe, have learned to read the intentions of the spiker and dive into position to receive the ball before it hits the sand (Figure 9-4).

Scoring

In the six-man game, it is preferable for the six starters to have a variety of serves to prevent the opponents from getting into a groove. In doubles, each player should have a variety of serves and use whatever type of serve that gives the opponent the most trouble. The *overhand floater serve* is the most accurate and should be hit at the seam between the players: short middle and particularly deep to tire the passer. The *overhand spin serve* and the *jump overhand spin serve* are very effective when serving into the wind because they drop quickly. The *sky ball* is most effective when the sun is directly overhead and the wind is blowing. The ball should be hit high in the air as shown in Figure 9-5a,b, and directed deep

Figure 9-5 *Sky Ball.* The ball is hit out of the left hand or tossed a few feet into the air and contacted with the cupped hand. This serve is difficult to field in a high wind or if the sun is directly overhead. (Gary Adams)

into the opponent's court. The serve should be directed to the opponent's weaknesses: serve a poor passer; serve a weak hitter; serve the partner of a poor setter; serve the player with poor endurance. After the serve, the player must get into his starting defensive position which is about sixteen to seventeen feet from the net and three to five feet from the sideline for both players.

Where the defense goes after that depends on the habits of the hitter and the location of the set. The defense should move to the area the spiker prefers based on the location of the set and the spiker's approach. If the opponents are siding out well, a *block* should be used to force the opponents to set further away from the net. The blocker and digger should coordinate their defense

Figure 9-6 *Team Defense.* All time basketball great Wilt Chamberlain blocks 6 ft. 5 in. Miles Papst crosscourt attempt while Mike Normand is prepared to dig a line shot. (Bob Van Wagner)

to channel the attack to the waiting digger. In Figure 9-6, the blocker takes the crosscourt angle while his partner stays on the line.

The other method is for the blocker to have the freedom to take the line or angle, and the digger has to react to the blocker. Very often the digger will be caught in a stride position using this tactic and will not be able to quickly change direction for a block deflection.

Side Outs

It is fairly easy for two players to cover the court indoors, but soft sand slows down even the quickest players. Serve reception re-

sponsibility will vary from team to team, and from match to match, but the starting body position is fairly standard: the feet should be placed a little farther than shoulder width with the weight on the balls of the feet, the knees slightly bent, and the hands outside and in front of the knees. Partners must tell each other if the serve is out and call for the serve. The better passer or better hitter may try to take most of the serves by loudly calling, "Mine!", particularly if the ball is served between the players. Since there is a lot of time to react to a sky ball, one of the players can pass all of the sky balls if his partner has difficulty with them. The normal procedure is for the crosscourt passer to take the middle of the court, because he has more time to react to

Figure 9-7 *The Pass.* Former UCLA All-American Singin Smith won the 1979 and 1981 World Championships with Kirch Kiraly and the 1982 Championship with Randy Stoklos. All three players were setters at UCLA. The high lateral pass demonstrated above is performed by tilting the front shoulder downward to present a broader rear forearm surface. (Ron Haase/Event Concepts)

the serve. Since the setter has to wait and see if he has to pass the ball (particularly if it served in the middle of the court), the passer should keep the ball from three to seven feet off the net, passing closer when

his partner has time to penetrate closer to the net.

The trend towards strict officiating of overhand setting by player-referees has reached the stage where only the best tournament players will take the ball overhand when the game is on the line. This trend was originated years ago by players with "bad hands" who had to bump set all the passes. This is unfortunate since most of our country's best male setters developed their setting technique on the beach and the new generation of beach players may not have the opportunity to develop their setting technique. The main problem in setting at the beach is moving quickly through the sand and in good position to face the target before the pass arrives. The ball should be set close to the net particularly if the opponent does not block. If the wind is blowing, it is a good idea to keep the set low, so the ball does not move around a lot and destroy the spiker's timing. For economy of movement (which is important in a gruelling two-day tournament), the ball should be set close to the setter. For example, if the passer receives the serve in the middle of the court and passes straight ahead, he would expect the set to be near the center of the court. All beginning players should use their hands to set whenever they can get into position to do so, or they will not learn this technique. Unless a spiker is very powerful and contacts the ball high enough above the net to bury the ball in the sand, it is best to place the spike in an open area of the court. There are only two opponents to cover 900 square ft., so if the spiker stays behind the set as shown in Figure 9-8, he will be able to see the opponent's court and direct the spike to an open area. Since the defenders usually protect the center of the court, the corners and short and deep middle are the best targets.

Figure 9-8 *The Spike.* Matt Gage, shown competing at the age of 33, keeps the ball in front of his attacking shoulder for maximum accuracy. He had already won 22 major tournaments by the end of the 1981 season. (Ron Haase/Event Concepts)

Winning

The foundation of winning is to *master the basic fundamentals;* no team has ever won an open tournament without excellent ball control. *Conditioning* is another very important factor; in a typical 64 team double-elimination tournament, the champion must play from seven to thirteen matches in two days. Each match in the Winner's Bracket is two out of three to 15 points, and Loser's Bracket matches are one game to 15 points. Of course, the competition gets better and the matches get longer as the tournament progresses. The Winner's Bracket Finals usually occurs in the hottest part of the afternoon when endurance and willpower are taxed to the utmost. The 1981 World Championship Winner's, Karch Kiraly and Singin Smith outlasted Andy Fishburn and Randy Stoklos in a three hour finals.

Most players train for an event like this by playing with their partner seven days a week against the best competition they can find. After practicing all day and being completely exhausted, I have seen Ron Van Hagen, at the age of thirty-seven, insist on one more game from his opponents. Although the sun was going down, Ron knew from years of experience he would be just as tired in the upcoming 1976 World Championships, where he seemingly chased down every loose ball and finished second. Since the better players generally train against each other, there are excellent matches all week long. The best teams are intimidating their opponents by beating them during the week, so they get used to losing. The best players never play at half speed. Of course, the psychological conditioning they are experiencing at the beach carries over to their indoor performance. Players who have a winning tradition on the beach know the importance of conditioning and hard work in getting to the top and strive to maintain their winning performance. The physical condition of a good beach players is very good from both an aerobic and anaerobic analysis. The athlete must explode out of the sand to get a good vertical jump. Since the upward acceleration phase of a typical vertical jump lasts for only 2–3 tenths of a second, the athlete must move quicker when competing in loose sand than he does on the gym floor; this quickness is carried over to the indoor game. It is impossible to have a good vertical jump in the sand without sharply pointing the toes at lift off. This important "follow through" of the ankle joint is valuable in adding inches to the indoor jump. While the rest of the country is training to jump on low speed machines which are supposed to simulate the vertical jump, athletes on the beach are exploding out of the sand using high speed muscle contractions to extend the limits of their muscular capacity (see Figure 9-9).

After the athlete masters the fundamentals and learns how to condition himself psychologically and physically, he must *choose the right partner.* Every player can play one side of the court at least a little better than the other side. Novices should play both sides until they realize which side is easier to spike and set from. If you are playing recreational volleyball, then you should choose someone with skills similar to yours that you are compatible with. If you want to win some tournaments, then you must choose a partner to play the side opposite your preference with the same goals as you. Most importantly, you have to choose a competitor who is good in tense situations and train with him until you know each other's every defensive move and offensive preference. If you are not a good

all around player, then your partner must compensate for your deficiencies. For example, if you are a poor setter, select a partner who can hit balls set away from the net; if you are a poor digger, select a partner with quickness and anticipation to cover the court while you block. Of course, the best teams have no apparent weaknesses, and that is why they win.

You can learn a lot once you arrive at *the tournament* by observing your opponents in actual competition during the preceding round. While you and your part-

Figure 9-9 *The High Dig.* Jumping quickly in the sand is difficult without a high speed contraction of the ankle joint. Notice how the toes are pointing towards the sand after the player takes off for the high dig. (Bruce Hazelton/Event Concepts)

ner are observing their techniques and tactics, you can formulate your game plan; always think of two or three ways to beat the opponent in case the first plan does not work. Particularly observe their defensive weaknesses, so you can side out well. Observe where your opponents like to hit different sets, so you can score easier; pay particular attention to the dink and off-speed shots that they use on a deep or bad set. Before the match, check the height and tension of the net and make adjustments if it is not adequate. Get a good warm-up and use the game ball during at least half of the warm-up period. Find out who the assigned referee will be in advance because, if a change is in order, it should be accomplished as soon as possible. Make up your mind whether to choose side or serve, de-

pending on the sun, wind, and your game plan. Once the match begins, do not ease up and let a poor team extend you because playing a short hard match is far less fatiguing than trying to save yourself for another match.

Beach Volleyball Popularity

Besides the obvious factors of climate, health, and year around court accessibility, there are other reasons that most of the best athletes in beach communities play volleyball. One of the reasons is that techniques are learned at the age of ten to twelve, and they are continually exposed to competition volleyball. The local rules inevitably state that to stay on the desirable court a team must win. Most of these communi-

Figure 9-10 *The Fans.* Each April through September, ninety official tournaments draw an estimated 300,000 people in California beach competition with crowds of 15,000 watching the pro tournaments. (Bruce Hazelton/Event Concepts)

ties are affluent because of the desirability of beachfront property, and some of the schools can afford to hire elementary physical education specialists who integrate volleyball into the required physical education curriculum. Former college players are also hired to coach volleyball clubs in the area. Later the high school coach has a large pool of athletes to select the school team from. These athletes have good all around ball handling skills and already have a broad base of competitive experience playing doubles.

Many coaches who have given clinics around the country will agree that they look in the schoolyards and playgrounds of America, and do not see groups of children playing volleyball. The reason is that volleyball is technically difficult and does not utilize the catching and throwing movements that are easily learned in basketball, baseball, and football where the children can achieve relative early success. Conversely, the children at the beach are invited by older siblings or parents to bump the ball around at the age of eight or so, are playing doubles with their dad or brother or sister at ten, and are competing against their own peers by twelve. By the age of thirteen to fifteen, they have been to volleyball camps and seen high school matches and are aspiring to be setters, middle blockers or outside hitters. The enthusiasm the children have for volleyball in the beach communities is unique in that they are introduced to the sport at a young age in a friendly environment. They are looking for improved performance and are receiving help from peers and older siblings when they start competing on the local courts. These children grow up and teach the game to their children, and the game is perpetuated.

10

Volleyball for Children

The popularization and improvement of volleyball in the United States largely depends on the correct introduction of the sport to children. We have strong age-group programs in the sports in which our country is successful at the international level.

The highest tempo of development of visual-motor reaction occurs during eight to twelve years of age.[1] "By the age of twelve a child has 92 percent of his gross body coordination, 83 percent of the finer eye-hand coordination, and 90 percent of his reaction time."[2] During the elementary school years, teachers and coaches need to teach children to move efficiently and quickly when playing volleyball and other activities. This is not accomplished by putting nine children on a team and playing mass volleyball

where the average child moves for two minutes during a thirty-minute period. Elementary school children learn skills by demonstration and drills, and not by explanations and being thrust into regulation games. In fact, if they are put in regulation game situations too early in their development, they will develop bad habits which will retard the learning process. Unfortunately, elementary classroom teachers are largely responsible for teaching physical education in the United States and, for the most part, do not teach volleyball or other movement skills in a sequential manner, as they are likely to do with the other subjects in the educational curriculum. Since children have traditionally not had many opportunities to play volleyball outside the school environment as they have in baseball, basketball, and football, they do not have any model or examples to follow when the elementary teacher gives them a volleyball and assigns two teams to a court. Consequently, power volleyball has been

[1]B. A. Podlivaev and O. K. Tarnopol's Kaya, "Speed Qualities In Young Volleyball Players," trans. Michael Yessis, *Soviet Sports Review*, Vol. 15, No. 2. (June, 1980): 94.
[2]John E. Anderson, Former Director of the Institute of Child Development and Welfare, University of Minnesota.

slow to develop in the United States because the basic skills and tactics essential to the sport are not usually taught to the children in the elementary schools. With the current trend of less funding to the public school sector, it is unlikely that there will be monies for elementary physical education specialists to teach the sport. Fortunately, there are some elementary age-group programs being established in volleyball where youngsters are starting to learn the game. If volleyball is taught correctly at an early age, interest among the young people will grow more and more as they mature. Volleyball is much more difficult to teach to older students and adults because they are self-conscious and afraid of looking uncoordinated and generally inept. Volleyball techniques are not easily mastered by people whose sports background has not incorporated similar movements. Children will readily attempt to learn the techniques of the dive and roll, but adults have a well-developed fear of going to the floor to retrieve the ball.

ELEMENTARY SCHOOL VOLLEYBALL

Although boys and girls can easily learn to play volleyball together at the elementary level their motivation for participation in the average class is different. Boys are primarily interested in strength, speed, and winning. The average girl is already interested in a healthy and beautiful figure and places more emphasis on social interaction. The better female athletes place more emphasis on mastering the techniques and will be persistant achieving their goals regarding technical skills. The age of twelve to thirteen is the best period for developing

speed qualities in female volleyball players.[3]

A Russian Program

An experimental group of eight to nine year old boys was selected by the Lesgaft Physical Culture Institute on the basis of their height and the parents' height.[4] These boys were significantly taller than their peers and their parents also surpassed the mean. "In the summer, the students went to a sports-health camp where twice a day workouts were conducted five days a week."[5] By the second year, they were working on jump sets and diving sets and had mastered the overhand floater serve. "Serving was executed with both the right and left hands. The left-handed serves were executed from a shorter distance (6–7 m. from the net)."[6] During the third year, they continued with the old skills and added backsets, serve reception, digging, diving saves, round-house serves, spiking with either hand and the one-man block. During the fourth year, they worked on play sets, the sidearm floater serve and advanced spiking techniques. In the fifth year . . . "starting from a foundation of already mastered technical skills, they studied individual, group, and team tactical interactions."[7] The Institute was very happy with the success of their thirteen and fourteen year olds, and they compared favorably to fifteen year olds in their traditional sport schools. The Russian National Junior Boy's Team won the World Championships held during the summer of

[3]Podlivaev and Tarnopol's Kaya, "Speed Qualities in Young Volleyball Players," p. 95.
[4]V. Popovsky, "The First Steps in Volleyball," trans. Michael Yessis, *Soviet Sports Review*, Vol. 15, No. 4 (December, 1980): 193.
[5]Ibid., p. 95.
[6]Ibid., p. 95.
[7]Ibid., p. 95.

1981 in Colorado Springs; our boys placed seventh.

The Japanese Program

After the International Volleyball Association developed Mini Volleyball, the Scientific Research Section of the Committee of Instruction and Popularization of the Japanese Volleyball Association carefully examined its possibilities. The Japanese have "taken a leading part in studying the volleyball rules for children and lead-up games that are considered a preceding stage of guidance to Mini-Volleyball. . . ."[8] The course of study for volleyball in the elementary schools of Japan develops the capacities of catching and throwing as the first step in a progression to the fundamental technique of the overhand pass. The overhand pass is developed by the practice of catching the ball in front of the body and immediately throwing it to a teammate over the net.

The following stages are recommended for teaching volleyball to children by Hiroshi Toyoda, the Chief of Scientific Research of the Japanese Volleyball Association:

1. Throwing and catching the ball.
2. Hitting the ball after bouncing it on the floor.
3. Hitting the ball without bouncing it.
4. A player is not allowed to catch the ball, but the criterion for a held ball is not too severe.
5. The criterion for a legally played ball is almost the same as that for the formal game.[9]

[8]Hiroshi Toyoda, "Report to the Council of Coaches: FIVB," *Technical Journal 1* (April 1974): 38–41.
[9]Hiroshi Toyoda, "Volleyball Coaching Seminar," *Technical Journal 1* (April 1974): 63.

LEAD-UP GAMES

Although there are many stages and styles of individual training for each of the principal lead-up games listed below, the main point to stress to children is to move quickly in front of the oncoming ball. When players reach the receiving area, the front foot should hit the floor first and point in the direction of the intended pass. It is very important to maintain a low body position in order to stop with good balance. The stop is made with the lead foot slightly forward and the trailing foot closing to maintain a balanced position. The teacher should be careful not to frustrate children during their initial training period by attempting to teach skills beyond their reach. Unless children feel successful and have fun while they are learning, they will lose interest. Too much drilling without motivating lead-up games and tournaments can quickly turn into drudgery.

The various lead-up games listed below are designed for the elementary school level.

Throwing and Catching

Net Ball. The game is played on a regulation court with a net or rope stretched across the center of the court. A team consists of six players or less when working with high ability groups of children; homogeneous groups may play with up to six on a side. Any player puts the ball into play by throwing the ball over the net from inside the court or behind the court. The ball can be contacted three times; it can be caught, but it must be released quickly. If a player touches the ball two times in succession, he commits a fault. If the ball flies out of the opponents' court or falls on the ground, a fault is called and the opponents' team is awarded a point. Balls that hit the net are always in play. A game is won when a team has scored 21 points.

Newcomb. This game is played on a regulation court with the height of the net from 5 to 7 ft., depending on the height of the children. The game is played with six players or less, depending on the abilities of those involved. Many physical education curriculum guides throughout the country list this game, which can be introduced in the second grade. Instructors may want to continue this game with low-ability fourth and fifth graders. All balls are allowed to be caught and quickly thrown to a teammate or into the opponents' court. Adult volleyball rules are observed, with the following exceptions:

1. The server may stand as close to the net as necessary to complete a successful serve. The teacher should encourage weaker youngsters to stand closer to the net.
2. A back-row player cannot throw the ball over the net. This rule is not in force when playing with four players or less.

Modified Newcomb. The rules are the same as Newcomb, but the ball that is returned to the opponents' court must be hit in a legal manner. A freer handling of the ball is allowed. The children line up in the M-formation to receive the serve, and the player who receives the serve may catch it and throw it to the setter in the middle-front court. The setter sets or lobs the ball with two hands in an underhand toss to one of the spikers who hits it over the net using any legal technique. The defense is also allowed to catch the first and second ball as long as the ball is hit into the opponents' court.

Hitting the Ball After Bouncing It

Bounce Volleyball. The game is played on a regulation court with six players per team. The ball is allowed to bounce and then play continues in a regulation manner. The server has two chances to hit the ball over the net, and weaker servers may stand as close as 20 ft. from the net.

Option Volleyball. This is almost the same game as bounce volleyball. A player is allowed to hit the ball with or without bouncing it. The ball may hit the floor once between hits by players on a team, but it must be returned to the opponents' court after three contacts. A game is 15 points with the teams changing sides when 8 points have been scored by one team.

Volley Tennis. The game is played on a tennis court with a tennis net with a team of six to nine players. The service is made from behind the end line and one assist can be made before the ball crosses over to the opponents' court. Although players are not allowed to catch the ball, they have the option of hitting it on the fly or letting it bounce once before playing it. The ball must be returned to the opponents' court after three contacts. This is a good game to use to emphasize the spike.

Modified Volleyball

Sitting Volleyball. A team consists of about nine players who all sit or kneel on the floor. A rope or net is drawn across the center of the court. The game can be played on mats and the size of the court is determined by the number of participants. Net height can be varied from group to group, depending on their strength. Service is made from behind the end line, using an overhand pass. Rotation can be used if desired.

Keep It Up. The game is played on a regulation court with four teams of two to four players. Each court is divided perpendicularly into two courts so that there are two separate courts on both sides of the net. A front-line player on a team puts the ball into play by using the overhand pass to direct the ball into one of the opponents' courts. If a team returns the ball over the net, the team is awarded one point. When an error is made, the team that made the error serves the next ball. There is no point awarded for serving the ball over the net. Each team is allowed three contacts to return the ball over the net.

Underhand-Serve Volleyball. The most difficult technique for children to master is an accurate pass of a hard overhand serve. To prevent a boring serving contest and to encourage rallys, an underhand serve into a smaller area of the court is used. The ball must be served into the badminton court which seems to be marked inside of every volleyball court in America. This gives the server an area 20 ft. wide and 22 ft. long to which to serve. The receiving team positions itself in the area of the badminton court for service reception. The percentage of well-placed first passes will increase immediately. Since the first pass is the key to the offense, better sets and spikes also increase significantly. After the serve is received, the boundaries extend back to the regulation court. The children play on a net that is lowered until the average child in the game can touch the top of the net with outstretched fingertips from a standing position. The lowered net will encourage spiking. Regulation rules are followed, but the criterion for handling the ball is determined by the abilities of the players.

Bonus Volleyball. The net height, serve, and criterion for ball handling is the same as in Underhand-Serve Volleyball. Points are awarded in the regulation way, with the following exception: If a team scores using a pass, set, or spike they are awarded 2 points. A game is won when a team scores 21 points.

Triples Volleyball. The game is played on a badminton court with a lowered net. The underhand serve must be used and all players can block and spike. Two players stay deep in the court to receive the serve and the third player stays at the net in the center of the court to set. Players rotate from the left-back position to setter to the right-back or serving position. To increase the movement of the players and to encourage spiking, the regulation court can be used after the serve is received within the smaller confines of the badminton court. As skill level increases, the standard court can be used with the overhand serve.

An instructor can devise modifications of the lead-up games to place emphasis on the fundamental techniques that need to be strengthened. It is important not to progress too quickly with games or children will not experience success and will feel that volleyball is too difficult for them.

MINI-VOLLEYBALL

The Trainer Commission Committee on Mini-Volleyball of the International Volleyball Federation developed rules recommended for adoption by all national volleyball associations in 1971.[10] These rules are for children from nine to twelve years of age and are for games played by two teams of three players each. The rules enable children to grasp the techniques, the elementary tactics and the abilities essential to the sport. Children are able to learn all this while they are actually playing. The rules for Mini-Volleyball are based on relevant experiences and on scientific publications of many countries.[11]

Rules

1. A team consists of three players; two substitutions per game are permissible.
2. The height of the net shall be 2.10 meters (about 6 ft. 10 in.) for both male and female teams.
3. The players of a team will position themselves within their courts in such a manner that there will be two "frontline players" and one "back-line player" at the time the ball is served. After serving the ball, the back-line player may not spike the ball from within the attack area or attempt to hit the ball in the attack area, unless the ball is below the height of the net.
4. The players of a team will change their positions upon receiving the ball for service (the right front-line player will become the back-line player and the left front-line player will now be the right front-line player).
5. A team wins the game when it scores at least 15 points and has a two-point

advantage over the opponents (15:13; 16:14, etc.).

6. A team wins the match when it has won at least two sets of the match (2:0 or 2:1).
7. The match is conducted by a referee. He takes care that the rules are not violated and ensures that the match will be played correctly and in keeping with principles of fair play. In doing this he has a pedagogic function.
8. The playing area shall be 4.5 meters wide and 12 meters long. A net divides the playing area in two equal parts. The spiking line is three meters from the center line.[12]

Offense

Because the backline player cannot spike in the official version of the game, it is usually advantageous for the front-row players to receive all the serves and for the back-row players to penetrate to the net in order to set. This allows the offense to be played with two attackers. If players cannot pass accurately, however, this system will not work.

It may be preferable to disregard the rule that does not allow the backcourt player to spike. Instead, a different formation and rotation can be used with two players placed deep in the court to receive all serves.

The third player on the team is placed at the net in the center of the court and has no receiving responsibility. This player's job is to set all passes to one of the other play-

---

[10]Horst Baake, "Mini Volleyball," *Technical Journal 1* (January 1974): 36–40.
[11]FIVB Trainer Commission Committee On Mini Volleyball, *Mini Volleyball Rules for Children From 9 to 12 Years of Age* (Leipzeig, 1971). Translation obtained from Michael Haley, USBVA Chairman of Collegiate and Scholastic Volleyball.

[12]4.5 meters by 12 meters is approximately 14 ft. 9 in. by 39 ft. 5 in. However, since most school volleyball courts have badminton courts marked within their dimensions, it is suggested that badminton courts be used for Mini- and Triples Volleyball. This gives an area of 20 ft. by 44 ft. with a spiking line 6 ft. 6 in. from the center line. Badminton courts can be used for children up to the seventh grade with good results.

ers to spike. All players are allowed to spike and to block, and players rotate from the left-back position to setter to the right-back, or serving, position.

Defense

Most children under thirteen years of age are not capable of executing strong spikes, so it is often best to position all three defenders back in the court to receive the spike. This also leads to long rallies and great concentration and pride in digging techniques by the participants. The enthusiasm that is evident when children complete these long rallies is very stimulating for the participants and spectators. When players are capable of strong spiking, they should be opposed by one blocker.

Global Mini-Volleyball

About 1962, the East German Volleyball Federation began to assign some of their top volleyball coaches to work with children under twelve years of age. They were soon confronted with arguments that power volleyball techniques were too difficult to teach to children because of their insufficient physical development. However, their immediate success caused mini-volleyball to spread throughout Europe. Today volleyball is an integral part of many national physical education programs and it is particularly strong in Eastern Europe and Asia. The first International Mini-Volleyball Championship took place in Bahrain in 1978 and has increased the interest of volleyball in the Arab countries.

Teachers and coaches begin teaching mini-volleyball to children who are eight and nine years old. This experience would be difficult to duplicate in the United States because the overwhelming majority of children do not receive regular instruction from a physical education teacher until they are in the seventh grade. The Chairman of the International Volleyball Council of Coaches, reporting on the East German Mini-Volleyball Championships, stated that "children possess already astonishing technical and tactical achievements, and their enthusiasm is enormous."[13] He gives several reasons for the quick and successful development of mini-volleyball: (1) Volleyball techniques are easier to acquire before puberty when the requirements of the game are modified to accommodate the age level. (2) The essential physical qualities of speed, mobility, and agility exist at this age or can be quickly developed. (3) Children are enthusiastic about the game and about competition. (4) The rich emotional content of mini-volleyball provides a strong attraction for children.

Children who train twice a week can learn the fundamental techniques in two or three months. After four or five months of training, they can successfully participate in formal competition. Mini-volleyball matches are decided by winning two out of three games, so children can play several matches on the same day without overstraining themselves. "For children, mini-volleyball is a complete, whole game, a struggle full of a sense of joy, an event and at the same time a lesson. It is of paramount importance to stimulate the interest and the enthusiasm, to learn the movements of the game, to develop the physical qualities essential for volleyball both for all mass games of entertainment and the elite volleyball."[14]

[13]Baacke, "Mini Volleyball," pp. 36, 37.
[14]Ibid, p. 37.

JUNIOR HIGH SCHOOL VOLLEYBALL

In a physical education class, intramural program, or extramural program at the junior high level, students should be given an opportunity to learn to set and to attack. Under our present system, players are labeled as setters or spikers and often fail to develop the fundamental techniques required to play the other positions. On our college teams, there are setters who are poor attackers and there are spikers who are poor setters. These players missed the opportunity in their development to become a complete player, capable of performing all techniques and of playing all positions.

At the junior high school level of competition, one position on the court should be designated as the setting position. For example, if a team is using a two-hitter attack, every player who rotates to the middle-front position should set the ball for the side-out attempt. If a team uses a three-hitter attack, the player in the right-back position should set. This six-six system of offense forces all players to develop fundamental volleyball abilities. On defense, the player should also play each of the six positions.

During the summer months, coeducational volleyball classes which meet daily for two hours for a five- to six-week period can be conducted as part of the school curriculum. The instructor can usually spend the first 20 minutes of class reviewing the previous day's progress and establishing points of emphasis for the current lesson. It is best to spend this time in the classroom where the students are not distracted by playground activities. The next 30 minutes should be spent on drills with no more than two or three students to a ball. When the players have learned a sufficient number of ball-handling drills, they should be moved from drill to drill very rapidly so that interest does not lag. Spiking and digging drills are introduced last because they are the most satisfying and provide the best motivation.

A 10- to 15-minute break can be taken at this point to allow the players to get drinks and a snack if desired. Many students prefer to work with the ball during the break in an unsupervised game of one-on-one or doubles. Others request help with certain techniques, particularly spiking. After the break the instructor can assign the class to various teams covering two to three courts, depending on the content of the daily lesson. Older boys and girls can be invited into the class at this stage to

Figure 10-1 *Net Height.* The height of the net should be lowered until the average participant can touch the top of the net with the fingertips of an outstretched hand while standing flat-footed on the court. This will allow young players to spike and attack block as shown above. (Gary Adams)

challenge the better players in doubles or mini-volleyball while the majority of the class plays the other modified games.

Because these classes usually play on the blacktop, the weather is a determining factor in the selection of the activity for the second half of the class. On particularly hot or humid days, the students can be divided into three teams to a court, so that they can rest between games. Three games of Underhand-Serve Volleyball can be played in 50 minutes, which gives every team two games. The more energetic players are allowed to play an unstructured game on the adjoining courts instead of resting. This type of practice is not designed to develop a school team, but rather to teach the fundamental techniques and to instill interest in the sport.

In Eastern Europe and Asia, children twelve to fourteen years old train a minimum of 10 to 12 hours a week after school if they are representing a school team. Studies conducted by a prominent coach in Bulgaria indicate children are capable of playing a five-game match at this age and on the following day are fully rested and ready to play again.[15] Children twelve to fourteen years old are in the bantam category in world competition and boys play on a net that is 2.20 meters high while the girls use the mini-volleyball height of 2.10 meters.

[15]Thomas Chakarov, "Some Questions of the Maximum Possibilities of Playing of Children in Volleyball," *FIVB Bulletin* 49–50 (March 1970): 27–35.

IV

ORGANIZATION

11

Coaching

MY COACHING PHILOSOPHY

Volleyball traditionally has been among the few sports that people still participated in for the pure joy of playing; that is changing at the college and national level. Many college men's programs have five full grant-in-aids. Title IX has increased the funding to Women's College programs and there are up to twelve full grant-in-aids for most Division I programs. Within the last decade benefits to the participant have become financial as well as social. Coaches are employed full time to coach volleyball in our colleges and our USA men and women teams also have full-time volleyball coaches. These coaches are under pressure to produce championship teams. This increased pressure to win which is so prevalent in our society is filtering down to the high school level. Of course the coaches and players are becoming better every year as the intensity increases, but let us keep in mind that the main reason for coaching and playing volleyball should be enjoyment.

Coaching philosophy is shaped through athletic experiences; we accumulate practical wisdom as we endure losses and are influenced by people and events throughout our careers. As an athlete I was influenced by my high school basketball coach, Bill Rankin, who was a former captain on John Wooden's UCLA Basketball team. Coach Rankin had a good sense of humor and managed to relate to us while working the team hard. We responded to him because he treated us fairly and truly enjoyed what he was doing. Under his direction we won the first conference basketball championship in our school's history. Sometime during that championship season I decided to become a coach. After playing college football and basketball my freshman and sophomore year, I transferred to UCLA and played six-man volleyball for the first time. As a senior I occasionally worked out with

Jerry Norman's freshman UCLA basketball team which practiced immediately before our volleyball team. I took a class from Jerry Norman, the UCLA Assistant Basketball Coach, and learned John Wooden's UCLA offense. I was amazed at its simplicity and asked to play against Coach Norman's freshman team to familiarize myself thoroughly with the offense. The next year I was working at a playground and taught the UCLA offense to a group of nine and ten year old boys who went on to win the Los Angeles County Pee Wee Basketball Championships. Two years later Coach Wooden won his first NCAA Championship with the same offense. I will never forget that it was so simple that a bunch of nine and ten year old boys could master it. In 1979 the UCLA Volleyball Team won their seventh NCAA Championship in the ten year history of NCAA competition with an offense that had three plays—an offense so simple that every summer we teach 800 campers to run it in five days.

I watched every home game during UCLA's 1964 basketball season and decided that the philosopher whom I admired the most is a coach and teacher of the highest order, John Wooden. Coach Wooden exemplified that rare person who was calm and patient enough under stressful game situations to make his judgments according to his philosophical beliefs. I tried to emulate his calm positive attitude by always thinking of the next play rather than becoming excited and making emotional decisions.

The interview below was taped and then compiled by Ron Salmons, whose son Steve was a great All-American middle blocker at UCLA. I think the answers to his questions accurately reflect my coaching philosophy.

Question: What do you feel is involved in being a winning coach?

Al Scates: It all begins with the selection of players the coach wants to use. Whether he's coaching a college or high school team, he has to recruit the players who will be suitable for his team. You want the best personnel . . . the people with the chance to have the best skills . . . the best physical abilities you can get.

If you have confidence in yourself as a coach, you recruit for potential physical ability and a winning attitude. It's important the athlete has a background of winning. If you take a player who has lost all his life, it's going to be a real battle to turn this person into a winner. The players you end up counting on must be tough in the clutch, those who know they can win.

Question: What about intelligence?

Al Scates: It certainly helps if a player is intelligent. That's another factor. But everyone doesn't have to be a genius. I doubt if the Russians are interested with intelligence at all. Yet they've had some great teams because of their physical ability. So physical ability is the paramount thing. That means having an explosive quality, the ability to move fast, jump high . . . these types of things.

Question: You've been very successful at recruiting. Are those the things you look for?

Al Scates: Yes, and I look so much for winning attitude. I can tell by looking at a player on the court if he thinks he's a winner or not. I can tell if he has the confidence—the *real* confidence—not the fake confidence. I like to watch him in crucial situations: That he *wants* the pass, he *wants* the set, he *wants* to hit the ball in the crucial situations when the team needs him. This is the kind of athlete I want.

Question: Does the act of winning lead to more winning?

Al Scates: Yes, you get used to winning . . . or losing. If you have a coach and a bunch of players who are used to losing, they're going to keep on losing. You turn it around by getting a new coach and new players in there who are used to winning. And once you start winning, it just perpetuates itself. We win at UCLA because we're *supposed* to win, we're *confident* we're going to win, and we train hard as hell because that's the way we *do* win.

Question: What effect does this have on opponents?

Al Scates: Psychologically, it's so important to beat everybody every chance you get . . . convince them they cannot win. Then when it comes time for the finals, they must overcome a losing attitude. You have the advantage. The National Team doesn't want to go out and play Japan or Cuba or any other team and experiment with a line-up just because the Olympics are a year away. What you want to do is go out and beat them. Period. That's the important thing. Never give them a chance. And that's why coming close to winning, but still losing, doesn't cut it. The next time you meet them it may be for a medal. Psychologically, they'll think they can beat you. And you're in trouble right from the start.

Question: How much of coaching is teaching?

Al Scates: They're the same thing. I don't know how you can separate the two. Coaching is constantly teaching and refining the technical skills of your players. Techniques are the building blocks. The players have to execute the basic skills you want them to before you can run any plays. I've always been a teacher. I really enjoy teaching . . . or coaching. It's the same thing.

I don't believe much in criticizing. I try to show a player how to do it right. When I see a player improve because of something I showed him how to do, it gives me a great amount of exhilaration. I really feel satisfied when something like that occurs. And that occurs all the time. I really get high on teaching. And that's what you have to do to have a winning team. It's all fundamental.

Question: To be effective in coaching, your players must have a respect for you, a willingness to listen. Why do you feel you've earned this respect?

Al Scates: In the beginning, I was a player and a coach at the same time. I could perform the skills and the players liked that. They knew I could do it, so they could do it. That was important. After that, I think it was my positive attitude. The most important requirement in coaching is to have a positive attitude. You have to be positive. If you walk out to the huddle and change a defense or you call a play—say like, "Run play four, set the ball to Jones"—first of all, you've got to know Jones believes he can do the job or you don't give him the play. Secondly, the *rest* of the team has to believe that this is going to work. If they believe, and you believe, nine-times-out-of-ten that will get you out of there. The key is you're always positive.

When a coach walks out there and starts chewing a player out for something he did, that is ridiculous. It's already history. The player knows he made a mistake. You don't have to tell him. What you have to do is get the players to leave that huddle on a positive note and think of what they're going to do *next*. That's the important thing.

You have to be honest with your players. You can't lie to them or you'll lose their respect. And you must be consistent, or you'll throw your players off. It's reached a point at UCLA where I can walk out there and I can tell my team to do anything. Even if I'm wrong it's going to work. Because I believe it's going to work. And they believe it's going to work. And if *they* believe it's going to work, it *will* work.

Question: You're noted for your unique style of giving your players a free hand, yet you maintain discipline on the team. How do you accomplish this?

Al Scates: I don't try to control the players. What they do on their own time is their business, as long as they don't embarrass the program. I treat them as adults. They are adults. When we go somewhere, I don't tell the players to be in at nine o'clock at night. I ask the Captain what time we should be in. He might talk it over with a few guys and *they* decide what to do. They have as much invested in the program as I do. They have plenty at stake. They have to have a chance to decide about their program. I give it to them. I'll take care of the tactical business on the court. All I want them to do is to show up ready to go, at practice and at the matches. In return, I'll be open and honest with them. And the rest of their life is up to them.

Question: Once your squad is set, do you have any philosophy about treating each member of the team equally?

Al Scates: Every man on a squad is unique. Each one needs to be recognized and treated as an individual if you expect him to play his best. I think it's up to the coach (and this is key) to work with the various personalities. The players are set in their ways. They're mature young men. I'm not going to change them. I don't want to change them. So, as coach, I must learn their individual strengths and develop them to their utmost.

But when it comes to handing out the benefits, the meal money, the accommodations, the jobs, the uniforms, and things like that, then everyone on my squad gets equal treatment. It's extremely important that each man feels he's a part of the team and being treated fairly. Each man must be treated with respect and dignity. I won't have it any other way.

But everyone on my team doesn't train the same. There are individual differences, and individual weaknesses which must be taken into account. So we physically train people differently. There are some exercises I won't have certain players do. Obviously, I want no one hurt. A team at full strength has the advantage. I'm proud of the relatively low number of injuries attributed to our policy of individually taking care of our players. This policy adds more fun to more players as they play the game, and it helps us to remain winners.

Question: The word is you have a "system" for winning. Can you tell us about it?

Al Scates: First of all, it's our team that does the winning. But as coach I must make decisions which affect our team. As background for making these decisions, I have three trained statisticians gathering special data at each of our matches. Then they give all the stats to me. I compile them and am the only one who studies them. I don't share my stats with anyone. I don't post them. I don't give them to the newspaper. If I have a player with bad stats and I want to play him, I'll play him. If he's a winner and helps the team win, that may be more important. There are always intangibles. The special stats are only for my personal use; our News Bureau compiles stats for the media and opposing coach.

Question: What is the purpose of gathering these stats?

Al Scates: I'm mainly interested in what my players do under stressful situations. Meaningful stats always come in the more meaningful matches. I'm not really interested in a player who can dominate weak teams. What I want is the player who will play best in the championship matches. The goal is to win, whether it be the NCAA Championship at the university level, or the Olympic Gold Medal for the National Team. These are the ultimate matches. And the coach must decide the best six players to be out there, who should be playing side-by-side in the rotation, and the three substitutes (one at each position) who are ready to go into the game at any moment. My stats help me make these decisions.

Question: Do you use stats in scouting competitive teams?

Al Scates: We often send statisticians to matches where a key team is playing someone else. We also have stats from when we play them. The more times the team plays the more stats I gather. When it comes time to play them when it counts, I develop a game plan they haven't seen before. This happened in 1981 when we played USC for the NCAA Championship. We knew from the stats they set two players 70 percent of the time. For the first time all year we had our two best blockers follow them around the court regardless of what side they went to. It was close, but we won the NCAA for the eighth time.

Question: What type stat charts do you gather?

Al Scates: The first is a *Sideout Chart* on both our opponent and our team. I want to know where each team hits the ball, what type set did they hit, and what kind of combination did they run. As an example of how I use this, if I have a player who everytime he gets a "X" set he always hits the ball to "area five" on the court, then I'll have to develop that player's capabilities so he can also hit the ball to "area one" on the court, or "area two" or "area four." So if teams are scouting us, we don't have a stereotype offense. I might not make this adjustment without the stats.

The second is an *Attack Chart.* It records our sideouts—that is, our first hit off the serve reception. This chart tells me the type of set that was hit and whether the hitter put it away, kept it in play, was stuffed, or made an error. This is divided into sections or areas of the court so we find out if our player is more effective from the left, middle, or right side. We then adapt our use of this player to best use his strengths. Half of this chart also has what we call "other hits." These are hits that are usually more difficult. For instance off the dig, where the setter must run to the backcourt and set high to the hitter, the blockers have plenty of time to get ready and the hit is more difficult. These stats tell me this. There may be a player who cannot hit well under these circumstances. With the stats, I know this and the ball is set to someone else who has better skills in this type situation.

The *Blocking Chart* is divided into end blockers and middle blockers, and records blocks, stuffs, deflections, and what combinations of people work well together. I grade each blocker. You'd be amazed at how important deflections are. They most often keep the ball in play and can be converted into points.

We sometimes keep a *Serving Chart.* It lets me know how many points each server scores. If we're not scoring off a particular man's service it may be because the front row is weak, but usually his serve needs some work. This chart also records aces and errors.

Question: Do other coaches keep stats?

Al Scates: I'm sure they do. I have written a book, "Winning Volleyball," which is now going into its third revision and has sold over 50,000 copies. The various charts are in the book. Of course they have to have people capable of recording the action, they have to be able to interpret the stats, and they have to know what decisions to make. I have records that go back several years that give me information of specific teams, countries, coaches and players. The more data you collect the more you know. I've found it gives me an edge in making decisions.

Question: It's said that "weak" coaches try to make up for their shortcomings by over-conditioning and over-practicing their players. Do you have any feelings on that?

Al Scates: I don't know about so-called "weak" coaches. I can only give you my thoughts. I do not believe a six-man team playing on hard floors should practice twelve months a year. It puts too much stress on the body, and no team is going to play well if they have several players hurting. A team should take two or three months off, then treat the rest of the year as a season. A goal should be set in terms of time and key matches when the team must be at its best. In these matches you want your team strong. But you also want your team fresh mentally and rested physically.

At the beginning of a season I like to work on conditioning and developing techniques. But I do them on separate days. I don't believe in practicing when the players are tired. It prevents them from developing their skills properly. I like a team to practice techniques—or to learn something new—when it's fresh. So on days we practice techniques, I make sure that's all we do. On other days, we just work on conditioning.

Once our team is in shape, we level off the conditioning work. Our NCAA championship is in May. In March, we stop all weight work and wind-sprints. We've found that the players' vertical jump actually increases about two weeks after we stop the weights, and will be maintained through to the championships in May. This discovery is one of the advantages of keeping detailed records on each player. Otherwise, we might have continued with the weights and sprints, leading to soreness, aches, fatigue and ultimately to injury.

Question: There are those who state that the importance of the coach is best dramatized in a five-game match. Do you feel that has any merit?

Al Scates: The coach is really important when two teams meet which have equal ability. The coach will decide who will win or lose the match in those situations. The five-game match that has been well documented is the 1976 match between Poland and Russia for the Gold Medal. The strategies the Polish coach employed against a superior physical Russian team were pretty

fantastic. I believe everyone agrees the Polish coach won the Gold Medal that day.

Question: What do you feel is the importance of having a qualified trainer with the team?

Al Scates: A winning team is a healthy team. I learned a long time ago that a good, consistent trainer is extremely valuable. The trainer gets to know the players very well, and he's a good source of accurate information for the coach. You'd be surprised how a player will confide in a trainer he respects. If something's bothering that player physically he might be afraid to tell the coach. He might be out there working hard on drills he shouldn't be working on. A good trainer will let you know. He has complete information on the condition of each man on the squad. As champions, I insist our teams have the very best in trainers available at all times.

There are a few areas that needed to be elaborated on or were not covered in the interview that are important to a team in achieving its goals:

1. **Leadership.** Leadership begins with an administrator who is interested and supportive of the program. The head coach should have good rapport with the administration and have the respect of the coaching staff and players. It is beneficial if the coach is an experienced competitor, is confident enough to teach outstanding athletes and has above average intelligence. The assistant and junior varsity coach should be loyal and share the philosophy of the head coach. They should be thoroughly familiar with the techniques and tactics to be taught to the athletes. The *captain* should be an outstanding player, intelligent and have the respect of the team.

2. **Organization.** There should be a continuity of staff and program from year to year. As assistant coaches move on to new positions players who have come through the program should replace them because they are familiar with the head coaches philosophy. At the high school level this means that graduating seniors who can fit assistant coaching into their college or job schedule should be encouraged to join the staff. At the college level the use of graduate assistant coaches is recommended. The season should be planned in advance so the players concentrate on conditioning and techniques before spending a lot of time on tactics. Later as tactical practices become necessary techniques and conditioning must be maintained. The long range goal of peaking for the championships must be primary when a team is a contender.

3. **Talent.** Every coach should try and select the best players available. Of course the philosophy, system of play and returning players will determine what characteristics a coach looks for in a player. Championships are often won by teams with simply above average talent playing together as an outstanding team. Teams with players that have outstanding size, quickness and strength often finish significantly below their team potential because they do not work together well.

4. **Practice.** Winning teams must make a committment on the practice floor. If the opponents have more physical talent, your team must practice harder and more often to defeat them. Teams that make such a committment in sweat and time do not lose easily. Through practice a team must be prepared for every tactic that the opponent can use.

5. **Annual training program.** There should be an opportunity for athletes to play volleyball during the entire year. Our team has a fall practice in October and November and then usually takes December off for final exams and vacation unless a foreign tour is scheduled. During the fall we practice techniques in the gym three times a week and work on conditioning (without a ball) two times a week. We play in about three "friendship" tournaments during this period against clubs and other universities. We stress physical conditioning during our preseason or preparatory training phase which is in January. During January we try and play six or seven practice matches and enter one or two college tournaments. Our competitive season is February through April and we usually play about two matches a week and practice three times a week. After the playoffs in early May the boys are on their own until October. We keep three nets up in the main gym for recreational play from May to September. Doubles tournaments run from May to September in Southern California and most of the boys compete every weekend in various tournaments. Of course the more talented players are recruited by our Junior and Senior USA Teams for international competition during the summers.

6. **Facilities.** The use of proper facilities at convenient times for the athletes are important. At least two indoor courts with quality nets are a necessity for a varsity and junior varsity program. Three courts are preferable if there are eighteen or more athletes involved in the program. Teams that practice in small gyms with low ceilings have difficulty beating compa-

rable teams when playing in large gyms.

7. **Team support.** Teams who go all the way win in their own gym. Strong support must be cultivated among the student body and community to help the team win the close match.

A successful season begins with a logical series of procedures that starts with selecting the squad, offense, defense, positions and player combinations. It is maintained by good teaching, intuition, accurate observation and hard training. It ends with the attainment of a common goal or the knowledge that you did the best you could to attain that goal.

SELECTING THE SQUAD

When the coach is anticipating a large turn out for the opening day of practice the returning players who are sure to make the team should be invited to practice at a later date. I often use the first week of practice to look at junior varsity and new players before asking returning varsity players to practice. Of course if you have a short pre-season you may not be able to afford the missed practice time.

Important Factors

There are a few factors that should be considered before the first day of try-outs:

1. Develop a depth chart of your returning players by position.
2. Determine any possible position changes for returning players.
3. Develop a position chart of your players by years of eligibility remaining.
4. Determine the number of players that would be best to carry during the pre-season and competitive season.

During the pre-season we like to keep between six and eight players at each of our three positions of setter, quick hitter and power hitter. We have three courts and can carry a maximum of twenty-four players in our program. Some years I like to drop to eighteen players before the competitive season and practice with the nine best players on the same court. If an upperclassman is not good enough to be among one of the twelve players suiting up for the varsity, then a freshman or sophomore should take his place on the squad of eighteen players. Only freshmen and sophomores who have a chance to play on the varsity in the future are kept on the junior varsity team. Through the years we have seen some great changes in players between the freshman and sophomore years and for that reason we like to keep players trying out for the team until we have a good insight into their potential. Of course the longer a player trys out the harder it is for the coach and athlete to come to an amicable parting. I believe in cutting the players personally at practice by discreetly taking them to one side while the try-outs are in progress and explaining to them why they did not make the squad. This gives the athlete an opportunity to ask questions and analyze his future intentions regarding the program.

Characteristics to Look for

The importance of these characteristics will vary according to your philosophy and system of play:

- Fighting spirit, desire, and determination
- Winning attitude and experience
- Coordination
- Intelligence
- Reach and vertical jump
- Quickness and speed

- Technical skill
- Strength and endurance
- Remaining eligibility
- Self-control

Try-Out Procedures

The first day the prospective players report at 3 PM ready to work out. They are dressed in their own volleyball gear and warm-up and stretch under the direction of a coach. At 3:30 PM they choose a partner and are directed to pass and set the ball in a variety of ball handling drills for about fifteen minutes. During this time the coach should talk to any prospects that are not familiar and ascertain how much eligibility they have remaining. This is important since you can afford to keep freshmen and sophomores with potential and teach them to play the game. While the players are engaged in ball handling drills it may be obvious that some poorly coordinated prospects can be released at this time, but this is not usually the case. At 3:45 PM players engage in pepper to warm-up their arms, and then at 3:55 PM we explain the spiking drill. During the try-outs we limit the drills to the fundamental techniques. At UCLA we concentrate on spiking the first day. Due to the large numbers of players trying out we run each drill for about twenty minutes so that all candidates will get several turns.

First Day

3:00–3:30 PM   Jogging, push ups, sit ups, dives, rolls, stretching.

3:30–3:45 PM   Ball handling drills in pairs.

3:45–3:55 PM   Pepper.

3:55–4:05 PM   Explanation and demonstration of spiking. Stress the following points:

1. Tell the athletes to wait and approach fast. Show them the four-step approach with the step close takeoff. Caution them to keep the ball in front of their attacking shoulder.
2. Watch for the heel, toe takeoff.
3. Stress the importance of using the arms to increase their vertical jump. Tell them to use a double-arm lift.
4. Show them the East German technique of spiking with the elbow high. Stress extending the spiking arm and contacting the ball high with an open hand near the apex of the jump.
5. Watch for a good wrist snap.
6. Stress upper body rotation into the ball on high sets.
7. They must attempt to hit every ball over the net regardless of the set. If they catch the ball they go to the end of the line.

4:05–4:25 PM   Spike four-sets and regular sets from area four.

4:25–4:30 PM   Break.

4:30–4:45 PM   Spike five-sets from area two.

4:45–5:00 PM   Use a straight approach and spike four-sets from area four. Practice the following spikes:

1. Spike deep line.
2. Spike deep crosscourt.
3. Spike crosscourt inside the ten-foot line.

5:00–5:15 PM   Use a straight approach and spike five-sets from area two. Practice these spikes:

1. Spike deep line.
2. Spike deep crosscourt.
3. Spike crosscourt inside the ten-foot line.

5:15–5:30 PM   Two ball, four corner setting drill.

This practice includes 40 minutes of ball handling drills and 65 minutes of setting and spiking. At the end of this practice I will know who the candidates for setter, power hitter and quick hitter are. Do not be in a hurry to cut people the first day. Players who are poor spikers may be lacking in several characteristics such as: coordination, reach or vertical jump, quickness and speed, technical skill and strength. Poor strength will effect the speed and vertical jump and can easily be improved upon. Good coaching can rapidly improve technical skill and vertical jump. Reach can be determined by noting the athletes standing touch along the net or using tests similar to Vertec testing described in the next chapter. Noting the size of the athletes feet and asking about the size of siblings and parents is also a good indication of potential growth and reach among younger athletes. The characteristic that cannot be improved from my experience is coordination. The coach must ascertain why a player is having problems and determine whether these problems can be improved upon enough to allow the prospective player to become a contributing member of the varsity before his eligibility expires. The selection of the squad is purely subjective and is only as reliable as the coach's analysis of a player's performance. If you are not sure about an athlete by all means keep him coming to practice until you are satisfied you can make the right decision. For example, in the fall of 1972 a player named Denny Cline showed up at the athletic department with his father and indicated he wanted to play volleyball at UCLA. After I looked at him in practice for a few days I decided he didn't have the armswing for an outside hitter; he was too short and did not jump well enough to middle block, and his hands were not good enough to set. He was

intelligent and learned quickly so I let him practice until the season began and then he became our statistician. During the summer Denny worked out hard and made a significant gain in strength and increased his vertical jump. I found out he had grown an inch and he seemed a step quicker, although I finally realized this step was due to anticipation. What Denny really excelled in was a fighting spirit and determination to excel. Once he started as a sophomore no one could get him out of the line-up. I came very close to cutting Denny the second day of practice; yet he started on three NCAA Championship Teams and was our 1976 captain. After that experience I prefer to keep a player until I am sure he cannot help the team. An exception is the clumsy prospect who is continually broad jumping into or under the net. It is best to cut this player before you introduce blocking drills to avoid injury.

All coaches are looking for tall, coordinated fast spikers with a good vertical jump. I want to point out that some players play taller than others. Do not be in a hurry to cut players because they are too small; take a look at their other characteristics first. One of the best women's team I have ever seen was the 1976 Japanese Women, who routed a much taller Russian Women's team to take the Gold Medal in Munich. One of the great setters at UCLA was 5'7" Toshi Toyoda, who made First Team All-American. In 1975, 5'10" Mike Normand was our most valuable spiker on an NCAA Championship Team. In 1980, our line up averaged 6'3" yet 5'10" Peter Ehrman made Volleyball Magazines First Team All-American and led UCLA in spiking percentage in most of our big matches. These players all had great fighting spirit to go with a winning attitude and winning athletic background. These characteristics are difficult to evaluate during the first day of try-outs.

Second Day

3:00–3:30 PM   Jogging, push ups, sit ups, dives, rolls, stretching.

3:30–3:40 PM   Pepper.

3:40–3:45 PM   Explanation and demonstration of end blocking. Stress the following points:

1. Start an arms length from the net so you can spike balls passed over the net.
2. Look at the setter and spiker in front of you to pick up any signals as to what play is going to be run. Do not look at your server.
3. Watch the pass and the approaching spiker in your zone; then see in which direction the setter releases the ball.
4. Watch the approaching spiker or spikers in your area. Keep your eyes open.
5. Move to the point of attack using the slide step and squat and keep your back straight.
6. Slide arms above and over the net.
7. Pike.
8. Keep hand spread 8 in. apart.
9. Read the spiker's approach, upper body, and armswing in that order. The ball will come into view.
10. If the ball goes by your block, turn in that direction as you descend.

3:45–3:55 PM   Hit four-sets from area four and block one time after spiking.

3:55–4:00 PM   Explanation and demonstration of digging. Stress the following points:

1. Keep the feet about shoulder width apart with your feet slightly turned in

"pidgeon toed" style. The knees should be bent and inside of the toes with the weight on the balls of the feet.

2. Get low and hop into the position where you think the ball will be hit just prior to the spiker contacting the ball. Be sure your feet are not moving when the ball is contacted.
3. Try to use the two-arm forearm pass.
4. Keep weight forward.
5. Give with a hard spike; do not follow through.
6. Try and keep your back straight and your hips under the ball, so the ball is dug high on your side of the court.

4:00–4:15 PM   Hit five-sets from area two; block one time and dig in area five, six, one, and two before returning to the spiking line.

4:15–4:30 PM   Spike close one-sets. Spike medium one-sets.

4:30–4:35 PM   Break.

4:35–4:45 PM   Crosscourt approach spike line from area four.

4:45–4:55 PM   Crosscourt approach spike line from area two.

5:00–5:30 PM   Meeting.

Review the try-out procedure. Emphasize important keys that will help the players improve their techniques. Fill out insurance forms and biography forms. Get the players addresses and phone numbers.

Third Day

3:00–3:30 PM   Jogging, push ups, sit ups, dives, rolls, stretching.

3:30–3:45 PM   Ball handling drills with partners.

3:45–3:55 PM   Pepper drill with partner.

3:55–4:15 PM   One- and five-sets versus one end blocker.

4:15–4:35 PM   Four- and three-sets versus one end blocker.

4:35–4:40 PM   Break.

4:40–4:45 PM   Introduce the fake X approach and spike for the area two spiker.

4:45–5:00 PM   Spikers run the fake X approach and hit a back two-set.

5:00–5:15 PM   Spike five- or two-sets from area two versus one blocker and four diggers.

5:15–5:20 PM   Explanation and demonstration of serve reception.

1. Get to the ball and stop.
2. When you're in the basic position your feet are about shoulder width apart with your feet slightly turned in "pidgeon toed" style. The knees should be bent and inside of the toes with the weight on the balls of the feet.
3. Use quick movement to get to the ball.
4. Face the target area.
5. Lock the elbows.
6. Make any necessary lateral adjustments with the arms.
7. Contact the ball on the forearms.
8. Do not swing the arms at the ball; most players use too much follow through during service reception or when digging a spike.

5:20–5:40 PM   Serve and receive.

Fourth Day

3:00–3:30 PM   Jogging, push ups, sit ups, dives, rolls, stretching.

3:30–3:45 PM   Ball handling drills with partners.

3:45–3:55 PM   Pepper.

3:55–4:00 PM   Explain and demonstrate how to play the middle-back defense. Emphasize that the line diggers move up for the dink when the end blocker covers the line. The center back only has lateral responsibility unless the middle blocker leaves a hole in the block. Only then should the middle-back player move in. He has no dink responsibility. The middle back steps towards the sideline when the line digger moves in for a dink. Emphasize that four diggers should be in the ready position facing the attacker when the ball is contacted. Walk everyone through the positions.

4:00–4:20 PM   Scrimmage. Side out players versus six scoring players in the middle-back defense.

4:20–4:35 PM   The coach in area two hits balls at a spiker in area four and a digger in area five. The setter penetrates out of area one and sets the spiker off the dig. Six defenders try to score against the attack.

4:35–4:40 PM   Break.

4:40–5:00 PM   Run the right X from area two and spike to area five.

5:00–5:10 PM   Run the right X from area two and spike to area one.

5:10–5:30 PM   Scrimmage. Side out team versus scoring team.

Fifth Day

3:00–3:30 PM   Warm-up and stretching.

3:30–3:45 PM   Ball-handling drills.

3:45–3:55 PM   Pepper.

3:55–4:05 PM   Dink and block two times from area two and area four.

4:05–4:20 PM   Run the X or fake X with an area two and three attacker versus three blockers.

4:20–4:25 PM   Break.

4:25 PM   Games.

The five-day try-out schedule shown above has been used to select players for the UCLA Men's squad. A try-out schedule for a high school girl's team should emphasize ball control drills such as serve reception, back-row defense, setting and serving. The college coach is usually looking for players to dominate the net, which is the easiest way to win. Coaches of younger players should place more emphasis on moving quickly and controlling the ball.

TEACHING

Most of the volleyball coaches in the United States are teachers during the school day and coach the team when the regular school day has ended. This is a logical combination of duties since the basic task of the coach is to teach fundamentals. The coach should explain and demonstrate the fundamentals himself if he is capable; if not he should have a model demonstrate. The important thing is the technique should be demonstrated correctly. Next the player should execute the fundamental while the coach identifies the key problem the athlete is having. The coach should show the athlete what he is doing wrong while verbally identifying the error. Next demonstrate the correct technique several times while discussing it with the athlete and have the athlete repeat the technique. Only after the key problems are identified and corrected can the coach move on to other smaller problems in the athlete's technique. Make sure you and your assistants are positive and show athletes how to correct problems in a friendly manner. Use a minimum of talking and utilize correct demonstrations done quickly. If criticism is given in a negative manner athletes are reluctant to try new techniques. After the athletes can execute the fundamental correctly the action must be repeated many times to become an automatic response. That is when the coach has to make the drill goal oriented. For example, the coach can use the ball bag or ball cart for targets in serving and spiking drills. Athletes can rotate from a digging rotation when a certain number of balls are dug. Use your imagination to make your drills interesting and change drills frequently.

SELECTING THE OFFENSE

I prefer an offense that gives everyone on the starting unit an equal opportunity to spike; this keeps players motivated and defenses guessing. The offense should be simple yet unpredictable. After a match the statistics should reflect a fairly even distribution of sets among the various spikers. The exception to this occurs when a team has a great spiker; in this case, the ball should be delivered to this player until the opponents can stop him. The offense should allow players to specialize by hitting certain sets from particular areas of the court, so that there is a better utilization of practice time and spikers can concentrate on hitting the sets that they excel at.

Four-Two Offense

The best offense for inexperienced coaches and players is the four-two system utilizing four spikers and two setters. The main advantage is that it does not require the accurate serve reception of the other two systems. It is the simplest offense and the easiest to learn although there are many innovative plays and alignments that could be added throughout the season. It is the only system that allows five people to cover the hitter on every spike if the offense is run in the traditional manner. Since the two setters are not required to spike it gives smaller athletes a chance for more participation. The obvious disadvantage is that there are three blockers defending against two hitters; this can be negated to some extent if the setters are taught to hit or dump a close pass. Since there are two setters, hitters must be aware of any differences in their delivery of sets. The setters in this offense are usually small and block poorly.

Five-One Offense

The best offense for many teams that have one exceptional setter is a five-one system utilizing five spikers and one setter. This system is advisable for teams that have a short season or little practice time because only one primary setter and a substitute have to be trained; the primary setters can devote almost all of their practice time to setting and the spikers can learn to develop their timing with one setter. At the upper level of competition five-one teams usually are strong blocking teams because there are opportunities to "hide" a tall player who has difficulty receiving serves. This offense is much more potent if a back-row spiker can be set when the setter is in the front court. Very few teams have players who can take off behind the ten-foot line and put the ball on the floor with regularity, however. The main disadvantages are that there are three rotations of a two-hitter attack. This is negated to a great extent if serve reception is accurate and the setter can jump-set or dump the ball on the second contact; this will force one blocker to stay with the setter and have the same effect as a three-hitter attack. When a starting setter is injured in this system it is always a tremendous loss; much more than the other two systems. Five-one systems are very

popular among national teams; the great Japanese setter Nekoda revolutionized combination play with two and three attackers and his exploits were well documented in print and film. Debbie Green and Dusty Dvorak are two outstanding setters who have run our USA Men and Women's team very effectively using this offense.

Six-Two Offense

The six-two system utilizes two setters who spike when they are in the front row. Since there are always three spikers in the front row with equal spiking opportunities it is easier to get one-on-one attack situations. A simple offense using only a few plays is sufficient to create one-on-one situations. The first team to go undefeated in NCAA competition was the 1979 UCLA Bruins (31–0), who used only three plays in their six-two attack. When fewer plays are used there is more practice time to perfect them. A big advantage of this system over the five-one is substituting. In the UCLA six-two system there are only three positions; setter, quick hitter and power hitter. The substitute setter, quick hitter and power hitter can go in the game at any time for either of two people and have exactly the same assignments on offense and transition. In a sophisticated five-one system every player has different side out positions and patterns of attack. At the international level this is not a problem since the players have a lot of time to practice. A disadvantage is that if the serve reception is poor the middle attacker cannot be set. Poor passing teams should not use the six-two system. The coach must plan the practices carefully to make sure the setters get enough practice time spiking and setting. Another disadvantage is that the coach must constantly monitor the setters to make sure

Table 11-1 *NCAA Men's Championships*

Year	Team	Offense
1970	UCLA	6-2
1971	UCLA	6-2
1972	UCLA	6-2
1973	SDSU	6-2
1974	UCLA	6-2
1975	UCLA	5-1
1976	UCLA	6-2
1977	USC	5-1
1978	Pepperdine	5-1
1979	UCLA	6-2
1980	USC	5-1
1981	UCLA	6-2
1982	UCLA	6-2
1983	UCLA	6-2

they are delivering the sets at the same speed height and general area of the court since spikers will be hitting sets delivered by both setters.

College and club coaches can recruit players for the system they like to use. At the high school level an experienced coach with good athletes should probably use the five-one or six-two depending on the technical skills of the players. A beginning coach or a coach with mediocre athletes should use the four-two.

The information below indicates that either the five-one or six-two offense can win at the higher levels of competition. Most of the better college teams are now using a five-one offense.

SELECTING THE DEFENSE

I prefer a defensive system that assigns each player one blocking position for three rotations and one backcourt position for three rotations. That enables the coach to drill the player on only two defensive positions instead of requiring the athlete to become proficient at all of the defensive positions. Many teams learn two or more basic defensive alignments and choose the defense that provides the best match up for a particular opponent. I prefer using only the middle-back defensive alignment and teaching our players to shift into alignments within this defense that incorporate the strengths of the middle-in and off-blocker defense. These defenses are discussed in Chapter eight and the reasons for using them are detailed. All three defenses are used at all levels of competition. In international women's competition the quick teams that rely on digging to score prefer the middle-back and off-blocker defenses; the Japanese Women's team is the best example. Taller slower teams who rely on their block to score often prefer the middle-in defense; the Russian Women are usually suited for this defense.

Individual players who have great anticipation should be given more backcourt responsibility. For example an exceptionally quick player such as Karch Kiraly who plays in area one in the middle-back defense can be responsible for all the dumps and dinks from the opponents front-court setter.

Our UCLA defense utilizes a quick transition from defense to attack and our personnel is selected with that quality in mind. Our setters are usually tall and capable blockers who can protect the net in area two for three rotations and are good right-side spikers. Our front-court setter always switches to area two to block even if he is hitting from the left side when our opponent serves. After the block our front-court setter will set the ball if the backcourt setter digs it or he will back off the net to hit a five-set. On a free ball situation the front-court setter will hit an X or fake X; he is told what to do by the backcourt setter who runs by him when penetrating from area one on the free ball situation. The backcourt setter always switches to area one on defense and tries to dig all balls to the frontcourt setter in area two. Our quick hitters all block the middle on every play when they are in the front-court. They always approach for a one-set during the transition from blocking to attacking. On those rare occasions that they slip or see they cannot approach for the one-set they must yell "NO!" to the setter so there will not be a broken play. Our scoring is built on our transition game to the quick hitter. Since our quick hitters are usually our biggest men we play them in the middle back where they have more time to run down spikes deflected by the block. They do not have any dink responsibility here, so they do not have to dive as much to retrieve balls. The key to dominating the net is to use quick big players at the quick hitter position. Our power hitters block in area four for three rotations and always back off the net to hit a four-set. If the ball is dug badly they will hit a high set. They will hit about 80 percent of their spikes on the left side during a match; the other 20 percent will be hit on the right side during side out situations. The power hitters are generally smaller and better diggers than our quick hitters so we play them in area five when they are in the backcourt. This allows them to play more balls since our opponents set most of the balls to their area four and usually hit crosscourt into our power hitters protecting area four and five. This tendency to set to area four increases at the high school level.

When we are practicing defense we are really practicing scoring. At least 30 percent of our spikes in a competitive match occur from a defensive transition; this includes side out attempts that are returned by the opponent as well as scoring attempts initiated by our serve.

MATCH THE PLAYER TO THE POSITION

If any changes in positions are going to be made with returning players, it should be accomplished as early in the season as possible. When we are teaching fundamental techniques such as spiking in the pre-season we have all of the players learn to spike all of the sets in our offense. Every player blocks in every position along the net and every player digs in every position in the backcourt. Besides deciding on positions for new players we should reassess the possibility of changes for returning players. If a spiker has good hands we may look at him during the setting drills. If we are seriously considering moving a spiker to a setting position we also look at him in scrimmage and game situations before making our decision. Besides physical ability there are certain attitudes and characteristics that I look for in each position. Our setter must be able to concentrate on the next play selection immediately, even after extremely adverse plays have occurred. He must have the confidence to use an overhand set on high spinning balls, on balls dug near the stands or beyond the back line. The setter should be able to analyze the game situation and feed the ball to his hot hitters and to the open man. Intelligence is important because the setter should be able to quickly read changes in the opponents blocking strategy and call plays and deliver the sets to take advantage of any soft spots in the opponent's defense. The setter should be in control of his emotions so he can listen to the coach during brief time outs and carry out changes in the game plan even though adrenalin is pumping through his system.

Our quick hitter should be able to jump and reach at least 11 feet and preferably 11 ft. 6 in. to present a good target to the setter. We like our setter to deliver one-sets from anywhere inside the 10-ft. spiking line to our quick hitter. Our quick hitters need a good vertical jump, so we can have a big target area for the setter. On close passes we do not want our opponents' middle blockers tip-toe blocking our quick hitters and moving to the outside for a two-man block. To prevent tip-toe blocking we deliver the one-set fast and high to force the middle blocker to jump; we can only set high and fast to the hitters who can reach high. I like our quick hitters to be physically intimidating; by that I mean having the strength, vertical jump, quickness and speed to "crush" the ball and cause our opponent to concentrate most of their efforts in stopping our quick attack. The most important job our quick hitters have is middle blocking; a good middle blocker really has to enjoy stuffing the ball back into the opponents court; a great middle blocker has got to love it. The middle blocker has to get into the flow of the game and read all the keys that can tell him where the ball is going to be set so he can get a step ahead of the setter. The middle blocker should be able to psychologically intimidate the opponent after he blocks the spike. The blocker can do this by knowing his opponents favorite shots; by studying him and then forcing him to hit shots that he does not use as effectively or as often to force mistakes. The middle blocker can afford to let the adrenalin flow and get excited about the match, the game and particularly the opponents next side out attempt. In those rare and beautiful occasions when the blocker is really "on" against a strong op-

ponent in an important match he can reach a state of concentration that enables him to see the opponents actions in "slow motion". He can be aware of every movement the spiker makes as he approaches; he can "read" his intentions and by watching his approach, takeoff, upper body, eyes and arm, he can tell exactly where the spiker wants to hit the ball and he can be there to deny him. I look for quick hitters who have the potential to reach this state of competitive euphoria.

When we look for power hitters, we are after a spiker who is willing to hit the ball hard and try to put the ball on the floor whenever the ball is set above the net. This player should be able to spike the ball from *anywhere* on the court. Intelligence and game sense are important here since the power hitter should be able to know when to hit off-speed shots, dinks and wipe-off shots. We usually do not deliver any play sets to this player except a few two-sets on the X and fake X. The power hitter must use variety on the close sets and be able to spike the deep sets hard. Since our quick hitters are usually just adequate passers the power hitter should be a good aggressive passer who can cover more than his own territory. It is certainly a plus if the power hitter is a capable blocker since his blocking assignment is in the seam of areas three and four, where he has ample opportunity to block quick hits and X's. This player should also be an agile and a good digger since he is usually positioned in area five and is expected to dig hard crosscourt spikes and cover dink shots that frequently occur over the area four blocker. Every coach should have a similar description of what requirements are needed to fill the position in their offense. New coaches must see what abilities their players have and then choose the offense to match their players abilities.

SELECT THE WINNING COMBINATION

The strongest combination of players are those who play the best as a unit against the strongest opposition. Once this combination is found they should not be broken up if they continue to win.

During the pre-season new players must play with the veterans to speed their development. During all the pre-season intersquad matches we keep track of the wins and losses; this increases the pressure which will be there during the season and makes the matches more important to the players. It will also give us an opportunity to see who the "winners" are; those players who play better under stressful situations and seem to be on the winning teams most of the time. We start putting the "winners" together on the same team and see how they work together. The best six players do not necessarily make the best team. The six players with the best statistics rarely make the best team.

A team needs a blend of many different things to be successful; these tangible and intangible items are only necessary on the court. A winning team needs to project a winning attitude, they have to be positive, even cocky; yet they must be willing to sacrifice their bodies, to dive to the boards, to grovel, to somehow come up with the ball and keep it alive. To be great, a team must work very hard and make such a committment in time and work that they are not willing to lose. They do not have to live together, eat together, party together or even like each other as long as they carry out their assignments on the court. The right combination will compliment each other; for example, the middle blocker who dominates the net will be protected in the back court by an aggressive power hitter who takes all the balls in the seam or area between them. At the net the

Opponents' Scouting Report

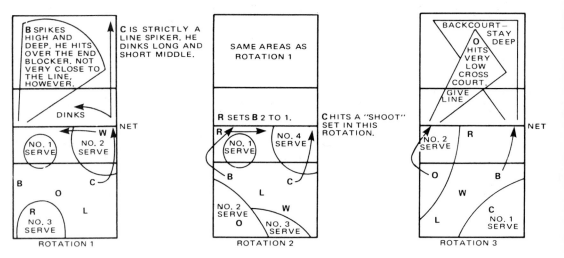

Diagram 11-1 *Opponents' Scouting Report*

middle blocker will reach over the power hitter and stuff a spike. The strongest combination will recognize the abilities of their teammates and will be willing to sacrifice for the team. When they are together on the court there must be a *combination* of aggression and calmness among the starters that keeps the team moving steadily until bursts of momentum rattle off points very quickly. The calm player should be the captain and preferably a setter. The aggressive players should be spikers.

SCOUTING THE OPPONENT

At the conclusion of the season I look at all the teams in our league and figure out who is returning and what the strength of that team will be. After the recruiting season is over, I look at who the new players are and rate the teams again. I pick the strongest team and try to play them as much as possible by entering the same tournaments they do. Each time we play an opponent my team tries to familiarize itself with their tendencies and my staff and I pick out the opponent's weak spots. We do not tell our players how to beat this opponent until we play them in a must win situation. We do not want to show them their weaknesses because they may be able to correct them by our next meeting. In non-league matches we use several different players to see who plays well against strong opposition. Meanwhile we are noting our own weak side out and scoring rotations and are improving them at practice.

Opponents' Scouting Report

An Opponents' Scouting Report (see Diagram 11-1) can be compiled from a rotation chart of the opposition. This report should be discussed with the team during the practice before and immediately prior to the

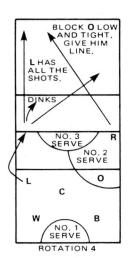
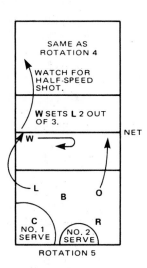
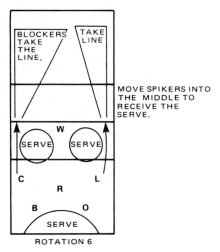

Diagram 11-1 *Opponents' Scouting Report (continued)*

match so that they will understand why defenses are being altered and why serves should be directed at particular areas of the court.

An explanation by the coach must accompany the brief notes on the charts if the game strategy is to be meaningful. The strategy determined from the Opponents' Scouting Report could be presented in this manner on the night of the match:

In Rotation 1, the best place to serve is to B's right, close to the net. B is their best spiker and receives significantly more sets than any other player. Although he is a good passer, he has trouble recovering to spike when he is pulled to his right and close to the net to receive the serve. It is to their advantage to start in this rotation because of B's spiking ability, and we assume they will start there tomorrow night. Therefore, Kilgour will serve to the opponent in this rotation and will practice serving to the three areas indicated in the chart.

C has rarely received a serve when he is in the right-front position and has not passed well from there. If B gets in a groove, we will serve to their right-front player. Be sure to serve very short or C will let the ball go to L, who is an excellent passer. R has trouble in the left-back position when he has to receive balls over B's right shoulder or O's left shoulder. He is an excellent passer if the ball is served directly to him. Becker will block the middle and Herring will block the line against B.

Since B hits very high and deep into our court, we'll attempt to soft block and to deflect the ball to our backcourt diggers. Herring can come off the line more than usual since B doesn't go inside the end blocker but prefers to hit over the block. We'll use the middle-in defense, with Kilgour playing behind our end blocker when B spikes. Do not play out-side the end blocker until B hits the line. Irvin will play middle-in although B will not dink unless he is in trouble. We expect Becker to deflect spikes to your area. Do not attempt to field the hard spike or you'll cut off Holtzman in the right-back position. Holtzman should receive most of B's spikes. Start deeper than usual because most of B's spikes hit a few feet from the backline. He hits with a lot of topspin and rarely hits out. The off-blocker will be Machado. When the set goes to B, get as far off the net as possible before B contacts the ball and then move forward. Machado should get off the net to the 12-ft. line near the sideline. Holtzman will be deeper than usual, and Machado will take some of his normal coverage; B will not hit the ball inside the 10-ft. line. The set will go to C about one-third of the time. Machado will block the line, even when he's blocking one-on-one. We may "cheat" Becker toward B and end up with several one-on-one situations here.

Irvin, be alert for the middle dink. The rest of the defenders keep normal spacing, but rotate to your left if there is no effective crosscourt attack by C.

The presentation of the defensive scouting report should be handled by the coach subjectively rather than relying on scouting charts and statistics. Within one match, a coach can pick out the ineffective blockers and pick up weaknesses in a team's defense. The defense can be easily identified during the match. However, identifying poor diggers and players who are habitually out of position can be done only if the team being scouted has strong opposition.

The best places to evaluate the blockers are above and behind the referee's stand and behind the blocking team's endline in the center of the court. By watching the match from both vantage points, the coach can see if the blocker reaches over the net. Lateral arm movement can also be evaluated. The backcourt setter on defense should be watched. Does he leave his position before the ball is spiked to run to the front row and set when the ball is dug?

Some players are too slow to cover dink shots and have a tendency to compensate by playing too close to the net where they cannot possibly dig a ball. Other players squat low to the floor before the ball is hit or stand flat-footed and do not react fast enough to dive forward to recover a short dink shot.

When scouting the defense, one should observe the following:

- The weak blockers
- The types or type of defense used
- The best areas to dink
- The poor diggers

THE MATCH

The Unsuccessful Coach

A coach can be a great teacher, a good organizer, and a thorough conditioner, but if he fails to select the best players to cover the proper positions, makes untimely substitutions, does not use his time outs correctly, and uses the wrong strategy, he will not be successful. Coaches whose teams fail between the practice session and the game can be classified in several categories.

The *indecisive coach* may have a good game plan with a lot of variables that never become clear to the team. After scouting the opposition and finding a player who cannot pass an easy serve, his instructions may be casually relayed as, "If you get a chance, serve to No. 10." Once the game begins, the indecisive coach may ask the

person sitting near him what to do next. The indecisive coach continually has substitutes warming up but can never find the strategic moment to put them in the game. He substitutes only if a player injures himself or asks to be taken out of the game.

The *over-enthusiastic coach* reacts to the play like an ardent fan. He moans, cheers, and yells at the officials, the opposition, and the players. During the time outs, he slaps his players on their backs and is terribly exhausted at the end of the match. He is so involved with the last play he cannot remember why his team won or lost.

The *morale crusher* is usually a strict disciplinarian and an ardent egotist. Mistakes are not allowed on his team; any offender is immediately removed from the game and given a stern lecture. The morale crusher's teams are characterized by a lack of aggressiveness because players are inclined to avoid the ball so they will not make mistakes.

The *faint heart* cannot bear to watch the action in crucial situations. Over-wrought with emotional involvement, the faint heart withdraws by turning away or lapsing into a stupor, while the team captain takes the responsibility of making the judgments when the going gets tough. This approach can be successful when the captain is more knowledgeable than the coach.

The *relaxed spectator* is thoroughly aware of what is happening on the court but believes in predestination. This coach rarely calls a time out or makes a substitution to stop the opponents' momentum because he believes the best team will always win.

The *athlete* is usually a coach who did not quite master the fundamentals of the game in his competitive years but still believes in demonstrating to his players exactly how to play the game. The athlete usually closely supervises all aspects of the team warm-up before the contest and personally sets all of his spikers prior to competition. Of course, setters do not touch the ball for 20 minutes before game time, but the coach gets a chance to maintain "touch" on the ball while giving last-minute encouragement to the hitters. Rival coaches notice that this team's setters always seem to make several errors early in the first game of their match.

Coach Percentage does not seem capable of grasping the psychological aspects of volleyball. Early in the first game, he may send in a serving substitute for a spiker who has just put away seven straight spikes and has sparked the team to a fever pitch. According to Coach Percentage, the spiker does not serve and pass as well as the substitute and should come out of the game. But he is a big part of the team's momentum and should stay in the game, by the time he returns to the game, he may lose his hot streak and be just another hitter. This coach will also take out the substitute who in three backcourt rotations has made three perfect passes and five diving saves while firing the team to great heights. The substitute is made to feel that regardless of how great a job he does in his speciality, he will never be given a chance to play more than a few rotations in a crucial situation.

The Successful Coach

Successful volleyball coaches who are capable of making the right decisions in competition seem to exhibit an outward calmness and assurance that draws the confidence of their players. All instructions before the game and during time outs are given in a positive, decisive manner, although the coach inwardly may be unsure of himself. Most important, the suc-

cessful coach learns to blend percentage volleyball with the psychology of the moment. He rarely interrupts or slows down his team's momentum to change strategy, to insert substitutes, or to call time outs. Conversely, he chooses opportune times to slow the momentum of the opposition by substituting players to force the opponent to change successful patterns of attack. Regardless of the situation, the coach can always take a few seconds to speak to the player being substituted out of the game. This habit of speaking briefly to players coming out of the contest often stops morale problems before they develop.

The successful coach knows the capabilities of his players and recognizes their limitations. He realizes that certain players need to be encouraged, whereas others must be calmed down so that rampant emotions do not adversely affect the tactics of the game plan. The successful coach knows that some starting players perform better after a brief rest on the bench, whereas others lose their touch and rhythm. To sum it up, the winning coach knows the capabilities, idiosyncracies, and limitations of his players and helps them to win matches by controlling the tempo of the game and by using their skills to the team's fullest advantage.

Pre-match Preparation

Always have something a little different planned for the big match; particularly when the opponent is stronger than your team. Of course this should be worked on in practice for several days before the match. It could be a switch to the off-blocker defense for a particular opponent spiker or a new offensive play or anything that would give the team a psychological lift. For example, if you have had some success running a quick middle attack and you believe your opponent will be keying on the middle you should tell your setters to use the middle as a decoy on good passes and set outside.

Team Meeting

If the match is at 7:30 PM the coach should call a 6:00 PM team meeting in a secluded room away from the opponents' dressing area. If your opponent is strong tell your players precisely how to beat them. Give your players a xeroxed copy of the Opponents Scouting Report and go over the proposed match-ups. Your players should know where and to whom they should serve, who the weak blockers are, what the opponents' defense is and where are the best areas to attack. They should be familiar with the spiking habits and patterns of their opponents and be given explicit instructions on how to stop their offense. If the opponent is weak, point out their strongest points and remind your team that they cannot improve unless they play up to their full capabilities. Do not tell your team the opponent is strong when they are not or you will lose credibility. The coach should be definite and positive in this final recap of game strategy.

Tell your players who the referee and umpire are and discuss any idiosyncrasies that they may have. For example, there still may be some referees who do not allow your front-court setter to dump the ball over the net in a fast downward trajectory; if this is the case your setter should be told before the match. Perhaps your assigned umpire loves to get in the game and make calls; in that case caution your players to watch for overlap violations. The setter is the player who should try various ball handling maneuvers when a new referee is on the stand. The coach should instruct his setters to set laterally early in the match to see if the

referee reacts adversely. Setting laterally is an integral part of any combination offense and should be established early in the game so the referee is used to it. When tried late in the game the referee may think it is a violation.

Let the team out of the meeting at 6:15 PM so they can be taped and on the floor dressed to play between 6:30 and 6:45 PM.

Warm-Up Period

Do not allow your players to touch the balls until they warm-up their bodies by jogging and stretching. It might be best to have a young or inexperienced team warm-up together. I prefer teaching the players a pregame warm-up in practice and then letting them plan their individual warm-up on the night of the match. Let your starters know that if they are not ready to play the first game they will be on the bench the second game. If you have a manager have him finish preparations for the match at least one hour before match time. This includes mopping the floor; putting up the net; putting out twelve warm-up balls; securing three game balls for the referee; opening and securing the locker rooms; seeing that the home teams' favorite music is being played; also hooking up the scoreboard. About fifteen minutes prior to the first game the manager should check the following:

1. Is the microphone working?
2. Are there towels in the visitors' and home locker rooms and on the benches?
3. Have the locker room doors been secured?
4. Are the referee, umpire, announcer, trainer, scorekeeper, and linesmen all present?
5. Does the referee have the game balls?

Watch your own team warming up. If it is an important match, you do not want your team to start warming up too soon because a long intense warm-up uses too much energy. If you are playing a weak opponent, insist on a hard warm-up and treat it as a work out since your team may not expend much energy during the match. In the sixties the Japanese girls teams used to begin warming up nearly two hours before they played our girls because the match would be over in about 45 minutes. Now that our girls can beat the Japanese their warm-ups are considerably shorter.

Watch the other team warming up to see if you can detect any individual weaknesses or changes in attack patterns since you have scouted them. For example, if the opponent's best spiker is a crosscourt hitter and he practices spiking every ball down the line, it probably is worth a few points to tell your end blockers to protect the line on a good set. If you have some impressive spikers who can jump high and hit hard, you may want your setters to deliver the ball on top of the net so they can bounce the ball into the stands or the rafters. This generally starts your team's adrenalin going and may cause your opponent to think more about your players than preparing himself for the match. Usually it is best for the players to practice the shots they plan on using during the game rather than getting into warm-up hitting contests. Of course the coach has to make sure that his players are getting an equal warm-up opportunity and share of the court. I can vividly remember the first time I warmed up against the Russian Men's Team. Their setters were standing in the middle of area three and another setter was in the seam of area two-three. They were setting their spikers about one foot over the net on our side of the

court and were pounding balls straight down or into our lone spiking line on the sideline. They were trying to intimidate us with their warm-up spikes and they did. Of course we could have placed our setter in area two-three also, but none of our setters would stand in that position without a helmet.

Sometime before the match the coach should check the game balls to see that they are the right brand and are inflated properly. There is a tremendous difference in the way various "approved" volleyballs react in competition. On a recent tour to Japan we were playing a match in an outlying city and I could not locate the game balls. Due to the language barrier and the nature of our "friendly competition," I did not demand to see the balls as I normally do and thus an interesting situation occurred. As the referee blew the whistle for the teams to shake hands and start the match I noticed a man running to the referees stand with a large cardboard box. The box was unsealed and out came three game balls which were given to the ball shaggers for the competition. We served first and All-American Steve Salmons served the ball fifteen feet; as it bounced under the net our blockers turned and stared at him in disbelief as he did a few arm circles to limber up his right arm. The opponent served to All-American Peter Ehrman in area five and he passed the ball about three feet; it landed in area five. At that point I took the game ball from my players and examined it; the ball was not familiar and seemed peculiar to the touch as if it were made of some synthetic material. The President of the Japanese Volleyball Association came onto the court and quickly ordered the designated ball for this competition to be put into play. Of course this whole procedure was quite embarrassing to the local host who apparently made an honest mistake. This problem would not have occurred had I checked the balls before the competition.

Turning in the Line-Up

The *starting rotation* is very important because of the various match-ups and mismatches that may occur. For example, a player may be convinced that he cannot handle an opponent's serve in the left-back position and will be useless if the coach matches him up with that server. Some blockers convince certain spikers that they cannot hit the ball past the block, and other spikers simply cannot be stopped by certain blocking combinations.

More than once crucial match has been lost by a coach leaving his line-up form within view of his opponents. As a precaution, line-ups should be personally handed to the scorer about 10 minutes before game time. He will check the line-up for form and record it. There should be no confusion about who will serve first because the referee or umpire should hold the toss of the coin well ahead of the time when line-ups are to be filled out.

It is good practice to jot down the opposition's starting rotation as the umpire lines up the team prior to the start of the game. In the first game, most coaches fall into the habit of either starting their best spiker in the left-front position, regardless of which team wins the serve, or of arranging their line-up so that their best server serves first. If their team wins the serve, the ace server should be in the right-back position; when the opponent serves first, the best server should start in the right-front position and rotate to serve first when the team gets a side out. Other common tactics include placing the best passer in the right-back position or starting a backcourt specialist in the right-back position.

After the line-ups have been turned in I like to look around the audience to see if anyone is arranging to video tape the match. I also look for coaches to see if any opponent is scouting us. If I do not know who the scouts are I find out, so we can keep track of what our opponents have seen.

After the teams have been introduced I like a brief huddle on the sideline just to review an important point or two before the competition begins.

DURING THE MATCH

As the match begins the statistician keeping the Rotation Charts sits on my left with the statistician keeping the Block and Pass Chart next to her. My assistant coach sits on my right with the statistician keeping the Attack Chart next to him. The assistant coach records the opponents starting line-up as the umpire lines up the team. He does this so he can identify the eligible spikers during each rotation our opponents make. This is accomplished by calling the numbers in to our players as we serve. This is important when the opponent is running a five-one offense and faking with a backcourt spiker.

Substitutes

In USVBA and NCAA men's competition a team is allowed six substitutions per game, and a player is allowed to start and reenter the game one time, providing the reentry is in the same position. A substitute is allowed to enter the game one time.

In NCAA women's and high school girl's competition a team is allowed twelve substitutions a game, and each player is allowed three entries in every game, providing the reentry is to the same position. If a game plan called for dividing one position between a strong spiker in the frontcourt and a strong digger in the backcourt, the player who can make the greatest contribution to the team should start on the bench, since the third time the player enters the game, she must stay in unless the coach wishes to put a third player in that position.

Starting players should be benched if playing poorly or losing interest.

Substitutes should want to be starters but must not be critical of players on the floor. Any player on the bench who is overtly critical of his teammates or is not ready and eager to play should not suit up. The substitutes should know their roles and follow the game situation closely so they will be prepared when they are called on. Substitutes can be used as messengers to change offensive and defensive tactics if the coach is not willing to use a time out or has no time outs remaining. While on the bench, the substitute should study the opposing players' assignments so he will be aware of with whom he will be matched. Serving specialists should study the opponents for passing weaknesses. Blocking and spiking specialists should study the opponents' favorite attack patterns and look for weaknesses in the defense. Defensive backcourt specialists should familiarize themselves with the oppositions' spiking habits. If the coach plans a line-up change for the next game, the new player should be inserted as a substitute in the current game, particularly if the present game is one-sided.

As soon as the coach perceives that a player is starting to lose his effectiveness, he should signal the appropriate substitute or substitutes to warm up on the sideline. Substitutes should also share in this responsibility and exercise on the sideline whenever they feel themselves getting cold. A common tactic is to direct the action to the player coming off the bench in an attempt to force errors before the substitute can warm up and get in the groove.

Time Outs

When the opponent scores three straight points a time out should always be called. Late in the game two straight points may be reason enough for a time out. If there are no time outs left a substitute can be inserted into the game to slow down the opponents' momentum. When your team calls the time out the coach should tell the setter what play to call and who to set the ball to if it is a good pass. If passing has been a problem, a correction in technique can be directed to the likely recipient of the next serve. A new receiving formation or an adjustment in the standard formation may be needed. The players should be reminded to talk to each other during serve reception and to back up the spiker to retrieve blocked spikes. In our league the assistant coach is allowed in the huddle with the head coach; the head coach should determine if the assistant is to be given time to speak as the coaches are approaching the huddle. If the opponent has called the time out the head coach should tell the server where to direct the ball. The middle blocker should be told which spiker is likely to receive the set and where the spiker likes to hit the ball. If your statistician is keeping a Side Out Rotation Chart on the opponent this information can be shown to the starting team. There are only 30 seconds al-

Figure 11-1 *Time Out.* Generally, time outs should be called when a team loses three consecutive points; when a player or players is upset; when the team is playing poorly; or when a change in tactics is in order. Time outs should never be called when a team has gained momentum. (Stan Abraham)

lowed for a time out so this brief interval in the competition should be well organized. A designated person should carry towels and liquid to the starting players who are not allowed to leave the court. This material is to be distributed by the trainer, assistant coach or substitute player so that it does not interfere with the head coaches instructions. A poorly organized huddle does not accomplish anything for the team. When the players are all talking at once and grabbing towels and drinks it is difficult to leave the huddle with the positive feeling necessary to maintain or turn the momentum.

Changing the strategy of the game during a 30-second time out requires a clear explanation of the most important variables in that particular game. The able coach will soon realize which players, if any, can contribute useful suggestions during time outs; he will quickly learn to evaluate and to put into action suggestions that will win games. It is advisable to have the statistician sit next to the coach so that the key statistics influencing the game can be quickly identified before the coach reaches the playing floor. The coach should not chastise a player or players during the time out but rather advise the team in a positive manner on techniques or a change in tactics. Some teams may not develop adequate leadership on the playing floor and must rely totally on signals from the bench to supplement important strategy contrived during the brief time-out period.

When the opponent calls a time out in order to break your momentum, the server should be cautioned to take a little off the first serve to make sure it does not hit the net or go out of bounds. Then the server can come back with a tough serve after the first point. Be sure to identify their key spiker and his hitting tendencies and to tell your team how to align the defense.

Strategy

Teams should change their strategy during the game to meet the situation. As the opponents' strengths, weaknesses, and strategy become evident, it is wise to make changes in play to take maximum advantage of the situation. Even the best game plans must be changed to counter strong players and alignments and to exploit weak spots of the opposing team. Strong blockers should be switched to positions where they can combat the strong spikes of the opposing team.

If the coach sees that a spiker is scoring by hitting the ball down the line, the blockers must be signaled to block the line and to force the opponent to hit crosscourt. At the same time, the backcourt defense should be realigned so that the best digger is assigned to the area where the block is channeling the hit. Many times an experienced captain can make changes when the ball is dead and prevent incurring a charged time out.

Occasionally, a team leader develops with the ability to choose an opportune time to switch defensive assignments during the course of a rally. Most players understand that a change in defense is in order if the opposition is scoring with the present alignment. However, very few players can choose the precise moment to move correctly. This type of player should be given the freedom to increase their range within the team defense. Usually this moment occurs when the opposing spiker is tiring or out of position for a set and likely to dink or use a half-speed shot.

When the captain is in the front row, the signal to change from one team defense to another can be signaled verbally or by hand. When the defense learns to play together as a cohesive unit, the backcourt can change alignment by letting the center-back player change positions during a rally, with the other backcourt players following his lead. The opposition will not recognize a defensive switch during a rally and will usually direct the ball to an area it has found open earlier in the game—only to have the ball passed by a newly assigned defensive player.

A strong outside blocker who has just blocked his opponent may sense that the spiker will not be set again on the next play. When this situation occurs, the blocker can take the initiative of changing assignments with a weaker teammate in order to align himself with the spiker who is going to receive the set.

The opponents defense should be identified the first time your team sides out so the spikers can attack the weak areas. If the opponent is switching defenses the coach should ascertain the pattern or situations when they will be in a specific defense. For example, a team may play a middle-in defense when a specific player is in the backcourt and change to a middle-back defense when that player is in the front row. Some teams only change defenses after time outs or when the captain runs to each player and tells him what defense to use. Your team should be informed as soon as possible each time a defensive alignment is changed by the opposition.

The opponent middle blockers should be watched to see if they are keying on your quick hitter on good passes; when this is the case your setters should be aware of this situation and set outside for one-on-one situations or set the second man through on the combinations, if you have this offensive capability.

Signals from the Bench

It is possible to send signals from the bench rather than using a time out to get information to the team. Hand signals are prefered because in noisy gyms the players cannot hear verbal signals. For example, if your bench is on the right side of the umpire your server is located forty-five to sixty feet away from you when behind the serving line, and it would be difficult to talk. If the coach is situated in a clear visual line with the server instead of sitting behind a

linesman it is easy to give the server signals which denote a specific target area of the opponent's court. The easiest way is to use the six areas of the court and raise the corresponding finger or fingers to the server: right back = area 1; right front = area 2; middle front = area 3; left front = area 4; left back = area 5; and middle back = area 6. If the coach wanted the right-front spiker served he would raise two fingers and the server would direct the ball to area two. Rolf Engen who coached several championship teams at Laguna Beach High School preferred to use only two signals: one finger for the left side of the court and two fingers for the right side. At the college level many players are capable of pinpointing serves and can be given double signals to hit the seams of areas. For example, if a quick hitter was receiving about the ten-foot line in area three and you wanted your opponent to set outside, the appropriate tactic would be to: signal for the server to serve area 3-6. When the server hits the quick hitter high and forces him to back up it often forces him to use a hurried approach and ruins the timing of the quick set. If the setter goes to him anyway there is a greater chance of error. If the setter goes outside there is a good chance of forming a two-man block on the spiker.

If the blockers will look at the coach for instructions, directions can be given by merely pointing the index finger crosscourt or towards the line indicating what zone of the net to protect. If the backcourt defense is trained to react to the block it would not be necessary for them to receive signals. Although I believe in letting the setters call the offensive plays, coaches could signal what hitter to deliver the ball to by raising two, three or four fingers to correspond to the spiker's position on the court.

Between Games

If a coach wins the first game, he usually keeps the same starting line-up or moves the rotation back or forward one position, depending on whose turn it is to serve. When the opposing coach loses badly, he usually starts new players or starts the team in different rotations to try new match-ups. When an opponent has been well scouted, it is always good procedure to have all of the opponents' rotations and your intended match-ups written down so that quick decisions about new line-ups or substitutions can be made.

The rest period between games is two minutes except for the interval between the fourth and fifth game which is five minutes. If the team lost the game, the coach may want to change the line-up to keep his best attacker away from the opponents' strong blockers. There is time to review the opponents' tactics with the team and to decide on any strategy changes for the next game. The coach should identify the hot hitters and have the setters give them the ball. The winning team often feels relieved and so may relax at the beginning of the next game. The coach should remind a winning team about this factor and encourage them to maintain their momentum into the next game. Before two minutes are up, the coach, manager, or captain should give the scorer the written form with the starting players in their starting rotations. If a team or coach is confused about the line-up, positions can be verified with the scorer when the ball is dead.

If conditions allow, the coach should talk briefly to the players being replaced. Many times players do not understand why they are taken out of the line-up, and a quick explanation can often prevent a misunderstanding.

AFTER THE MATCH

Usually a coach likes to talk to his team after the match. If this is the case the team should meet in a closed locker room to discuss the match. If the team played well and still lost, the coach should praise the team's effort and try to get the players thinking positively. If the team won and played poorly, the group should be reprimanded and be asked to work to improve themselves during competition. After the team meeting has been concluded the locker room should be opened and reporters and other selected people allowed in.

I prefer to use a different approach. If we are at home or away and we win, I let the players stay on the floor and chat with their friends and reporters and shower at their leisure. I think this is particularly important at away matches so the players can savor the victory and enjoy their surroundings. I want them leaving the opponents gym thinking it is a fine place to play the match and looking forward to the next visit.

If we lose at an away match we move to the locker room quickly and shower. I do not want them to discuss the reasons for our loss with friends or reporters on the floor. Usually we will not have a team meeting but will shower and leave quickly. I prefer to discuss our shortcomings at our next practice session and tell them how we will solve any problems we experienced during the match. By delaying the analysis of a defeat until the next day I find that we can be more objective and less emotional. If the defeat was particularly bitter, I may have a few words with the players to calm their emotions and to make the defeat a positive learning situation; but the bulk of the discussion will be withheld until the next practice day. If we lose at a home match, I give the players a minute or two to talk to their parents and girl friends and then get them to our locker room. I may have a few words with the team but will reserve most of the comments until the next practice session.

12

Conditioning and Training

For our sport, it is easiest to think of *conditioning* as increasing the energy capacity of muscle with an exercise program that does not utilize a volleyball. I think of *training* as a program that develops an athlete's skill and maintains the energy capacity of muscles through drills utilizing a volleyball. Conditioning should be emphasized more in the pre-season and training in the competitive season. Training takes place during the entire season, but is emphasized more in the final competitive season. Volleyball conditioning and training should emphasize the type of strength and speed work that is described under the sections of this chapter entitled interval training, weight training, depth jumps, and vertec jumps.

Most of the high school coaches in this country have severe time constraints on the length of the season and practice time, and many do not use a conditioning program. To a great extent, this was the case at the college level during the early and mid-1960s.

It was possible to win a championship with great talent or superior tactical maneuvering, but this is no longer the case. Through conditioning programs volleyball players have become faster and are jumping higher than in the past. If goals are set high, then strength, speed conditioning, and training are necessary. The type of program a coach develops should depend on the skill of his players, the length of the season, the duration of the matches, the style of play used, and finally "peaking" or planning when the team should have its best performance. This will be discussed in more detail under the section entitled season overview.

The following conditioning and training programs are applicable to both men and women. Although women adjust to conditioning programs as well as men, women have larger stores of adipose tissue that gives them a smaller portion of strength in relation to their body weight. The strength of women is less than that of men because of this larger store of fatty tissue and their smaller heart size in relation to their body weight. Women are capable of training with weights and of gaining considerable strength without showing the marked increase in muscle size found in men because they lack the male hormone testosterone.

Many physiologists and doctors believe that menstruation does not inhibit motor performance; there is a general consensus among volleyball coaches, however, that the intensity of the training should be determined by the woman athlete during her period of menstruation.

ENERGY SYSTEMS

The Anaerobic Systems

For a muscle to contract, it must be supplied with energy or adenosine triphosphate (ATP). There are three energy systems that supply ATP to the muscle cells and the particular system or systems utilized depends on the time it takes to perform the activity. A system that is used in strength and speed activities lasting from zero to thirty seconds is called the ATP-PC or phosphocreatine (PC) system. This system is triggered almost immediately and attains maximum production in about five seconds because it uses high energy phosphates already in the muscle. The PC system is *anaerobic* as it increases the energy capacity without oxygen. Since most rallys in volleyball last between eight and ten seconds, the PC system is always used as long as phosphocreatine is stored in the muscles. At the start of a game, players have enough phosphocreatine stored in the muscles to manufacture ATP for a few spikes or blocks and then are allowed to rest when the ball becomes dead. In most volleyball games, the ball is dead for a longer time

than it is in play. In well organized competition where a three-ball retrival system is used, there is still an eleven or twelve second interval between serves. In poorly organized competition, this interval between serves is greatly increased. During this relief interval when the ball is not in play, a portion of the muscular stores of ATP and PC that were depleted during the rally will be replenished. However very little is restored under ten seconds and only 50 percent is restored in 30 to 45 seconds. During a two-minute break between games 100 percent of the PC system will be restored.[1,2] Of course, the same result occurs when a spiker is taken out of the back row and rested for a few rotations. The PC system can be used over and over again, if given rest intervals.[3]

As a match progresses, a few players may show signs of fatigue; this may be a sign that the lactic acid or LA system has been in use with the PC system. When the PC system is used up, the LA system for ATP replenishment predominates. Its maximum power is available after thirty seconds of continuous activity, although the LA system will contribute after fifteen seconds of activity and is anaerobic.[4] Lactic acid breaks down sugar stored in the muscle allowing ATP to be manufactured.[5] An athlete knows when the LA system has been used, because excessive amounts of lactic

[1]Daniel Rivit, "Training Instructions For Physical Conditioning of Volleyball Players," *Canadian Volleyball Association Volleyball Technical Journal*, Vol. V, No. 1 (Feb. 1980), p. 87.
[2]Edward L. Fox, Ph.D., and Donald K. Mathews, D.P.E., *Interval Training Conditioning For Sports and General Fitness*, (Philadelphia, London, Toronto: W. B. Saunders Company, 1974), p. 27.
[3]Ibid., pp. 25–27.
[4]Rivit, "Training Instructions For Physical Conditioning of Volleyball Players," p. 87.
[5]Fox and Mathews, *Interval Training*, p. 12.

acid occurring in the blood stream cause muscle soreness. The players who are most likely to complain about muscle soreness after a long match are middle blockers and primary attackers because they jump more than the other players, and are more likely to use the LA system earlier in the competition. "High intensity efforts requiring one to three minutes performance times primarily draw energy from the LA system."[6]

Of course, since very little of the PC system is restored during the normal ten-second intervals occurring in the latter stages of a long match, the LA system may play an important part in the source of energy for volleyball players. A team that plays only a two out of three game match in one day would likely get most of the ATP they need from the PC and LA systems. This would depend on the intensity of the match and the rest intervals between serves. At lower levels of competition, it is conceivable that 90 percent of the energy could be supplied by the PC system and only 10 percent by the LA system, as suggested by Fox and Matthews.[7]

The Aerobic System

The third system is the oxygen or aerobic system, and it provides the highest amount of ATP during endurance events which are comprised of long duration, low intensity efforts. The oxygen system converts sugar and fats in the presence of oxygen to ATP. Norman Gionet, a research physiologist from Canada, presents a new viewpoint about the aerobic system in a well-documented article entitled, "Is Volleyball An Aerobic or An Anaerobic Sport." Gionet as-

sumes volleyball is intermittent work alternating work periods of high intensity and complete or mild rest periods extended during the match. Gionet stresses the importance of the cardiovascular system and suggests that volleyball is 50 percent aerobic.[8] This is in contrast to Fox and Matthews, who do not think volleyball is aerobic at all. Of course, Fox and Matthews only list one volleyball source: *Power Volleyball* by Slaymaker and Brown.[9]

In a Russian study entitled, "The Factorial Structure of Special Endurance of Volleyball Players," the authors reported that both anaerobic (PC and LA systems) and aerobic capabilities play a significant role in the special endurance of volleyball players. They also concluded that "most important in the special endurance of volleyballers is a lactate anaerobic capacity," which refers to the PC system.[10]

The rest of this chapter will describe conditioning and training methods that have proven successful for various volleyball teams.

FLEXIBILITY EXERCISES

Flexibility or stretching exercises should be in every practice session and before every match. Before attempting stretching exercises, players should jog to warm up their muscles. Slow stretching is suggested to prevent the player's muscles from tearing during warm up. Explosive stretching ex-

---

[6]Ibid., p. 12.
[7]Ibid., p. 184.

[8]Norman Gionet, "Is Volleyball an Aerobic or Anaerobic Sport," *Canadian Volleyball Association Technical Journal*, Vol. V, No. 1 (Feb. 1980), p. 35.
[9]Fox and Mathews, *Interval Training*, p. 218.
[10]N. I. Volkov, N. A. Belyaev, and Y. I. Smirnov, "The Factorial Structure of Special Endurance of Volleyball Players," trans. Michael Yessis, *Yessis Review of Soviet Physical Education and Sports*, Vol. 13, No. 4 (Dec. 1978), p. 86.

ercises before the match begins will cause injuries that show up during competition.

Because muscles strains and pulls in the back and legs are relatively common volleyball injuries, it is recommended that the following exercises be included in workouts and pregame warm-ups.

1. **Trunk Twister.** Stand with feet spread shoulder-width apart and twist the body from side-to-side. Do not move the feet.

2. **Alternate Toe-Toucher.** Stand with feet spread more than shoulder-width apart and alternately touch toes with fingers on opposite hands.

3. **Groin Stretcher.** Spread legs considerably more than shoulder-width apart and alternately squat over one leg while fully extending the other leg.

4. **Crossover Toe Touch.** Cross legs in a fully extended standing position. Bending forward slowly from the waist, touch the ground.

5. **Tail Gunner.** Position body in a full squat. Hold toes of both feet with the fingers. Without releasing toes, slowly attempt to extend legs fully.

6. **Quadriceps Stretch.** Start from kneeling position, with hands on soles of feet. Slowly move the back of the head toward the ground.

7. **Crossover Toe Touch.** Lie flat on the back, hands outstretched at right angles to the body. Slowly raise one leg up and over the body to touch the palm of the opposite hand.

8. **Toes Over Head.** Lie flat on the ground on the back and slowly raise legs up and over the head until toes touch the ground. Touch toes of both feet to the ground over the left and right shoulder. This is an excellent stretching exercise for preventing the lower back muscles from tightening up.

INTERVAL TRAINING

"Interval training, as the name implies, is a series of repeated bouts of exercise alternated with periods of relief. Light or mild exercise usually constitutes the relief period."[11] "The relief interval avoids excessive production of fatigue products."[12]

When volleyball is played by skilled players, it is a game of brief high intensity effort. The average rally lasts between 8.6 and 10.5 seconds; an exceptionally long rally may last up to 30 seconds.[13] According to Fox and Matthews, whose book is widely quoted in a review of the literature, "activities . . . performed at maximum intensity in a period of ten seconds or less derives energy (ATP) predominately through the ATP-PC chemical system."[14] During rallys that last longer than ten seconds, a middle blocker that is transitioning from defense to offense would normally use up his small quantities of ATP and PC that are stored in the muscles. Through interval training programs, greater cellular storage of ATP and quite possibly PC can be accomplished to increase the capabilities of an athlete. Due to the length of the rallys in volleyball, the work intervals during conditioning need not last longer than thirty seconds, and the emphasis should be on short high intensity work intervals of about ten seconds. "This type of work interval will bring maximal increases of all energy systems in the shortest period of time."[15] In other words, there is a positive correlation between aerobic and anaerobic capabilities.

[11]Fox and Mathews, *Interval Training*, p. 21.
[12]Ibid., p. V.
[13]Jean Claude Lecompte and Daniel Rivit, "Tabulated Data on the Duration of Exchanges and Stops In a Volleyball Game," *Canadian Volleyball Association Technical Journal*, Vol. IV, No. 3 (1979), p. 87.
[14]Fox and Mathews, *Interval Training*, p. 10.
[15]Ibid., p. 42.

Therefore repeated sprints of ten second durations can also increase the ability of an athlete to play an intense five game match.

When the UCLA Volleyball Team started using an interval training sprint program during the 1975–76 season, it was designed to develop the ATP-PC system that is the major energy supplier of the muscles that are used in volleyball. We believed that by conditioning this system, we ensured greater storage of chemicals in the muscles; consequently our athletes could play longer with the speed of movement and explosive effort necessary for maximum performance. We have used the UCLA Sprint Schedule in the next section of this chapter without modification for several years, and have found that even though we do not run any distances over seventy yards, the endurance of our players is excellent as measured by the results of five game matches.

Sprint Training

The sprint will be run from a full running start, rather than a standing start to alleviate the possibility of muscle pulls. The athlete will jog, then run to attain full speed at the starting line and hold that pace during each sprint to gain maximum improvement in the energy system of the muscles. Besides improving the anaerobic systems, we are also developing the aerobic or oxygen energy system that becomes more important as the duration of the match increases. The maximal stroke volume of the heart is higher during the relief interval than the sprint. The higher the maximal stroke volume, the greater the capacity of the oxygen system and the endurance of the athlete. No student/athlete is allowed to participate in this program until he has passed a physical examination conducted by one of our team doctors.

At UCLA, we run the sprints on the grass in thick training shoes. We do not sprint or jump train in thin soled volleyball game shoes, because of the possibility of foot, knee, and lower back injury. If inclement weather does not allow you to run outside and there is not surface available with enough bounce to it, the bicycle ergometer or bicycle could be substituted for sprinting.[16] On conditioning days, we do not touch a volleyball but sprint, endurance jump, and weight train. Before the sprinting begins, the players stretch, jog one mile, and stretch again. The first four sprints are run easily to prevent injury. A coach should never work on technique training after sprints, because the muscles will not respond well, and everyone will become frustrated. Some coaches have their team sprint train after technical training, however.

A few weeks before the team starts practice, I send the returning players a letter which explains exactly the type of training and conditioning programs we will be using for the coming season and why we are using them. I think this is necessary at the collegiate level, particularly if your athletes are majoring in physiology, kinesiology, or are pursuing any type of pre-medical course. The explanation of seventy yard sprints and the schedule is reproduced below.

UCLA 70-Yard Sprints. Quick high intensity work intervals will guarantee maximal increases of all energy systems. You can determine if the work rate is sufficient enough to maximally tax the energy systems by determining the exercise heart rate. Immediately after running eight 70-yard sprints or one set, the heart rate should be 180 to 190 beats per minute. To determine

Table 12-1 *UCLA Sprint Schedule*

		Rules
1. Wed. 9/30	1 SET 8 + 1	1. Your heart rate should be 180 to 190 beats per minute after sprinting.
2. Mon. 10/05	1 SET 8 + 2	
3. Wed. 10/07	1 SET 8 + 3	2. Your heart rate should be 150 beats per minute between repetitions. (Vary the speed of your jog or walk to get 150 beats.)
4. Mon. 10/12	1 SET 8 + 4	
5. Wed. 10/14	1 SET 8 + 5	
6. Mon. 10/19	1 SET 8 + 6	
7. Wed. 10/21	1 SET 8 + 7	3. Rest between sets until your heart rate reaches 125 beats.
8. Mon. 10/26	2 SETS 8	
9. Wed. 10/28	2 SETS 8 + 1	
10. Mon. 11/02	2 SETS 8 + 2	
11. Wed. 11/04	2 SETS 8 + 3	
12. Mon. 11/09	2 SETS 8 + 4	
13. Wed. 11/11	2 SETS 8 + 5	
14. Mon. 11/16	2 SETS 8 + 6	
15. Wed. 11/18	2 SETS 8 + 7	
16. Mon. 11/23	3 SETS 8	
17. Wed. 11/25	3 SETS of 8 70-yard sprints three times a week	

a. If your heart rate does not reach 180 to 190 beats per minute after 8 sprints, add 1 or 2 sprints. Maximum of 10 sprints per set.

b. If your heart rate still does not reach 180 to 190 beats per minute after three sets, start another set.

the heart rate count the pulse for 10 seconds immediately after the sprint by lightly touching the cartoid artery in the neck with the fingers, or holding the hand over the left breast.[17] After the first four warm-up sprints, the remainder should be run in 9 to 10 seconds. Before the next sprint in a set, the heart rate should return to *150 beats per minute*. The *recovery* period or relief interval is important to *restore the muscles energy systems that were depleted during the exercise.* Jog slowly back to the starting line during the relief interval so that your heart rate will drop to *150 beats* per minute between sprints. The purpose of the recovery phase is to replenish the energy stores in the muscle that were depleted during the exercise and to offset fatigue by delaying the accumulation of lactic acid. The conditioning we are striving for in our interval training provides the muscle with a greater production of ATP, which is stored in the muscle cells. During the first few sprints, an athlete has enough ATP-PC stored in the muscle for high intensity work lasting 10 seconds or less. PC is the prime energy substance for ATP formation in volleyball.

Between sets of eight, wait until your heart beat reaches 125 beats per minute. This will allow you to run the next set with maximum speed for the entire seventy yards.

USA Men's Pre-Season Sprint Schedule. This sprint program was designed for athletes who were not already participating on a college team. Nine to ten weeks were given to the athletes to meet the goals of time and quantity of this program. The athletes were not in camp so this program was sent to their homes by letter. The letter read: "Those of you who are not playing in college should also add a running program to your schedule. Run four times a week: twice a week do five sets of 10 repetitions of 55 yd. dashes; and twice a week do three sets of 8 repetitions of 110 yd. dashes. In other words, run every other day alternating the distance! You should run one 55 yd. dash every 28 sec., at virtually 100 percent effort. After you run ten dashes, rest for 90 seconds and then begin the next set. One 110 yd. dash should be run every 65 seconds. Rest for three minutes between sets of 100s. If you have not been doing anything up to now, then start slowly.[18]

Circle Drill

When volleyball is played by skilled players, it is generally thought to be a game of brief high intensity effort. As noted earlier, the average rally lasts between 8.6 and 10.5 seconds, and an exceptionally long rally may last up to 30 seconds.[19] In an interesting Russian article entitled, "Energetics of Volleyball," the authors characterized volleyball as multiple repetitions of high-intensity work alternated with brief intervals of low-intensity work.[20] They stated that, "Our

work was designed to determine physical development and functional condition (aerobic and anaerobic capabilities) of highly accomplished volleyball players; to study oxygen and energy costs of play components; and to determine the contribution of different energy sources in volleyball depending on the athlete's maximum anaerobic and aerobic capabilities."[21] The study was done in the laboratory, workouts, and competition, and included heart rate recording, maximum oxygen uptake, and gasometric analysis. "The mean VO_2 max was 5077 ml/min, or 60.2 ml/K_9," which in a review of the literature was higher than hockey, tennis, and basketball players, but less than soccer players.[22] They found that "the highest values for oxygen and energy cost were noted in the spike (and) there is a great difference in the amount of effort applied in executions of the elements in volleyball, the spike being the most oxygen consumptive and general movement on the court being the least oxygen consumptive."[23] This study agreed with others in the review of the literature in that the main source of energy comes from the anaerobic systems (63.2–79.3%), but it also stresses the importance of the aerobic system "because speed of formation and liquidation of oxygen debt depends on the power of the respiratory processes."[24] The ability for effective play depends heavily on the speed of oxygen debt recovery which, in turn, is determined by the degree of aerobic capacity."[25] The longer the competition, the more important the aerobic system would become. Some of the tournaments in this country become endurance contests when

[16]Brian Jones, "A Physical Training Program for Volleyball," *Volleyball Technical Journal*, Canadian Volleyball Association, Vol IV, No. 2 (1979).

[17]Fox and Mathews, Interval Training, pp. 46, 47.

[18]Doug Beal, "Letter to National Men's Volleyball Team Candidates," Jan. 22, 1981.

[19]Lecompte and Rivit, "Tabulated Data on the Duration of Exchanges and Stops In a Volleyball Game," p. 87.

[20]A. F. Rodionova and V. A. Plakhtienko, "Energetics of Volleyball," trans. Michael Yessis, *Yessis Review of Soviet Physical Education and Sports.* Vol. 12, No. 4 (Dec. 1977), pp. 98, 99.

[21]Ibid., p. 98.

[22]Ibid., p. 98.

[23]Ibid., p. 98.

[24]Ibid., p. 99.

[25]Ibid., p. 99.

a team has to play up to fourteen games in one day to win the championships.

To increase the aerobic system and to strengthen the muscles used in the various techniques, we use a circle drill which uses multiple repetitions of high intensity work alternated with brief intervals of low intensity work. High intensity work includes simulated spike and block jumps, short sprints the width of two volleyball courts, quick sit ups, and push ups.

The low intensity work includes jogging, skipping, side steps, and jogging with the arms fully extended. At UCLA, we begin with a twelve minute circle drill and gradually work up to a peak of forty-two minutes. The repetitions on the schedule indicate the number of times each exercise is carried out. For example: in Session 1, the athlete will perform two sets of five maximum spike or block jumps as directed by the leader of the exercise. This activity will be repeated two times for a total of twenty maximum jumps in a twelve minute period. By Session 5, the athlete will execute a total of 30 maximum jumps, or three repetitions in twenty minutes. By Session 20, the athlete is performing 180 maximum jumps, 300 sit ups, and 300 push ups. The push ups and sit ups are done in sets

Table 12-2 *UCLA Circle Drill Schedule*

Session	Time	Repetitions	Activity
1	12 min.	2	jog and intersperse: 4 sprints (length); 2
2	12 min.	2	sets of 5 maximum jumps; 5 dives (3
3	16 min.	2	push ups after each dive); 5 rolls to
4	16 min.	2	alternate sides.
5	20 min.	3	
6	20 min.	2	jog and intersperse: 6 sprints; 2 × 10
7	20 min.	2	maximum jumps (1 set of block jumps
8	24 min.	2	and 1 set of spike jumps); 10 dives (5
9	24 min.	2	push ups after each dive); 10 rolls to
10	26 min.	3	alternate sides; 25 sit ups.
11	30 min.	2	jog and intersperse; 8 sprints; 4 × 10
12	30 min.	2	maximum jumps; 10 dives (10 push ups
13	32 min.	2	after each dive); 10 rolls to alternate
14	42 min.	2	sides; 50 sit ups.
15	35 min.	3	
16–21	30 min.	2	10 sprints; 6 × 10 maximum jumps; 10
17–22	30 min.	2	dives (10 push ups after each dive); 10
18–23	30 min.	2	rolls to alternate sides; 10 sit ups after
19–24	30 min.	2	each roll.
20–25	25 min.	3	

Jogging includes skipping, side steps, cross steps, running backward and jogging with arms up.

of ten to emphasize speed and explosive effort. At volleyball camps, we have run modified daily circle drills with 300 campers participating with 35 coaches on a grass field. Of course the activity in the circle drill must be taught individually before the group circle drill commences. The circle drill must be modified to fit the beginning strength and aerobic condition of a particular group. Make sure the group does some preliminary stretching and jogs several times around the gym before any explosive activity is undertaken. At the conclusion of the circle drill, jog slowly and warm down by walking a few laps around the gym before breaking for water. After the water break, stretch thoroughly and begin ball handling drills and commence with the practice. Do not run an intense circle drill with heavy activity when the practice will be centered on technique training because the athletes will not be able to perform well. Always run a light circle drill the day before competition.

Interval Technique Drills

When practicing volleyball techniques using the interval training method, more work can be done with less fatigue, because the rest interval slows down the accumulation of fatigue products in the muscles. This in turn allows the anaerobic energy systems to be partially restored before the next set. The overload principle tells us to increase the number of repetitions within a given set and the number of sets as the athlete becomes better conditioned. Digging, spiking, and blocking drills can be used as the techniques to be practiced. Serving and passing techniques do not require enough of an energy expenditure and, thus, are not suitable for interval training.

Drills for Technique Training (Anaerobic). When structuring practice sessions, always schedule technique training early in the practice while muscles are still fresh. The emphasis during technique interval training should be on executing the fundamental as correctly as possible. When spiking, the player should wait for the set and approach late and fast. When blocking, the player should squat low and explode into his jump. While digging, the coach should force the players to dive or react quickly, and get to their feet and react again. The coach should stop the exercise when the players' reactions slow down noticeably. The work interval should be ten to twenty seconds, and the relief or rest interval, two minutes. The relief interval of two minutes or longer should restore the entire amount of ATP-PC to the active muscles if the athlete comes to practice well-rested. When the relief intervals are under two minutes, the LA system will start supplying energy and the accumulating lactic acid will prevent the athlete from training as long or as well. Technique interval training is time consuming, and not very manageable for a large squad.

Drills for Game Emphasis (Anaerobic and Aerobic). The average rally and interval between serves are about ten seconds. For specificity of training, the work and rest interval should be ten seconds, or about the same as game conditions. This type of training is suited to partner drills; while one partner is working, the other is resting. The intervals can be continued until the heart rate is 160 to 180, or the players reach the point where they cannot execute the techniques correctly. Once again spiking, blocking, and digging drills are to be used with two people alternating between activity and rest until completion of the drill.

Of course, scrimmages with extra balls at each service line provide the same specificity.

Drills for Endurance (Anaerobic and Aerobic). These drills are not recommended for players who have not been examined by the team doctor. The exercise period is approximately one minute with a 45 to 90 second rest with light movement. The exercise should be strenuous enough so that immediately after the exercise, the pulse rate is 180/min. for players twenty to twenty-nine, and up to 190/min. for younger players. At the end of the rest period, the pulse rate should be about 125 beats per minute. It is helpful to have a coach with a stopwatch check out the pulse rate of each player until the player can reliably determine his own rate. We use a ten second count multiplied by six. When the pulse rate at the end of a 90-second rest period is more than 140/min., the athlete should stop. We have substituted the drills below for sprints in the winter and spring. The NCAA Men's Championships are in May, and we stop sprinting at the end of November.

1. **Repetitive Spiking.** Player A and B can be spiking from area two and four. The coach passes the ball to the setter in area three and controls the tempo of the drill by the number of passes he makes in one minute. Player A spikes and backpedals quickly for another approach, while player B is spiking. Player C and D help feed the ball (light movement) to the coach during their rest period, and then take their turns spiking while players A and B feed balls to the coach. This is repeated until the conclusion of the drill.

2. **Rapid Fire.** During a "rapid fire" spiking drill, three spiking lines are formed in area two, three, and four,

and the spikers quickly pass the balls they are holding to the setter in rapid succession. First, a player from area four, three, and then two, spike, and the sequence is quickly repeated. Player A blocks every spiker for one minute, and then rests while player B does the blocking. This is a very strenuous and competitive drill that we use at most of our practice sessions. When we are still using sprints three times a week, we limit the players to a few repetitions of this drill two days a week.

3. **Dig and Spike.** Another favorite is to start our "power hitter" (area four specialist) on the attack line about eight feet from the sideline, and have a coach hit crosscourt spikes and dinks to area four from a table on the other side of the net. The spiker digs the ball to the setter, who sets the spiker and the action is quickly repeated. The other power hitter in area five is getting light rest by digging every other spike. He remains in area five until they switch assignments. The same drill is used for our setter who blocks in area two. He digs the crosscourt spike to the other setter coming out of area one and receives a back set. The setters change places after about one minute and the drill is repeated.

4. **Transition.** A great transition drill for middle blockers utilizing the entire starting line-up can be set up as follows: Two coaches stand on tables close to the net in area two and four and alternate calling "Set," and spiking the ball off the middle and end blockers fingertips to one of the other four players. The middle blocker turns in mid-air as he is descending, to watch the dig and trys to get a good approach and hit a one-set. After he spikes, a coach yells "Set," and he runs to area two or four to block, and then spikes again. After about one minute of this,

he rests by digging balls in area six while the other middle blocker takes his place at the net. The coach continues flip-flopping the front and back players, along with the middle blockers, to keep everyone interested.

5. **Digging.** If digging is to be emphasized, two players can both work, while the other pair shags. Pair the players up by defensive assignments, and have them start at the assigned position. Both players can receive 15 to 20 balls apiece in one minute. The coach keeps them apart by hitting to different areas of their assigned position, and stressing that they return to their starting position after every dig. After one minute, the next pair comes into the court and the resting pair pick up balls until it is their turn again.

WEIGHT TRAINING

"Strength is the ability a muscle group has to exert force against a resistance in one maximal effort."[26]

A good vertical jump during the spike and block depends on strength, speed, and technique. "Understandably, one of the most crucial factors in successful development to increase speed of jumping ability is solid strength preparation."[27] Most of the best players are characterized as having explosive leg strength. Volleyball weight programs should increase the strength of the muscle in such a way that the ability of the muscle to contract at a much faster and explosive rate is achieved. To increase speed while strength training, the athlete

has to concentrate on fast powerful movements even when he is fatigued. Lifting heavy weights very slowly can have a negative effect on movement speed and the ability of a muscle to react explosively. Speed training requires the movement of light loads at a high velocity compatible with correct technique.

Turi Verkhoshansky, who is considered as one of the world's foremost authorities on speed-strength development, states "An excessive amount of strength work, executed over a prolonged period of time, reduces movement and a muscle's ability to display explosive efforts. A cyclic wavelike increase and decrease in the amount of strength work provides the same wavelike, but steady increase in movement speed and explosive muscle strength."[28] Strength work should decrease before an important match to allow the body to recover. After high volume strength work, a brief period of active rest may increase speed-strength by ten to fifteen percent.

The most emphasis on strength training should be at the beginning of the season. Equal attention should be given to all muscle groups including the "core" muscles which are centrally located in the body.[29] A discussion of weight-training procedures for increasing the height and quickness of the vertical jump is necessary for players who are new to the team. The athlete who can lift the heaviest weight will not necessarily jump the highest in game competition; a weaker athlete may be able to contract his or her muscles faster. In speed movements, such as jumping to spike or to block a volleyball, the athlete who effects

[26]Fox and Mathews, Interval Training, p. 270.
[27]Evgeny Fomin, "A Jump Above the Net," trans. Michael Yessis, Soviet Sports Review, Vol. 14, No. 4 (Dec. 1979), p. 186.

[28]Yuri V. Verkhoshansky, "Special Strength Training," trans. Michael Yessis, Soviet Sports Review, Vol. 16, No. 1 (Mar. 1981), p. 7.
[29]Bob Gadja, "Core Training: A Subset of Stabilization Training," Journal of the National Volleyball Coaches Association, Vol II, No. 1 (Mar. 1981) pp. 66–74.

the greatest force in a brief interval achieves the most success.

Serious players lift weights to increase the height of their vertical jump and to sustain maximum jumping ability throughout long matches and tournaments. The low squatting position of backcourt players tends to sap vital leg strength and to decrease the height of the jump in net play—unless the legs are thoroughly conditioned. When weight training to increase vertical jumping height for the spike, the player should squat just as low as he would in competition. Slow-motion films or video tape may be used to determine knee angle and foot spacing. If the spiker is using the correct technique, the feet should be almost parallel. The legs should be extended as quickly as possible so that the muscle fibers are used as they are in competition. Players with strong backs and arms may add a further refinement by jumping with a barbell held behind their neck above the shoulders. The jump should be made as quickly as possible, and the arms should push against the barbell to prevent the neck from supporting its weight. The back should be kept straight to prevent muscle strain or tear when the athlete lands on the floor. The shock of returning to the floor must be absorbed by a controlled squatting action to prevent damage to the supportive structure surrounding the knee joints and vertebrae.

As additional strength is gained, more weight can be added to the program to ensure continued gains. Increasing the weight gradually is mandatory to prevent excessive stretching of ligaments surrounding the joint.

Safety Rules and Procedures

All lifts should be done with smooth, rhythmic, powerful motions with full ex-

tension of the involved limbs. Lifting for strength and quickness involves a maximum effort in short bursts over an extended period of time. The beginner must use light weights until the proper technique is established. Most coaches use a three-day-a-week program of lifting on alternate days to allow for the removal of waste products from the muscle before strenuous lifting is resumed.

The execution of an exercise from the starting position back to the starting position is called a *repetition*. A *set* is a given number of repetitions. There are usually two to three minutes of rest between sets. Warmup exercises are always performed before weight training to increase circulation, to elevate body temperature, and to stretch the muscle fibers. By increasing the rate of circulation, the muscles are given increased oxygen to perform the heavy tasks and are able to carry away the by-products of the exercise at a faster rate. A rise in body temperature and moderate stretching of the muscles also helps to prevent strains and tears in the muscles and supporting structures.

A few simple safety rules and procedures will prevent injury: 1) always warm up before beginning to train with weights; 2) learn the correct technique from a qualified instructor; 3) never lift a bar without collars; 4) do not train near other objects or people, or walk close to a person who is training; 5) use chalk to keep your hands dry; and 6) always use a spotter on difficult or heavy lifts.

Players with a history of knee problems should not weight train unless they are allowed to do so by an orthopedic specialist. Many doctors feel that weight training strengthens the muscles around the knee joint and makes it more stable. Their recommendation usually depends on the condition of the player's supporting knee joint structure. Since tremendous stress is placed on the back, the student athlete with back problems should not weight train until a written recommendation is received by the coach from the doctor. All athletes who perform squats should use a weight belt that supports the lower back.

Lifting Technique for Squats

To do squats properly, remember the following points:

1. Squat as low as required for the specific technique for which you are training. The coach can use slow motion films or video tape to decide

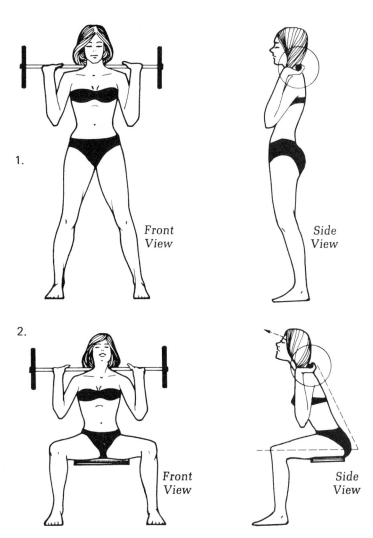

Diagram 12-1 *Half Squat.* The head should be kept up and the back straight during this exercise to prevent muscle strain.

which angle to use in the block and the spike. Do not squat beyond a 90° knee angle when using heavy weights.

2. Position a bench under your buttocks to prevent dipping below the 90° angle of the half squat. Do not relax when touching the bench if you are performing half squats. Use a power rack, which guides the barbell and prevents injury to the athlete's back.

3. Balance the barbell on the base of the neck and push up hard with the hands to release some of the pressure on the neck.

4. Keep your head up and stare at a point 10 ft. up on the wall. Holding the head up during the lift helps to eliminate back strain.

5. Inhale deeply and lower yourself to the desired squat position. Explode or jump to a standing position and exhale.

USA Men's Strength Workout

This program was mailed to the USA Men's National Team candidates in late January in preparation for competition beginning in early June. It was to be done three times a week in conjunction with interval sprint training. It is a good all around body strengthening program.

1. Do the circuit first. Go through the four exercises and repeat three times.

2. Then go on to the weight activities. The squats should be done first one day, and last the next.

3. The other exercises should be done in sequence; then go back and do the second set of all of them.

4. If you are doing intervals, forget the twelve minute run.

Circuit:
   Abdominal curls: 3 sets × 20 reps (slow, steady, sustained)
   Back hyperextensions: 3 sets × 10 reps (3 count hold at top of each rep.)
   Forearm curls: 3 sets to failure, each arm
   Reverse forearm curl: 3 sets to failure, each arm

Squats: 5 sets × 25 reps   (Add weight
      5 sets × 15 reps   each set—the
      5 sets × 10 reps   weight should
      5 sets × 10 reps   be heavy
      5 sets × 6 reps   enough each set so that the prescribed number of reps is all that can be done at that weight.)

Leg extensions: 3 sets × 10 reps

Toe raises: 3 sets × 10 reps

Leg curls: 3 sets × 10 reps

Bench press: 3 sets × 10 reps

Military press: 3 sets × 10 reps

Lat pulldowns: 3 sets × 10 reps

Parallel bar dips: 3 sets × 12 reps

Chins (palms facing away): 3 sets × as many as possible

Pushups: 2 sets × 30 reps

Squat jumps: 5 sets × 30 jumps (10 lbs. in each hand—one minute rest between sets)

12 minute run (A run will help to alleviate some of the soreness and develop cardio-vascular endurance for when practice begins.)

Basic Leg Program

1. To gain additional strength and speed, squat six to ten times with the maximum amount of weight that you can move at a high velocity compatible

with correct technique. Lift three sets. Extend your legs as quickly as possible. Add more weight as soon as your muscles can handle the additional load. Men may squat with as high as 100 percent of body weight while women may go as high as 75 percent of body weight.

2. To develop speed and the ability to jump quickly, perform three sets of ten explosive jumping squats with one half of your body weight.

3. To build and maintain the endurance to stay in a low defensive position, perform 25 consecutive half-squats with 50 percent of your body weight. Lift three sets.

Cuban Women's Jump Training

In an article entitled, "Our Secrets? Please!", published in a Russian journal in 1979, Euchen Jorque, the head coach of the Cuban Women's Volleyball Team, comments on his team's jump training methods.[30] Since the Cuban women won 'the 1978 World Championship with a phenomenal display of jumping ability, there has been much interest in their jump training methods. Jorque states that "in regard to physical preparation and structuring of blocking, our team takes its example from the Europeans and primarily from the Soviet Union."[31] There is the opinion around volleyball circles, including some prominent USA coaches, that "Cuban players have an innate ability to jump high—an ability that is evident even when the players don't do any training. It is difficult to say what role heredity plays in the unique jumping abil-

ity of our players (There is no scientific data on this account.). However, in my view, there is no other team that invests as much time and effort in physical preparation as the Cuban Team"[32] Jorque then cites some examples: "Peres, already a mature player and member of the national training squad, increased her jump by 20cm, thanks to training, and now reaches the mark of 3m 20cm;" that is almost an 8 in. increase to a height of 10 ft. 6 in. high."[33] He then reports, Diego Lopera, of the men's team, increased his jump by 23½ in. and reaches 12 ft. 5 in., "in four years of persistent work."[34] He refers to other equally awesome examples such as the maximum height that can be touched by the hand is 10 ft. 9 in. by Nelly Barnet, and that Anna Ibis Dias has a 37¾ in. vertical jump.

Jorque cautions, "don't hurry. Remember that Cuban players achieved their impressive results after many years of training. Excessive loads can easily inflict irreparable damage to the body."[35] The Cubans do "nothing mysterious or secret in our workouts. Barbell work remains the foundation of jump training. We try to tailor weight training exercises as close as possible to playing conditions; therefore, our women almost never do full squats, but stick basically with half squats."[36] Jorque respects individual differences among his players, which is an important factor in becoming a successful coach. He states, "Workouts with weights require utmost precision. It is necessary for the coach to have a delicate feel for the capabilities of his players, and to know when the exer-

---

[30]Euchen Jorque, "Our Secrets? Please!," trans. Michael Yessis, *Soviet Sports Review*, Vol. 14, No. 2 (July, 1979), pp. 101–103.
[31]Ibid., p. 101.

[32]Ibid., p. 101.
[33]Ibid., p. 102.
[34]Ibid., p. 102.
[35]Ibid., p. 102.
[36]Ibid., p. 102.

cises will bring real benefit and when they may be harmful. We usually work with weights for several months prior to competition, although this rule is not mandatory for everyone; the body's reaction to heavy weight training is highly individual."[37] I have seen more than one player injured because on arrival to a national team, they were put into the full conditioning program that the rest of the team had been using for several months. Instead of worrying about being tough and treating everybody equally, coaches should place more emphasis on individualizing their programs, particularly when it comes to weight training.

Jorque puts great emphasis on endurance as evidenced by the following: "Jump training is not evaluated by how high the player can jump five or even twenty times, but by how high he soars above the net during a whole match lasting 2–2.5 hours. Often the outcome of a match is not decided until the end of the fifth game, when a wholly fatigued sportswoman has to again summon all her strength and deliver several accurate hits."[38]

The Program
1. For leg strength use half-squats with 85 to 95 percent of one's personal best. Jorque gives no recommended repetitions or sets.
2. Imitation jump exercises with weights. Again, Jorque quotes no weight repetition, nor sets. The weight should be light enough so the athlete can jump explosively.
3. For endurance, execute repetitive jumps back and forth over one barrier. The height should be set at 6 in. below the player's maximum jump. Four

sets of 30 repetitions. Elastic is the safest type of barrier. It is best to avoid hard unyielding surfaces when doing repetitive jumps.

4. The women also endurance jump 120 times in succession attempting to jump within seven to twelve inches of their personal best. A target could be touched with the spiking hand for this exercise. Jorque states, "We do exercises for jumping endurance both in the preparatory period (long before competition), and for several days before the competition starts. All depends on the physical condition of the players."[39]

A Russian Leg Program

As an aid to Russian coaches, physiologists publish articles that have been tested under "laboratory" conditions with athletes from various sports. In an article entitled "How to Develop Jumping Ability," a two part program is discussed. The author cautions that "one should approach training with utmost care and get preliminary medical advice, or at least workout under a coach's guidance the first few times."[40] The beginning period of training for leg strength includes 10-12 workouts at a rate of two to three workouts a week.

The following systematic recommendations are given for weight training: "for development of maximum leg strength, use weights that permit one to perform 3–5 repetitions to exhaustion (inability to complete another repetition); for development of speed strength, exercises are executed at a fast tempo with weights that permit one

[37]Ibid., p. 102.
[38]Ibid., p. 102.

[39]Ibid., p. 103.
[40]V. Petrov, "How To Develop Jumping Ability," trans. Michael Yessis, *Yessis Review of Soviet Physical Education and Sports*, Vol. 13, No. 1 (Mar. 1978), pp. 6–8.

to execute 8–10 repetitions; for development of strength endurance, one should use a weight such that the exercise can be executed 15–20 times to exhaustion."[41] When the author does give recommended starting weights, they are for adult male athletes. For women, beginners, and teenagers, start at one-half the recommended weights, and then follow the recommendations above. At the beginning of training, emphasis should be on strength development. The author states that in order for the strength exercises to be explosive, "one should use special means of developing jumping ability, including jumps for maximum height and distance; hops on one leg; leaps from foot to foot; jumps on two legs, jumps to reach a basketball rim, tree branch, and so on".[42]

Beginning Period (10 to 12 Weeks)

1. Half squats with 88 to 132 pounds. One set with knees together. Second set with knees apart. Third set with knees spread wide.
2. Squats with barbells (88 to 132 pounds) on the shoulders with the heels on a 2 in. block. Keep the shoulders back and the spine straight. Wear a weightlifting belt, and use the assistance of a spotter on both sides.
3. Squats with a barbell (88 to 110 pounds) lowered behind the back. Novices support the barbell with straps on the shoulders.
4. Knee joint extensions while sitting with 13 to 22 pounds attached to the foot. Sit to avoid stress on the spine.
5. Lunges with one leg forward using an 88 to 110 pound barbell on the shoulder to "strengthen the ligaments and tendons of the leg and im-

prove joint mobility."[43] Use eight to ten repetitions.

6. Leg presses on a machine. If there is no machine available, use two partners and lie on the back and extend and lower the barbell until the knees almost touch the chest.
7. One legged squats with an 11 to 22 pound weight belt around the waist or dumbbells held with arms extended downward.
8. While lying on the back, open and close the legs while they are in a vertical position. Wear weighted boots. This exercise is for the adductor muscles of the thigh.
9. Stretch the anterior thigh muscle by squatting without resistance, strongly tilting the trunk backward. Put your hands on the waist, with a 2 in. block under the heels.
10. The following exercises are performed for the posterior thigh muscles:
    a. Flexion of the leg at the knee (knee joint flexion) in a standing position with resistance of 6 to 11 pounds attached to the foot.
    b. Same exercise while lying on an incline board.
    c. Use counter action from a partner while lying face down on an incline board rather than use weight boots.
11. After lying face down and fastening one's feet behind a soft roller, execute trunk raises by using the strength of the knee joint flexors.
12. "The gastrocnemius muscle and primarily the triceps surae, ensure the height of the jump."[44] A simple exercise to aid the development of the triceps surae is toe raisers. Place a barbell (66–88 pounds) on the shoul-

---

[41]Ibid., p. 6.
[42]Ibid., p. 8.

[43]Petrov, "How To Develop Jumping Ability," p. 8.
[44]Ibid., p. 7.

ders with the toes on a 2 in. block. The block is used because "repeated contraction of the triceps muscle, without its subsequent stretching, may lead to lessening of foot mobility".[45] "Because of the peculiarity of the triceps surae muscle, exercises for development of their strength are distinguished by a large number of repetitions . . . from 20 to 25."[46]

In an article entitled, "A Jump Above The Net," another Russian reinforces the importance of the speed of contraction of the foot plantar flexors and jumping ability and prescribes the same exercise done rapidly six to eight times using ten to fifteen repetitions.[47]

Next Stage

1. One- or two-legged squat jumps with an 11 to 15 pound weight belt to improve explosive strength.
2. Depth jumps from 30 in. After about one year of workouts, the height can be increased to 39 in. to 42 in. "The most effective method of developing explosive leg strength is an active push-off after a depth jump. Studies have shown that as compared with the traditional methods, this method is 1.5 to 2 times more effective."[48] Depth jumps will be explained in the next section.

DEPTH JUMPS

The two phases of jumping are the amortization or setting and shock-absorbing phase, and the push-off or takeoff phase.[49,50] "In the amortization phase, the player is "crouched," the body's center of gravity drops downward, the knees are bent at an angle of from 111 to 128 degrees, and the muscles execute so-called 'yielding' work (eccentric contraction)."[51] Recent studies have shown that the height of the jump is limited by the strength which the leg extensor and spinal extensor muscles "demonstrate during their stretching, i.e., during their work in the eccentric ('yielding') regimen (ER)."[52] "Jumpers must execute such work under the influence of a kinetic energy reserve (acquired during the run-up) at the start of the take-off, in the so-called amortization (shock-absorbing set) phase."[53] The forces exerted on the muscles during the eccentric regimen "can display 1.2–1.6 times more than its usual maximum. In other words, in ER work a muscle is able to display a supermaximum strength (SMS)."[54] The eccentric contraction of the muscle must be strong enough to prevent excessive flexion during the amortization phase of the takeoff. "If excess flexion of the support leg in this phase is prevented, then the final phase of the take-off–the so-called push-off–is executed successfully."[55] "In the phase of active takeoff, the player's center of gravity is elevated over the support base; at the moment when the feet leave the ground the knees are bent from 187 to 205 degrees. Maximum muscular efforts are required at the moment of

[45]Ibid., p. 7.
[46]Ibid., p. 8.
[47]Fomin, A Jump Above The Net," p. 187.
[48]Petrov, "How To Develop Jumping Ability," p. 8.

[49]Fomin, "A Jump Above The Net," p. 184.
[50]L. I. Dursenev and L. G. Raevsky, "Strength Training of Jumpers," trans. Michael Yessis, *Soviet Sports Review*, Vol. 14, No. 2 (July 1979), p. 53.
[51]Fomin, "A Jump Above The Net," p. 184.
[52]Dursenev and Raevsky, "Strength Training of Jumpers," p. 53.
[53]Ibid., p. 53.
[54]Ibid., p. 53.
[55]Ibid., p. 53.

switching from one movement to another, i.e., switching from one "regime" to another—from eccentric to concentric work."[56] Traditional strength programs have been aimed at achieving strength in the concentric contraction of the muscle used in the takeoff. Depth jumps concentrate on building strength in the absorption or eccentric phase.

In the first of three studies reported in an article entitled, "Strength Training Of Jumpers," Dursenev and Raevsky used novices to "depth jump" up to 19 times in one practice session at heights of 6 ft. 6 in. or more.[57] Normally athletes have depth jumped from heights of 29 to 43 inches. Subjects usually depth jump into a sandpit or soft mats. "In these conditions, the athlete acquires the ability to display brief (in the range of 0.037–0.061 seconds) muscle tension during which force reaches values that are fantastic at first glance. It fluctuates from 1500–3500 kg, i.e., exceeds the athlete's weight by 20 or more times. These values are achieved for a period of from 0.028 to 0.065 seconds. A person is not able to achieve such strength in other exercises; hence depth jumps can be excellent stimulators of muscle strength for jumpers."[58]

The second experiment compared subjects depth jumping from heights of 29½ to 43 inches with subjects jumping from heights of 6 ft. 6 in. or higher.

"The data from the experiment substantiate that depth jumps (2 m and up) are significantly superior . . . "[59]

The third experiment was arranged to establish what height depth jumps would provide the best increase in strength. One group executed depth jumps from heights of 8½ ft. and the other group from 9 to 10½ ft. "The experimental data show the greater effectiveness of using depth jumps *from maximum possible height* in order to increase SMS. However, it was seen that in the second half of the experimental period the maximal-height group executed their depth jumps without desire, sometimes under pressure from the instructor."[60]

In a review of the literature, I have not been able to find a study on the condition of supportive tissue around the ankle and knee joints, nor the trauma upon the lumbar area of the spine after prolonged bouts of depth jumps. I have not used depth jumps at UCLA, nor with any other team I have coached. However, it seems to be effective in increasing the vertical jump.

Beginning Depth Jump Program

1. Jump from a table 2 ft. 6 in. to 3 ft. 6 in. high onto a thick soft mat, and immediately explode upward to touch a target with the spiking hand. The target height can be individualized at 1½ in. below the maximum jump reach. Work up to three to four sets of ten repetitions. Start at a height of two and one half feet.

VERTEC JUMPS

At UCLA, the men and women's volleyball teams use a practice device called a Vertec to evaluate and develop jumping ability. The original program we have used had players work on Vertec in pairs during our practice session in the gym. The two players alternately perform sets of 10 jumps until they

[56]Fomin, "A Jump Above The Net," p. 184.
[57]Dursenev and Raevsky, "Strength Training of Jumpers," pp. 53–55.
[58]Ibid., p. 54.
[59]Ibid., p. 55.
[60]Ibid., p. 55.

touch an assigned target height twenty times, or complete five sets of ten jump trials, whichever occurs first.

The resting partner resets the Vertec and records the number of touches his partner makes during each set. Upon completing their bouts or sets, they rejoin the drills in progress, and two more players take their place.

Before beginning the drill, each athlete must determine his maximum spike reach. We do not jump train the athlete until he has warmed up and stretched for at least thirty minutes.

The athlete then takes five jumps at the Vertec, using his normal spike approach, which can vary from ten to fifteen feet. The coach may want to observe this test to make sure the athlete is using the correct technique to obtain his maximum vertical jump.

In Figure 12-3, note that Steve's knees are bent at approximately 120° and his center of gravity is behind the heels. Spikers should keep their center of gravity behind the heels to help transfer their forward momentum into a vertical rather than horizontal jump.

After Steve descends, the displaced vanes will indicate how high he reached. In this test Steve reached 11 ft. 3 in. Since his standing reach is 8 ft. 1 in., that gave him a 38 in. vertical jump—very good for an ath-

Figure 12-1 *The Approach.* All-American middle blocker Steve Salmons is on the second step of his four-step approach. The first step was taken with the right foot. (Terry O'Donnell)

Figure 12-2 *The Step Close.* Steve is moving fast by his third step. The trailing left foot will close on the forward foot in what is commonly known as the step close. (Terry O'Donnell)

Figure 12-3 *Amortization.* The trailing left leg has already closed on the lead foot as the arms have extended backward to approximately shoulder height. The arms will then swing down and forward in an arc as the weight shifts forward to the toes. The leg muscles are stretching at this instant. (Terry O'Donnell.)

Figure 12-4 *Takeoff.* Steve's legs and ankles have forcibly extended, moving him into the air as his arms thrust upward. Notice that the powerful contraction of his plantar flexor muscles have pointed his toes toward the floor. This final quick push off the floor is most important to vertical height. (Terry O'Donnell)

Figure 12-5 *Apex of Jump.* Steve fully extends his right arm to contact the Vertec at the highest possible point. Note that the left arm has moved down to elevate the right shoulder. (Terry O'Donnell)

Figure 12-6 *Contact.* The vanes on the Vertec are displaced by Steve's fingers making contact. The height of the jump depends on the speed of the approach, a quick coordinated takeoff, and speed and strength of the muscular contractions. (Terry O'Donnell)

lete who weighs over 200 pounds. Our best jumper–who is 6 ft. 3 in., 185 lbs.–touches 11 ft. 6 in. and has a 41 in. vertical jump.

Jump Training for the Spike

Once the maximum reach has been established, all the vanes below the assigned target vane are retracted and the athlete starts the training program.

Most of our athletes are able to touch the target vane set 1½ in. below their maximum jump reach, seven out of ten times. Others are capable of six to eight touches out of ten trials at a target 1 in. below their maximum height.

Superior jumpers may require the target vane to be set 2 in. below their maximum in order to touch it six to eight times in a set.

After the first bout, the coach will have to make slight adjustments in the target height for some athletes. As the athlete increases his maximum vertical jump, the height of the target that produces six to seven touches out of ten trials provides the proper motivation for the athlete.

Bouts 11 to 20 have the player performing rapid double spike jumps, i.e., two approaches in rapid succession. For example, the player approaches, takes off, touches, lands, rapidly backpedals for another approach, and jumps again.

We use sets of five double jumps until the target vane is touched twenty times. After the twentieth bout, we retest and repeat the program at the increased test height.

Jump Training for the Block

Since blockers must often jump without taking a step in order to defeat a quick play, we also work on jumping without any approach. Note: Our athletes can come within 3½ to 5½ in. of their running jump reach from a standing start.

We use the same procedure of five jumps to determine each athlete's maximum standing jump, and set the Vertec one inch below that maximum for training.

Bouts 1 to 10 have the athlete performing single jumps without an approach. Bouts 11 to 20 have him jumping twice in rapid succession, using five sets of double jumps, until he touches the target vane twenty times.

Training Schedule. We alternated spike-training and block-training workouts. If your team works out five days a week, you can spike-train on Monday, Wednesday, and Friday the first week, and block-train on Tuesday and Thursday.

The following week you can block-train on Monday, Wednesday, and Friday, and spike-train on Tuesday and Thursday. The Natural Vertec Jump Training System (NVJT), described above, improved out athletes' jumping ability from 1½ to 7 in. with an average of 2½ in. after seven weeks. Coach Andy Banachowski obtained similar results with the UCLA Women's Volleyball program as well.

Last season we used a new NVJT system that was tested by the UCLA Men's Basketball Team with an average of 2½ in. of increased height.

The New NVJT Program

The new program only takes an athlete two minutes during the practice session and is easier to implement than the original program. The program is to be used three times a week during the pre-season and competitive season. It should be performed during the early stages of the regular practice session after the usual stretching and warm-

Figure 12-7 *Standing Reach.* This information is more important than the athletes' height because it also measures the length of the arms. There can be a 3 to 4 in. difference in standing reach between athletes of the same height. (Terry O'Donnell)

up drills. It should not be performed when the player is cold or towards the latter stages of a hard practice. In addition to the jumper, there should be a manager or coach to adjust the Vertec, to reset the vanes in between jumps (as described below), and to record the peak height scores on a data sheet. During the first workout, the athletes two-handed standing reach will be recorded as shown in Figure 12-7. This height will later be subtracted from the athletes' best vertical jump to compute his maximum vertical jump. Next adjust the Vertec, so the top vane will be 3 to 6 in. above the individual's peak-height capability. The athlete now performs three progressive preparatory jumps using the standard four-step approach as shown in Figure 12-8. The first jump is easy and should be approximately 12 in. below the peak height; the second jump should be 6 in. above that; and the third effort is near maximum. At this point, all the vanes up to and including the final vane touched should be rotated toward the jumper; therefore, only higher touched vanes will project forward and can be reset quickly between jumps. At this point, the athlete takes a minimum of five maximal jumps trying to exceed his best preparatory jump height. He will try to touch three vanes (1½ inches) above the peak preparatory jump height, and then try to touch a higher vane on each of the succeeding efforts. The athlete will take approximately ten seconds between jumps. If he is still improving in jump height with the fifth effort, he will continue until he does not touch any higher vanes in two successive efforts. The athlete should be reminded that to make a higher jump, he should be moving faster when he leaves the floor. Those athletes that have a below average jump should watch the better jumpers train. It is important that the athlete goes back into the team drills and

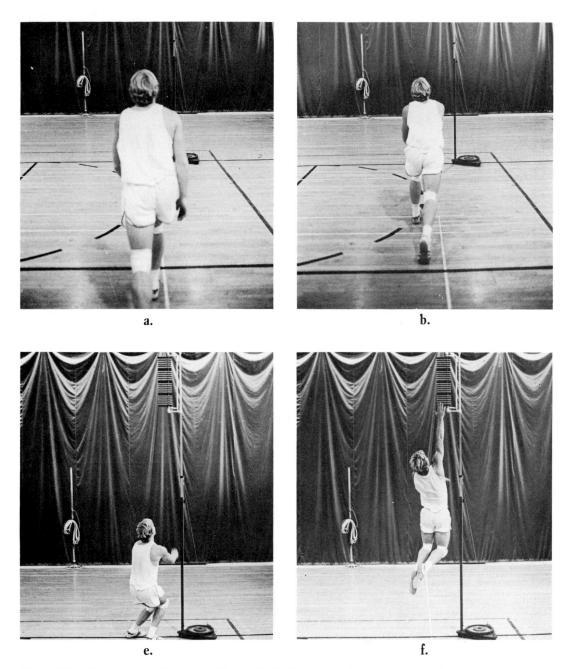

a.   b.

e.   f.

Figure 12-8 *Approach and Jump.* In Figure 12-8a, b, c, d, the four-step approach is shown. In *a,* the first step is taken with the right foot; in *b,* the second and larger step is taken with the left; in *c,* the player jumps into the third step with a vigorous push off his left foot; and in *d,* the final step has been taken with the left leg. In *d,* the player is in the absorption or shock absorbing phase; in

c.

d.

g.

h.

e, he has already started upward with a vigorous arm swing. In *f* and *g,* the player continues straight up with very little forward momentum. This was possible because he blocked his forward progress by putting his left foot forward and kept his center of gravity (buttocks) well-behind his heels. (Terry O'Donnell)

tries to attain his peak jump height every chance he gets. A maximum effort in NVJT and practice will combine to increase the vertical jump.

SEASON OVERVIEW

The emphasis a coach or player should put on conditioning and training should depend on several factors, with *length of season* being one of the most important.

There is a great difference in the rules various state, local, and (to a lesser extent) national sports governing bodies place on the length of the volleyball season. In many Southern states, high school girls' teams are not allowed to practice as a unit until two weeks before their first match. At the other end of the spectrum is NCAA men's volleyball where some teams begin training in September for the Championships held the first weekend in May.

In the former example, the girls should begin training to increase skill and energy capacities at the same time to enable the team to become ready for the competitive season. In NCAA men's competition, the pre-season is usually a minimum of seven to eight weeks, and conditioning is normally emphasized more than technical skill for the first two months.

Another important factor is the *length of the matches* held during the season. If a league plays two out of three game matches, then endurance would not be emphasized nearly as much as if the matches were three out of five. *Skill-level* is another important variable; a coach with well-trained players returning can afford to emphasize conditioning in the pre-season, while holding special training-sessions for the rookies. A coach with an inexperienced or poorly skilled team should use all available time

for training, because it will not matter what condition a team is in unless it can serve and pass the ball. The *style of play* determines the level of conditioning needed to successfully carry out the offense and defense. For example, a four-two system without combination plays does not nearly require the energy expenditure of a six-two or five-one system with its complicated transitions between offensive and defensive positions.

Consideration must be given to *peaking the team* for the championships at the end of the season. This is best accomplished by emphasizing conditioning in the pre-season and early competitive season, and then maintaining energy levels by specialized drills in the competitive season.

It is not good practice for a coach to pick a training and conditioning program from a book, another team, or the national team, and incorporate it in its entirety. The individual strengths and weaknesses of each potential contributing player on a particular team must be taken into account before the annual conditioning and training program is formulated.

Through the year, I have seen coaches injure their players because they didn't know how to alternate work and rest effectively. Unlike teams in Eastern Europe, who have team doctors to collaborate with the coach, our coaches have had the total responsibility of judging when to ease up in training and conditioning.[61,62] Most school programs can be divided into summer, pre-season, competitive season, and final competitive season.

[61]Dr. Gabriel Cherebetiu, "Collaboration Among The Doctors, The Coach, and The Player," *Canadian Volleyball Association Volleyball Technical Journal*, Vol. V, No. 2 (May 1980), pp. 5–11.
[62]Dr. Horst Baacke, "Cooperation Between Coach and Doctor," *Canadian Volleyball Association Volleyball Technical Journal*, Vol. VI, No. 1 (May 1981), pp. 9–11.

Summer

At the top level of play, there should not be an off-season, but a transition to a different program. The best player's development is on a constant basis: year-round indoor or outdoor courts should be available, so athletes can play against others of their same and higher ability. By providing opportunities for constant play, young people will be motivated to take up the sport. This is happening right now all over the country in women's volleyball. During the summer months, tournaments should be held by recreation departments or private groups; outdoor doubles tournaments are particularly popular in Southern California with an estimated 14,000 people watching the finals of a recent Santa Barbara beach tournament. College and high school players have many opportunities to play in summer leagues, and those players with exceptional ability have the opportunity to represent various areas of the country or even the United States in competition.

If rules limit the program to a short pre-season, then the coach should prescribe an individualized conditioning program for the players before they report for practice. If the pre-season begins in the fall, the coach should meet with the individual players before they leave for summer vacation and develop an individualized program that takes into account the age, physical condition, experience, and skill level of each athlete, so that the player will have a personalized plan of improvement.

The attitude of the players during the individual conference cannot be overlooked. Players must want to develop strength, endurance, flexibility, and speed and to learn the basic theories of conditioning in order to train effectively. Explanations of the cardiovascular and respiratory systems and principles of strength, endurance, flexibility, and speed training are invaluable to the athlete.

Pre-Season

The pre-season is that time of the year that competition does not count for league standings. Practice matches and tournaments are usually played in the latter part of the pre-season. The coach should take inventory before the pre-season based on the returning players' previous training and conditioning loads, their technical and tactical skills, experience, and the physical condition they are likely to report in.[63] It is important not to start with too heavy a load or injuries will occur. To prevent injuries, you should know the activities of your players during the summer or off-season to gauge your practice load during the first week. The weights or loads, sets, and repetitions listed in this chapter may be beyond the capabilities of a particular team or individual, and adjustments have to be made. Whenever technical skills are adequate, the pre-season should emphasize conditioning on two to three days when following a five-day-a-week training schedule. Since most teams have a lot of players try out, they should train at least three days a week in the gym until the team has been cut to the desired number of players. A coach should select personnel while training in the gym and not during the conditioning days. In fact, when anticipating a large turn out during the pre-season, it is best to schedule the first five days of practice in the gym, so that the size of the squad can be reduced before conditioning begins. When conditioning, remember to emphasize speed-strength work, as that is most

[63]Charles H. Cardinal, "Annual Training and Competition Plan," *Canadian Volleyball Association Volleyball Technical Journal*, Vol. V, No. 2 (May 1980), pp. 59–63.

applicable to volleyball. The length and load of the conditioning is not as important as correct technique.

The early pre-season program that has worked well for the UCLA Men's Team consists of conditioning on Monday and Wednesday, training in the gym on Tuesday, Thursday, and Friday, and playing in tournaments on Saturdays. We do not play any five game matches during this period. The emphasis during this early pre-season is conditioning and improvement of technical skill. The coach must be careful to slowly build up the conditioning load, or the athlete will be too fatigued on Tuesdays and Thursdays to properly work on fundamental technical skills. There will also be a feeling of boredom for the veteran players if the conditioning and training has been the same year after year.[64] A sample program is presented below:

Monday and Wednesday Conditioning

1. **Warm-Up.** Meet outside on the grass if weather permits, and warm-up by stretching easily before jogging a mile, and then stretching thoroughly.
2. **Sprints.** Next follow the UCLA Sprint Schedule explained earlier in this chapter to develop power. Remember that maximum speed-strength efforts are anaerobic and can only be performed for a maximum of ten seconds, which is why a 70-yard sprint has been selected. If the sprint schedule is followed and enough sets are run, the athletes will begin to improve the cardiovascular system and increase the aerobic capacity which will maintain performance in a long match.

3. **Jump Training.** After sprints, jump training over elastic or the "snake", as it is commonly known, comes next. Zigzag a 25-ft. length of elastic between six to twelve players at varying heights and use a 2-ft. takeoff imitating spike jumps and block jumps while "following the leader" of that particular set of jumps. This drill can be very interesting and competitive if the leader is imaginative.
4. **Weight Training.** Use one of the programs in this chapter or use your own. The USA Men's Strength Workout is an example of the type of program that emphasizes total body strength. A total body program provides the necessary base for leg work.
5. **Power Training.** Use explosive Vertec jumps described earlier in the chapter.

Tuesday, Thursday Training. The emphasis on Tuesday and Thursday is on serving, passing, setting, spiking, blocking, and digging techniques. The same techniques must be worked on constantly throughout this period using different drills and introducing new learning situations early in the practice. Do not make the mistake of attempting to condition the athletes during these two days of practice, because they will not be able to achieve good results with their technical training. To begin the practice, use light stretching followed by a light to medium circle drill, and more stretching. Next, move to partner ball handling drills and a spiking drill such as "rapid fire." Player specialization drills come next, i.e., middle blockers can work on blocking moves, setters on setting, and outside blockers on ten foot spikes. Introduce any new technique or variation thereof that pertains to the whole group while bodies and minds are still fresh. In the pre-season,

---

[64]Yuri V. Verhoshansky, "Special Strength Training," trans. Michael Yessis, *Soviet Sports Review*, Vol. 16, No. 1 (Mar. 1981), pp. 6–10.

Figure 12-9 *Jumping the Snake.* When players are endurance training by jumping over elastic, they should wear thick shoes and land on a soft surface such as a lawn or a board floor that has some give to it. (Norm Schindler)

I like to work on one main technique the entire practice using a variety of drills.

Friday Training. By Friday, the players should have recovered from Wednesday's conditioning, and be ready for a strong practice. The problem with using sprints to condition is that they exert such a maximum anaerobic effort from the athlete that the recovery is often slow and players may be sore for Tuesday and Thursday workouts. This is a problem that is worth dealing with, however, since sprints develop speed and strength very effectively. Of course, conditioning could be held on Tuesday/Thursday which we are going to try this season. A heavy workout can be scheduled on Friday if there is no Saturday competition. We also scrimmage on Friday and work on tactics such as team offense and defense. After offensive and defensive assignments are learned, we also try various player combinations in practice games. If there is a tournament on Saturday, we have a light circle drill and concentrate on serving and passing drills.

The pre-season schedule that is outlined above is for a school team and usually averages about twelve hours a week, not including the Saturday tournaments. Ideally the team would work out at 3 P.M. daily, because that is the most convenient time for student-athletes. If you stay with this schedule for about eight weeks, you will have had 16 days of conditioning and 24 days of training. At this time, the coach can have made the final cuts and should know his starting line-up. The team defensive and offensive systems should be familiar from the Friday scrimmages and the Saturday tournaments.

From a strictly conditioning standpoint, it would be better to have a three-day-a-week program on Monday, Wednesday, and Friday. If your team's technical skills are outstanding, then it would be better to go to the three-day-a-week conditioning program. The players' speed-strength would be significantly better after an eight week program and would last longer, particularly if the next phase of the season included a high power output during practice sessions. The UCLA Men's Team has used both a two and three day conditioning program during the last ten years, and have found the two day more favorable, because the three-day program was incompatible with the technique work that had to be taught and improved on before the competitive season commenced. The muscles should not be fatigued when practicing technique, and that is why I favor a two-day-a-week conditioning and a three-day-a week technique program during the pre-season for school teams. As soon as the pre-season conditioning program is over, the athletes will feel stronger because their muscles have recovered and their power will increase by ten to fifteen percent. During the two-day-a-week program, the pre-conditioning jump is usually the lowest; the mid-period slightly higher; and the post-period, the highest. In a three-day program, the pre-conditioning jump is higher than the mid-period because the muscles are fatigued, and the post-period jump *significantly* higher than the pre-conditioning tests. The significantly higher jump after conditioning for eight weeks is due to the "delayed training effect," and

must be maintained during the competitive period. At the college level, the women's competitive season usually begins at the end of September and culminates in mid-December. A conditioning program begun in late July or early August and maintained for eight weeks will carry a team through the championships if the team trains heavily three times a week during the competitive season. Of course, most NCAA Division I Women's Teams now stay together until the USVBA Women's Championships in May. Coaches peak their team in December for the NCAA Championships, then start again in January playing in USVBA competition. This is their time for increasing speed and strength work.

Competitive Phase

The competitive phase begins when standings are kept for league play or selection to regional and national tournaments. Team members should know who is in the starting line-up and whom they will be playing next to on offense. Up to one-third of the practice at this stage should be devoted to team tactics. During the competitive season the players need heavy practice or competition that overloads their anaerobic and aerobic systems at least three times a week.

Individual and team weak points in competition should be worked on in practice. Players should be shown the charts and statistics on their performances, and drills should be developed to minimize their errors. Drills and scrimmages vary according to the imperfections discovered in the last match or tournament. The finer points of team tactics, such as backing up the block and switching from offense to defense, should be stressed.

Physical conditioning should not be isolated from fundamental techniques and playing tactics during the competitive phase.

Physical, technical, and tactical training must be developed concurrently for best results. The amount of time allotted to specific areas of training is dependent on the stage of the season and the progress of the individuals and team. The coach must be flexible enough to adjust practice schedules to the progress of the team's development.

During the competitive phase, the substitutes should become *specialists*. Often a single player can fill many specialized roles. Teams at all levels could use the following specialists:

1. A player who can serve for points in critical situations. Often this player is also a backcourt defensive specialist who can rest a starter for three rotations. It is a bonus if the serving and backcourt specialist can fire the team up and spur them to perform beyond expectation.
2. A setter with good ball handling skills who can perform well off the bench. This player can also double as the serving specialist.
3. A spiker who can come off the bench and side out when the team is in trouble.
4. A middle blocker who can block for points and intimidate the opposition.

Specialists should not be selected until it becomes obvious that they will not earn a starting position. For example, if a player is too small to spike effectively and cannot handle the ball well enough to set, he can still contribute to his team's success by perfecting his serve, pass, and backcourt defensive skills.

Substitutes should know the positions that they might be required to play and should receive extra practice in their specialties during the competitive phase of the season. This differs from the pre-season when all players participate in the same drills.

During the competitive stage of the season, it is important that maximum workouts do not occur the day before the match or tournament. Maximum practice sessions should occur twice a week if a match or tournament is scheduled; three times a week if there is no contest during that week.

Final Competitive Phase

Before a championship tournament, it is often helpful to simulate practice sessions with the schedule that will occur in the forthcoming competition. For example, in order to win a championship, a team must play three matches on Friday and two matches on Saturday. Since most teams are accustomed to a light workout on Friday and a heavy tournament schedule on Saturday, they may have difficulty in playing at a high level on both days unless the intensity of prior training is equal to the stress encountered in the championship event.

The coach must constantly be on guard against players *"going stale"* because practices are too frequent and prolonged. If this situation occurs, the coach should vary the drills when planning practice sessions at the conclusion of a long season so the players will be *mentally* ready for important matches or tournaments. Scheduled practices may be cancelled if mental fatigue takes hold.

Schools and college teams often find that they have lost their momentum after a final exam period because practices were held on a volunteer basis for student athletes who could spare the time from their studies. During the first week after exams, the coach must decide whether to take a long- or short-range view toward planning practices. Should he attempt to regain his players' technical skills through rigorous practice of fundamentals, or should he stress offensive and defensive tactics to use for the next match? It is best to take the long-range view by emphasizing techniques if the team has a good chance of qualifying for the playoffs.

WEEKLY AND DAILY PRACTICE SCHEDULES

It is best to outline the weekly practice sessions in advance and to develop plans for the next daily session in detail at the conclusion of each practice.

Weekly Practice Schedule

Workouts scheduled for maximum intensity should be followed with practices of less intensity.

Repeated drills are necessary to create a conditioned reaction. For example, if a player has to think about diving to dig a spike, he will move too late to reach the ball. When a player has dived to retrieve balls thousands of times in practice, he will automatically dive for a ball in competition. There is little development or improvement without repetitive training. It is the coach's responsibility to utilize varied drills that develop the same techniques through repetition.

Daily Practice Schedule

Practice Outline for the Competitive Phase

1. Warm-up (30 min.)
   Jogging and stretching
   Partner drills with emphasis on passing and setting
   Pepper drill

2. Technique (60 min.)
   Drills to correct individual weaknesses
   Setting and attacking
   Blocking
   Digging
   Serving and receiving
3. Tactics (30 min.)
   Offense
   Defense
4. Scrimmage (20–40 min.)

While some coaches may prefer to work from a simple practice outline, others may choose a more detailed practice plan. The practices should be evaluated and dated for the coach's reference throughout the season. Whole sections may be omitted from certain practices, particularly during the competitive phase when practice sessions should be used to strengthen weak points that show up in competition.

Detailed Practice Outline for the Competitive Phase

1. Warm-up (30 min.)
   Jogging and stretching
   Setting
   Blocking
   Dives
   Rolls
   Pepper
2. Technique drills (60 min.)
   Attack and setting drills
   Left
   Right
   Dinks—L, M, R
   Deep sets—L, R
   Four-sets
   Three-sets
   One-sets
   Middle two-sets
   Right two-sets
   Five-sets
   Right X and fake X

Tandems
High middle
Blocking
    3 attackers *v.* 3 blockers
    2 attackers *v.* 3 blockers
    1 attacker *v.* 1 blocker
    2 attackers *v.* 1 blocker
Digging
Serving and receiving
    In frontcourt
    In backcourt
    Team receiving

    In middle-front court
    Pass and hit—one-sets
3. Tactics (30 min.)
    Offense
    Defense
    Game preparation
        Back-up spiker
        Free ball
        Down block
        Special
4. Scrimmage (20 min.)
    Offense and defense scrimmages

13

Charts and Statistics

It is very important to keep charts and statistics on your own team throughout the entire season so that problem areas can be identified and corrected in practice and strong points can be emphasized during future matches. It is also important to scout all of your opponents and become familiar with the plays they like to run and to identify the poor passers and blockers and the individual spiking tendencies.

CHARTS TO USE DURING THE MATCH

At UCLA we use three statisticians during our matches. The head statistician keeps a Rotation Chart on our team and our opponent; the second statistician keeps a UCLA Attack Chart; and the third statistician keeps a UCLA Passing and Blocking Chart. During the match I have three charts that give me information on UCLA and one chart that shows us where to serve and block

the opponent. Each statistician uses a different color pen for each game and keeps the statistics on the same piece of paper for the entire match.

Rotation Chart

The Rotation Chart shows the coach who the ball was served to and rates the reception of the serve a plus, zero or minus. A plus indicates that the setter can deliver a one-set to our quick hitter. A zero indicates that the setter can only deliver a set to either of the outside spikers; a minus indicates that the player passed poorly and the ball could only be set to one hitter. A fourth symbol could be added at the high school level to indicate a double hit or passing error. When the serve reception occurs in the seam between two positions the statistician attaches an arrow to the symbol indicating which player received the serve. There is no provision for rating the set on this chart; the statistician tries to indicate

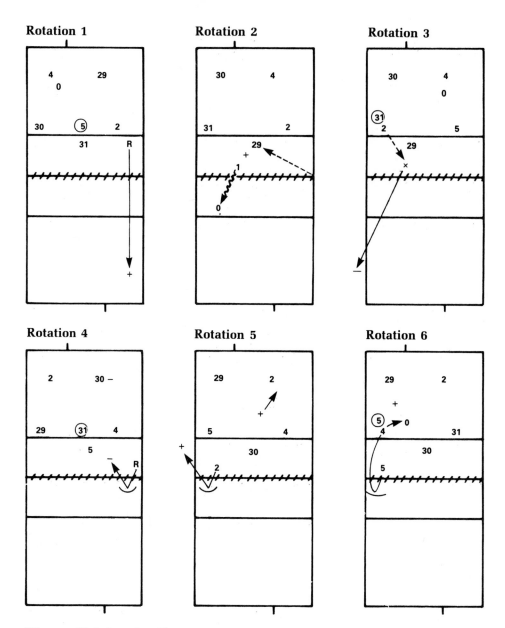

Diagram 13-1 *Rotation Chart*

the spot on the court that the spiker contacted the set by starting the arrow at that point on the chart. The type of play set that was delivered is indicated by putting a small number on the chart at the point of contact. The flight of the spike is indicated by a solid line with the result of the spike indicated at the end of the arrow by a plus, zero or minus.

In rotation one on the Rotation Chart (see Diagram 13-1), Number 4 passed the ball adequately; it was set high to Number 2 about 8 feet from the net near the sideline and he put the ball away for a side out. The R next to player Number 2 indicates it was a regular or high set and the arrow diagramming the direction of the spike starts near the attack line so we know the set was about eight feet from the net. There is a plus at the end of the arrow which indicates the play ended in a side out. In rotation two the dotted line indicates that Number 29 moved from the area four to area three to pass the serve and the plus indicates a good pass. The one indicates a one-set and the wavy line means a dink shot. The dink was kept in play by the defender because there is a zero at the end of the arrow. This chart is designed to evaluate the pass and first side out spike only, so we cannot tell from this chart who won the rally. In rotation two and five we do not record the position of the setter who starts in area four close to the net. There will be many symbols in this area by the end of the match and it is understood that the setter is in this position when the ball is served. In rotation three the dotted line tells us that Number 2 crossed behind our quick hitter and hit an X-set out of bounds, which is indicated by the minus. In rotation four Number 30 passed the ball badly and the set was high to Number 4, who spiked into the block

and was stuffed for a point. The block is indicated by the solid line on the opponents side of the net; the minus indicates the spikers teammates did not retrieve the blocked spike. In rotation five the ball was passed well by Number 2; the setter delivered a two-set to Number 5, who hit the ball off the blockers hands for a side out. In rotation six, Number 4 spiked a five-set into the block and it rebounded back into the spiker's court, where it was played by a teammate.

The purpose of taking a side out chart is to let the coach know what hitters are hot in each rotation and what types of sets are being put away. It also identifies poor passers and shows the serving tendencies of the opponents. When the coach calls a time out he should take the chart into the huddle with him and show the players where the opponents are likely to serve; the coach may elect to shift the receiving formation a step or two in that direction. The setter should also be told who the most effective hitter is and what type of sets he has been putting away. Of course it takes several rotations for trends of this sort to develop. In a competitive game we will average between seventeen and twenty-one rotations and our opponent will average one point on about 50 percent of their rotations. Therefore there are usually between four and six passing and spiking entries on each rotation at the end of our first game. Of course if your opponent makes a lot of serving errors there will be fewer entries. A statistician who makes the symbols small enough should be able to record a five game match (up to 130 rotations) on the side out chart and still have the coach understand it. The most valuable chart we keep is the Rotation Chart on the opponent. When the opponent calls a time out we take this chart into our huddle and show the server exactly where the passer has been having trouble receiving the serve. Also, we definitely show the blockers and diggers the opponents' spiking tendencies and tell them how to stop their offense. I always tell my statisticians to point to the rotation our opponent is in as they hand me the chart, so I can save a few valuable seconds in the brief one-half minute interval allotted for time outs.

Attack Chart

I divide the Attack Chart into two parts: the First Side Out Spike and Other Spikes. The first side out attempt is recorded on the top half of the page and is the spike after the serve reception. This is usually a very controlled situation compared to other spikes which usually occur in a rapid state of transition from defense to offense. The left-side spiker can be set on any kind of pass whereas the middle spiker can only be set on passes inside of the attack line. The right-side spiker requires a good pass to be set in the UCLA offense. On 70 percent of the side out plays he is approaching for an X or fake X set which is difficult to connect on when the setter is more than five feet from the net. Therefore the middle spiker and right spiker are being set off of good passes and the setter is delivering almost all the bad passes to the left spiker, who was kept wide for such occasions. Therefore our power hitter is spiking against a two-man block and a defense that has time to set up correctly.

First Side Out Spike Chart. The First Side Out Spike Chart is located on the top half of the Attack Chart (see page 219). Looking at the distribution of sets we see that 30 percent of the balls went to the left-side

spikers and the spiking efficiency was only .081 from the left-side. To compute the spiking efficiency use this formula:

$$E = \frac{U - M}{A}$$

where:

E = spiking efficiency.

U = unreturnable balls that the spiker has hit—these spikes are in the plus column.

M = mistakes, or balls blocked for a point or side out, and balls hit into the net or out of bounds—these spikes are recorded in the minus column.

A = attempts, or number of balls that the spiker hits or dinks—these include all balls recorded in the plus, zero or minus column.

Thirty-seven percent of the first side out sets were delivered to the middle spiker for an outstanding spiking efficiency of .434. Thirty-three percent of the sets were delivered to the right side and 36 of the 41 sets were X or fake X sets. Due to space limitations the First Side Out portion of the Attack Chart is totaled for easier reading, but the original chart which was used during the match recorded the type of set under the appropriate plus, zero or minus column. The type of set possible with our offense is in parenthesis above the plus, zero and minus columns. By recording the set it enables the coach to see what plays are working well during the match so this information can be relayed to the setters. Looking at the right side spiking column we see that there were 41 attempts. Our statistician recorded 21 X sets for a .333 spiking efficiency; 14 two-sets were delivered for a .429 spiking efficiency; there were

Chart 13-1 *UCLA Attack Chart*

Date 5/5/79   Team UCLA   Scores 12,15,15,15   Rator Kinnison
Place UCLA   Team USC   Scores 15,12,11,7   Event NCAA Championships

First Side Out Spike

Player	Left Spiker (R, IV, III, II) +	0	−	Middle Spiker (R, I, II, III) +	0	−	Right Spiker (R, V, II, I, X) +	0	−
1. Salmons				11	6	2	4	1	2
sub									
2. Amon				11	5	0	4	2	3
sub Gulnac				0	1	0			
3. Ehrman	5	3	3				2	0	0
sub									
4. Keller	1	4	3				3	1	0
sub Mica	6	2	3				2	2	1
5. Kiraly	1	2	1	0	2	2	2	1	1
sub									
6. Smith	1	1	1	2	4	0	5	4	1
sub									
Total attempts	14	12	11	24	18	4	22	11	8
Spiking efficiency	37	(+3)	.081	46	(+20)	.434	41	(+14)	.341
Distribution of Sets	30%			37%			33%		

5 five-sets delivered for a 000 spiking efficiency and one regular or high set that was put away for a 1.000 efficiency. In this particular match it was evident that on good passes the setters went to Amon and Salmons in the middle and ran the X and fake X enough to prevent two attackers from keying on the middle spiker. The analysis of the right side setting indicated we did not have to set five-sets and regulars to the right-side attacker because the combination of the right-side spiker breaking behind the middle attacker was all the offense we needed. It was also evident from looking at our left-side spiking efficiency that whenever we passed badly and our setter had to set the left spiker the opponent had a much better chance of scoring. This is usually the case unless there is an outstanding spiker on the left side who can put a deep set down against a two-man block and a ready defense.

Other Spikes Chart: The Other Spikes Chart shows a marked difference in the spiking efficiency of some athletes in comparison with their first side out spikes (see page 293). For example under controlled conditions Amon spiked 16 one-sets and put 11 on the floor when siding out and was not stopped. When in transition the Other Spikes Chart shows that his results were average. In side outs, Mica was average; yet under Other Spikes in transition situations he put seven of nine spikes away. The important thing this chart can tell us is to be specific when telling your setters who to give the ball to. For example, after a few games had been played in the match the hot hitters had emerged and directions to the setters were given as follows:

Give the ball to Salmons whenever he is in the middle regardless of how many blockers are keying on him. Feed Amon ones on side out situations. Keep running Xs and fake Xs on side outs. Give the ball to Mica and Salmons on scoring opportunities.

Passing and Blocking Chart

One statistician can easily keep this chart (see pages 294-295). The passing is recorded by noting the area of the court where the passer received the serve in the appropriate plus, zero or minus column. The key explaining the procedure is at the bottom of the chart. Upon reviewing the passing we see that 85 percent of the time the setter could deliver a combination play to the quick or right hitter; only 15 percent of the time did the setter have to set outside. The backcourt substitutes Brown and Saunders passed four pluses and one zero. Mica who played the second through fourth games for Keller passed ten out of eleven pluses. USC served thirteen balls to Keller the first game, and when he went out they concentrated on serving to our middle blockers Amon and Salmons; this was a good tactic since our power hitters Ehrman and Mica passed 29 out of 30 balls perfectly. Kiraly and Smith only received in the front row and passed six pluses in six attempts. The good passing caused our opponent to serve increasingly harder serves which contributed to eleven USC serving errors: 8 percent to UCLA's three errors. In reviewing the blocking on the same chart, we see that UCLA had fourteen play ending or plus blocks; twenty zero or deflected blocks that were played by either team; and only two minus blocks where nets, foot faults or touching the antenna occurred. At 5 ft. 10

Chart 13-2 *UCLA Other Spikes Chart*

Player	Left Spiker (R, IV, III, II) +	0	−	Middle Spiker (R, I, II, III) +	0	−	Right Spiker (R, V, II, I, X) +	0	−
1. Salmons				11	6	0			
sub									
2. Amon				8	3	4	0	1	0
sub Gulnac									
3. Ehrman	9	2	4						
sub									
4. Keller	1	1	1						
sub Mica	7	1	1						
5. Kiraly							1	1	0
sub									
6. Smith							1	1	0
sub									
Total attempts	17	4	6	19	9	4	2	3	0
Spiking Efficiency	27	(+11)	.407	32	(+15)	.469	5	(+2)	.400
Distribution of sets	42%			50%			8%		

Chart 13-3 *UCLA Passing and Blocking Chart*

Date 5/5/79 Team UCLA Scores 12,15,15,15 Rator Rabe
Place UCLA Team USC Scores 15,12,11,7 Event NCAA Championships

Serving Order

Player	Passing +	Passing 0	Passing −	End Blocking +	End Blocking 0	End Blocking −	Middle Blocking +	Middle Blocking 0	Middle Blocking −
1. Salmons	29	5	1				7	7	0
sub Brown	2	1	0						
2. Amon	27	6	1				1	6	0
sub Saunders	2	0	0						
3. Ehrman	19	0	0	1	1	2			
sub									
4. Keller	9	3	1	2	0	0			
sub Mica	10	0	1	2	3	0			
5. Kiraly	4	0	0	1	3	0			
sub									

in., Ehrman was not an effective blocker against the taller USC team and probably 6 ft. 8 in. K.C. Keller should have been substituted back in the front row for Ehrman for certain blocking match-ups. Keller had two plus blocks in the first game. Salmons had half of the teams' stuff blocks and certainly was the dominant force at the net during that match. Amon was not having a great night blocking with one plus and six deflections, but we could not afford to substitute him out because of his outstanding side out spiking. Smith and Kiraly did not have many blocking opportunities as USC was running most of their plays to the other blockers. Four to five plus blocks a game against a strong opponent such as USC would be normal instead of the three to four we averaged here. We had been averaging five blocking errors a match with USC and we wanted to cut back on our net violations. By not blocking as aggressively as

Chart 13-3 *UCLA Passing and Blocking Chart (continued)*

| Date 5/5/79 | Team UCLA | Scores 12,15,15,15 | Rator Rabe |
| Place UCLA | Team USC | Scores 15,12,11,7 | Event NCAA Championships |

Serving Order

Player	Passing +	Passing 0	Passing −	End Blocking +	End Blocking 0	End Blocking −	Middle Blocking +	Middle Blocking 0	Middle Blocking −
6. Smith	2	0	0						
sub									
Totals	104	15	4	6	7	2	8	13	0
Percent	85%	12%	3%						

\+ = a pass that can be set into a "one" play
0 = a pass that can be set to either end spiker
− = an ace or pass that can only be set to one spiker or a pass that must be set by a spiker
Record the area of the court the passer received the serve.

Net

4	3	2
5	6	1

\+ = a stuff block
0 = a deflected block that is played by either team
− = a net violation or foot fault

we had been we only had two net violations for the match.

AFTER THE MATCH

As soon as the match is over the statisticians compile the Attack and Passing and Blocking Charts and one of the coaches picks up the official scoresheet.

Spiking Total

The Spiking Total is compiled from the Attack Chart (see pages 296-297). Notice that there were 124 side out spikes for a .298 spiking efficiency. There were only 64 other spikes, but the efficiency was an outstanding .438. The total efficiency was .346. Another way to compile spiking statistics is called the attacking average, where the pluses or kills are divided by the total number of attempts.

Attacking Average And Efficiency

The average is always higher than the efficiency because errors are computed as just another attempt. Efficiency is a better way of evaluating your spikers' performance but

Chart 13-4 *UCLA Spiking Total*

| Date 5/5/79 | Team UCLA | Scores 12,15,15,15 | Rater Kinnison |
| Place Pauley | Team USC | Scores 15,12,11,7 | Games 1–4 |

Serving order

Player	First side out			All other spikes			Composite		
	+	0	−	+	0	−	+	0	−
1. Salmons	15	7	4	11	6	0	26	13	4
sub	26	(+11)	.423	17	(+11)	.647	43	(+22)	.512
2. Amon	15	7	3	8	4	4	23	11	7
sub	25	(+12)	.480	16	(+4)	.250	41	(+16)	.390
3. Ehrman	7	3	3	9	2	4	16	5	7
sub	13	(+4)	.308	15	(+5)	.333	28	(+9)	.321
4. Keller	4	5	3	1	1	1	5	6	4
sub	12	(+1)	.083	3	-	.000	15	(+1)	.067
5. Mica	8	4	4	7	1	1	15	5	5
sub	16	(+4)	.250	9	(+6)	.667	25	(+10)	.400
6. Kiraly	3	5	4	1	1	0	4	6	4
sub	12	(−1)	−.083	2	(+1)	.500	14	-	.000

Chart 13-4 *UCLA Spiking Total (continued)*

Date 5/5/79   Team UCLA   Scores 12,15,15,15   Rater Kinnison

Place Pauley   Team USC   Scores 15,12,11,7   Games 1–4

Serving order

Player	First side out			All other spikes			Composite		
	+	0	−	+	0	−	+	0	−
7. Smith	8	9	2	1	1	0	9	10	2
sub	19	(+6)	.316	2	(+1)	.500	21	(+7)	.333
8. Gulnac	0	1	0	-	-	-	0	1	0
sub	1	-	.000	-	-	-	1	-	.000
9.									
sub									
10.									
sub									
11.									
sub									
Totals	124	(+37)	.298	64	(+28)	.438	188	(+65)	.346

Chart 13-5 *Attacking Average and Efficiency—NCAA Championships Individual*

Player	Pos.	Att.	Kills	Avg.	Err.	Eff.
Salmons	Q	43	26	.605	4	.512
Mica	P	25	15	.600	5	.400
Amon	Q	41	23	.561	7	.390
Smith	S	21	9	.429	2	.333
Ehrman	P	28	16	.571	7	.321
Keller	P	15	5	.333	4	.067
Kiraly	S	14	4	.286	4	.000
Gulnac	Q	1	0	.000	0	.000

By Position

Position	Att.	Kills	Avg.	Err.	Eff.
1. Quick	85	49	.576	11	.447
2. Power	68	36	.529	16	.224
3. Setter	35	13	.361	6	.200

Team

Att.	Kills	Avg.	Err.	Eff.
188	98	.521	33	.346

P = Power hitter and area four blocker
Q = Quick hitter and area three blocker
S = Setter and area two blocker

is a little more difficult to explain to the fans. Averaging relates to baseball and is easy for Americans to understand.

Using the Scoresheet

Unfortunately there are still different scoresheets and different symbols in use throughout the country, though they all tell the story of what happened during the match. The coach should always get the scoresheet or a copy of the scoresheet from the official scorer. I use the scoresheet to find out how many points we scored and gave up in each of our rotations and whether we score more points than we give up in a particular rotation. One of our seasons goals is to give up less than .5 of a point each time our strongest opponent rotates to serve against us.

Chart 13-6 *UCLA Points Given Up By Rotation Versus USC*

Event	Match I t. finals		Match II league		Match III league		Match IV t. finals		Match V NCAA		Season totals		
Date	3/3		3/7		3/31		4/7		5/5				
	Att.	Pts.	Att.	Pts.	Att.	Pts.	Att.	Pts.	Att.	Pts.	No.	Pts.	Avg.
Rotation I	11	8	9	3	8	10	11	11	17	15	56	47	.84
Rotation II	11	4	9	7	8	6	9	2	17	6	54	25	.46
Rotation III	11	3	8	4	8	2	8	0	17	8	52	17	.32
Rotation IV	11	4	7	3	8	2	8	6	16	6	50	21	.42
Rotation V	11	0	7	3	7	1	8	4	16	8	49	16	.33
Rotation VI	12	9	7	1	6	6	8	7	15	2	49	25	.51
Match Totals	67	28	47	21	45	27	52	30	98	45	310	151	
Match Average	.42		.45		.6		.58		.46		.49		
Results	3 - 0		3 - 0		3 - 0		3 - 0		3 - 1		15 - 1		

UCLA Points Given Up By Rotation Chart. This chart records the totals for five matches against the team we had to beat in the NCAA Finals. The Att. under the date on the chart stands for the number of times the opponent rotated to serve and attempted to score against us that match.

Look at the Match I totals and see that the opponent scored 28 points in 67 rotations. Under Rotation V the opponent had eleven service opportunities and failed to score. Our worst rotation was VI where the opponent scored nine points in twelve attempts. According to the scoresheet of Match I, the scoring for Rotation VI went like this:

		Att.	Pts.
Game 1	0,1,0	3	1
Game 2	0,0,0,2,0,0	6	2
Game 3	1,3,2	3	6
		12	9

The raw data from the scoresheet was compiled into attempts and points for the chart. Once rotations are identified that are giving up the most points, the coach should concentrate on correcting the problem in that rotation. For example Rotation I was a problem for us the entire season averaging a point loss of .84 each time the opponent rotated to serve. As the trend continued serious consideration was given to changing our line-up to correct the problem. Since we had not lost a match and the other rotations were going extremely well I decided not to change our line-up and take a loss in that rotation.

Match Scoring Differential. The Match Scoring Differential can be used to determine what rotation to start in (see page 299). After the first match of the season the coach should take the information from the scoresheet and decide who the first server

Chart 13-7 *Match Scoring Differential*

	Points against			Points for			Differential
	Att.	Pts.	Avg.	Att.	Pts.	Avg.	
Rotation I	11	11	1	11	6	.55	−.45
Rotation II	9	2	.22	10	8	.8	+.58
Rotation III	8	0	.0	8	6	.75	+.75
Rotation IV	8	6	.75	7	13	1.85	+1.1
Rotation V	8	4	.5	8	6	.75	+.25
Rotation VI	8	7	.88	8	6	.75	−.13

will be in the next match by looking at the scoring differentials in each rotation. Looking at the chart we see that the obvious point to start is Rotation II because Rotation II, III, IV and V show a plus differential and V is almost even. Rotation I is a minus .45 and should be the last rotation; during a three game match the team would usually be in that rotation at least three fewer times than some of the other rotations.

SEASON STATISTICS

During the season I like to keep tabulating statistics on various techniques by player and opponent.

Block Points

The Block Points statistics are tabulated from the Blocking Chart kept during the match (see page 301). Most coaches are concerned solely with stuff blocks and errors. The point system we use gives one-half point for zero blocks that are played again by either team; one point for plus or stuff blocks; and we subtract a point for minus blocks or errors. Salmons was our best blocker and averaged 6.91 block points per game. Amon our other starting middle blocker averaged 4.42 points per match. The leaders should be the middle blockers because they have more opportunities. Following the middle blockers should be the area two blockers (or setters in our system), who were Kiraly at 3.17 and Smith at 2.3. This type of chart can be kept on digging, spiking, passing, setting or spiking.

Composite Attack Chart

The Composite Attack Chart is used either for a particular opponent or for season op-

Table 13-1 *Block Points*

Name	Year	Matches	Number	Average
1. Salmons	JR.	24	166	6.91
2. Amon	JR.	24	106	4.42
3. Kiraly	FR.	23	73	3.17
4. Keller	SR.	23	52.5	2.28
5. S. Smith	SR.	20	46	2.3
6. Ehrman	SO.	17	35	2.06
7. Rofer	SO.	10	22.5	2.25
8. Mica	SR.	15	21.5	1.43
9. Gulnac	FR.	7	17.5	2.5
10. A. Smith	SO.	2	4	2.0
11. Timmons	SO.	3	2½	.83
12. Dolby	SO.	2	1½	.75
13. Saunders	FR.	1	1	1

Chart 13-8 *Composite Attack Chart Versus USC*

First Side Out Spike

Position	Player	Left Att.	Left Eff.	Middle Att.	Middle Eff.	Right Att.	Right Eff.
Setter	Kiraly	13	.154	13	−.385	18	.388
Setter	Smith	11	.364	16	.125	22	.500
Quick	Salmons			49	.408	25	.360
Quick	Amon			53	.509	28	.142
Power	Keller	49	.204			22	.772
Power	Mica	23	.391			11	.182
Power	Ehrman	22	.364			9	.556
Totals		118	.280	131	.344	135	.440
Distribution		31%		34%		35%	

Chart 13-9 *Other Spikes*

Player	Left		Middle		Right	
	Att.	Eff.	Att.	Eff.	Att.	Eff.
Kiraly					10	.300
Smith	3	.333			17	.353
Salmons			56	.571	1	1.000
Amon			47	.255	2	.500
Keller	30	.167				
Mica	29	.345				
Ehrman	31	.613				
Totals	93	.376	103	.447	30	.344
Distribution	41%		45%		14%	

ponents to determine the areas of the court or situations where individual spikers are the most effective. This information is to be used by your own setters and like all of the charts we have seen thus far it is not for public information. Information like this could be very valuable to your opponents becuase it would tell their blocker who to key on. After compiling this chart the coach would know which of the three hitters at the net had the best spiking efficiency in each of the six rotations.

Side Out Spiking Efficiency By Rotation

The coach can develop a Side Out Spiking Efficiency By Rotation Chart to give to the setters before an important match. The setters should identify the most efficient hitters by position. For example, in Rotation II the setter would want to give more balls to Kiraly and Salmons than to Keller who is hitting .204. In Rotation III the setter should set Keller, who is hitting .772, even though the other hitters have a good effi-

Chart 13-10 *Side Out Spiking Efficiency*

	Area 2		Area 3		Area 4	
Rotation I	Amon	.142	Kiraly	−.385	Keller	.204
Rotation II	Kiraly	.389	Salmons	.408	Keller	.204
Rotation III	Keller	.772	Salmons	.408	Smith	.364
Rotation IV	Salmons	.360	Smith	.125	Ehrman	.364
Rotation V	Smith	.364	Amon	.509	Ehrman	.364
Rotation VI	Ehrman	.556	Amon	.509	Kiraly	.154

Chart 13-11 *Player Statistics*

Player	Position	Serving			Serve Rec.			Attacking					Stuffed Blocks	Saving Digs
		Atts.	Ace	Err.	Atts.	Err.	Avg.	Atts.	Kills	In Play	Err.	Eff.		
Olbright, Dave	Setter	303	21	12	28	5	821%	331	154	111	66	266	34	76
Smith, Singin	Setter	228	13	8	111	9	919%	406	188	158	60	315	36	81
Rolles, Scott	Setter	41	5	6	11	2	818%	51	25	14	12	254	2	12
Rabe, Doug	Middle Blocker	242	15	13	306	45	853%	315	152	121	42	349	68	68
Salmons, Steve	Middle Blocker	217	9	16	284	46	838%	409	207	142	60	359	103	58
Amon, Rick	Middle Blocker	11	0	1	29	8	724%	14	7	4	3	286	3	8
Ehrman, Peter	End Blocker	262	22	14	255	31	878%	364	173	98	93	220	18	99
Giovanazzi, Greg	End Blocker	181	13	23	233	26	888%	246	110	75	61	199	22	46
Keller, K.C.	End Blocker	45	5	6	39	8	795%	73	34	27	12	301	10	25
Brown, Dave	Specialist	47	3	6	45	7	844%	2	1	1	0	500	20	20
Team Totals		1577	106	105	1341	187	861%	2211	1051	751	409	290	296	493
			6.7%	6.7%					47.5%	34%	18.5%			

ciency rating also. Smith was the setter in Rotation I, V and VI and was responsible for memorizing those spiking efficiencies. Kiraly was the setter in rotation II, III and IV and was responsible for those rotations. The substitute setter had to remember the best hitters in all six rotations since he could substitute in for either setter.

Player Statistics

Player Statistics are for the fans because they are readily understood (see page 303). A good serving team should have about as many aces as errors in the serving column. A team that serves aggressively will make more errors than a team who merely serves to put the ball in play. Serve receiving is averaged by subtracting the errors from the good passes and dividing by the total number of attempts; teams running combination offenses should be more concerned with the percentage of plus passes that can be set into a "one" play. The attacking column is valuable for the coach but it is not specific enough to plan tactics with. The stuffed blocks column do not count deflections, which can be converted to points. The saving digs column only records hard hit spikes or dinks. Routine easy balls are not counted.

Appendix

SCHEDULING TOURNAMENTS AND MATCHES

Major domestic tournaments have borrowed some aspects of major international or world tournaments by scheduling single round-robin tournaments in "pools" or separate brackets. For example, if twenty teams were competing in a tournament, they would be divided into four pools of five teams apiece. The top four teams would be placed in separate pools as well as teams five through eight. The placement of the rest of the teams would depend on their luck in the draw. If the tournament were scheduled to run for one day, the teams would play a two-game round-robin schedule; the top two finishers would compete in a single elimination finals and the rest of the pool would be eliminated. Winners and runners-up would then be seeded into an eight-team single elimination bracket for the championships.

Most of the players, officials, and fans in the United States are in favor of changing the structure of volleyball competition from tournaments to *leagues*. Since 1963, the California Intercollegiate Volleyball Association (CIVA) has been conducting *league matches* between schools that have relative playing ability. Publicity and attendance at CIVA matches have improved tremendously over the years. Fans have identified with a college team, and crowds of 3,000 to 8,000 have seen matches at some of the larger campuses. Local papers publish stories before and after the match and CIVA standings are publicized.

This collegiate league has drawn excellent athletes, a great number of spectators, and additional money to support the program. Recently, radio and television have covered the more important matches.

The organization of CIVA is quite simple. Varsity matches are played at 7:30 PM and consist of three out of five games, with no time limit on their completion. Players go all out and the fans leave at the end of the match in anticipation of the next league contest.

The commissioner of the league draws up the yearly schedule and handles all conflicts that may occur. Eligibility rules do not present a problem because all athletic departments file with the commissioner a certificate of eligibility of their team members, according to NCAA rules and regulations. The commissioner then forwards a copy of each competing school's eligibility report to member coaches. If an eligibility question arises, the commissioner contacts the athletic director at the involved school.

A head referee is selected to assign officials to all league matches. Each member school pays one fee to the commissioner at the beginning of the season and he pays the assigned officials.

As soon as several strong teams have developed in a district, it becomes necessary to hold a district tournament to qualify teams for the national tournament. The initial selection of teams for the district tournament is made by a district advisory committee, which submits its recommendations to the National Volleyball Tournament Committee. The advisory committee uses the following criteria to select teams for the district tournament:

Won-lost record
Strength of schedule
Eligibility of athletes for the National Volleyball Championships

DEVELOPMENT OF VOLLEYBALL RULES

The basic features of the original rules for volleyball, written by William Morgan in 1895, are listed below:

Net height: 6 ft. 6 in.
Court dimensions: 25 ft. × 50 ft.
Any number of participants allowed.
Length of game: nine innings; each team allowed three outs per inning.
Continuous air dribbling of ball permitted up to a restraining line 4 ft. from the net.
Unlimited number of hits allowed on each side of court.
A served ball could be assisted across the net.
A second serve was allowed (as in tennis) if the first serve resulted in a fault.
Any ball that hit the net (except on the first serve) was a fault, resulting in a sideout.[1]

Obviously, drastic changes have occurred since Mr. Morgan demonstrated the game to his YMCA associates at Springfield College. The following chronology lists the changes that have taken place and govern the game as it is played in the United States today. Some of these changes were withdrawn for a number of years but were reinstated at a later date:

1912

• 6 players on each team

1915

• Official timer

1916

• Official game: 15 points
• Two out of three games determine a match
• Height of net: 8 ft.

[1]William T. Odeneal, "A Summary of Seventy-Five Years of Rules," in Martin D. Veronee (ed.), *Official Volleyball Guide, 1970* (Berne, Indiana: United States Volleyball Association, 1970), pp. 149–54.

- Player rotation: each player serves in turn
- Any serve that touches the net or any outside object to be considered out of bounds
- Ball not allowed to rest in a player's hands
- Playing the ball a second time (unless played by another player) prohibited
The rules were published in a separate book, *Official Volleyball Rules.*

1920

- Ball may be touched by any part of body above the waist
- Court size: 30 ft. by 60 ft.
- Before crossing net, ball may be played three times by each team

1922

- The centerline was added to court markings under net
- Official scorer
- Double foul defined and written in rules

1923

- 6 players per team, 12 players per squad
- Players are given numbers
- Player in right-back position serves

1925

- Umpire
- Player must obtain referee's permission to leave court
- Ball must cross net over sideline
- Each team allowed two time outs per game
- Team with a 2-point advantage wins a 14-14 tie game

1926

- Court measurement extended to *outside* edges of boundary lines

- Length of net: 32 ft.
- Game forfeited if either team is reduced to less than 6 players

1932

- Centerline extended indefinitely; player allowed outside of court to play the ball
- Vertical tape marker put on net over sidelines

1935

- Players required to wear numbers on shirts
- Touching the net becomes a foul

1937

- If ball is driven into net and causes net to come into contact with player, it is *not* a foul

1942

- Forfeited game score considered 15-0

1948

- Service area: right third of court

1950

- Clarification of a held ball stipulates that the ball must be clearly batted

1952

- Players allowed to warm up during time outs

1954

- Players must remain in position until ball is struck for serve

1956

- Players may stand anywhere on court, provided they are in rotation order

- Teams allowed to change courts during third game of a match if the ball has been in play for 4 minutes, or if one team has scored 8 points

1962

- Players not allowed to grab officials' platform to halt themselves from going over centerline

1965

- Players may cross the extension of the centerline, if they do not attempt to play the ball
- Illegal to screen receivers from server

1968

- Minimum ceiling height: 26 ft.
- Lines added to outline 10-ft. serving area on right side of court
- Spiking line moved from 7½ ft. to 10 ft. back from net; backline spikers allowed to land in front of spiking line, if they jump from behind the line.
- Blockers may reach across net, if they do not contact ball until it has been attacked
- An individual blocker may contact ball twice in succession
- Players may follow-through over the net when returning the ball

1969

- Blocking permitted by frontline players only
- If two opponents simultaneously hit ball above net, the player behind the direction of the ball is considered to have touched it last
- If two opponents hold ball simultaneously, it is a double fault and a play-over

1970

- Umpire's duties increased at discretion of referee
- Injured player must be replaced by a substitute immediately
- No change in line-up allowed after team has been signaled to take the court

1971

- Blocking rules clarified and interpretations refined
- Any ball, except the served ball, may be played off the ceiling, fixtures, or other obstructions if these intrude on court's height; however, no such ball may rebound into opponents' court
- Ball declared dead if it comes to rest or is wedged in ceiling or other obstruction
- Height of net for elementary school children: no lower than 6 ft.
- Coed play: one backcourt player may also block when there is only one male player in a frontline position

1972

- Linesmen can assist in calling contacts with the ball if so instructed by the referee
- Any ball contacted by blocker(s) on the opponent's side of the net is considered to have crossed the net

1973

- Ball is out of bounds when it touches a net antenna or passes over the net not entirely within the net antennas
- Linesmen shall visibly signal the referee when the ball does not cross the net entirely within the net antennas
- When the ball is served, all of the backcourt players in the court must be completely behind all of the frontcourt players in the court

1974

- Net antenna mandatory
- A player shall not contact any part of the net antenna while the ball is in play
- Five-minute intermission before the fifth game of a match; at this time, a toss of coin shall again be made to determine choice of serve or playing area

1975

- During play any part of a player's body may touch the center line. In addition, only a player's foot or feet may contact the playing area on the opposite side of the centerline, providing that some part of the encroaching foot or feet remains on or above the centerline at the time of such contact

1976

- The captain is the only player permitted to address the referee or umpire during the progress of a game
- A player may reach under the net to retrieve a ball that is still in play by that player's team

1977

- The USVBA adopted the rules of the International Volleyball Federation
- The court shall be 18m long by 9m wide (59 ft. × 29 ft. 6 in.)
- The attack line shall be 3m (9 ft. 10 in.) from the net
- The service lines shall be 3m apart
- The length of the net shall be 1m (3 ft. 3 in.) wide
- Round net posts are preferable and fixing the posts to the floor by wires should be avoided
- The height of the net measured from the center of the court shall be 24m (7 ft. 11⅝ in) for men and 2.24m (7 ft. 4⅛ in) for women. The ends of the net cannot exceed regulation height by more than 2cm (¾ in.)
- The antennas shall be placed on the net 9m apart directly above the sidelines
- A team is allowed six substitutes a game; the player starting the game may be replaced by any substitute and reenter the game once. Only the original starter may replace a substitute
- A substitute who already played cannot reenter the same game unless through accident or injury, a team is reduced to less than six players
- Coaches and managers shall not contest the decisions of the referee during play
- The linesmen signal the referee when an "out" ball is contacted by a player of the receiving team
- The ball must be tossed or released from the hand for the serve
- Any player who blocks the ball shall have the right to make the next contact, such contact counting as the first of three
- Crossing the vertical plane of the net with any part of the body to distract the opponent constitutes a fault
- Six ball retrievers will be utilized using a three ball system
- When the server tosses the ball in the air but does not hit it and it touches some part of the server's body before it bounces, it constitutes a side out

1978

- A ball that touches the net outside the antenna is considered as being out
- The serve can be blocked over the net by one or more front line players
- Disagreements with the interpretation of the rules must be brought to the attention of the referee and solved immediately

1979

- If an illegal substitution request is discovered by the scorer, the request will be denied without penalty
- If a blocker reaches over the net outside the antenna and contacts the ball, it is a fault

1980

- It is legal to have one foot in the bleachers as long as the other foot is in contact with the floor when playing the ball
- Coaching during NCAA play is allowed if not done in a disruptive manner
- The playing captain may request permission for the coach to speak to the first referee during the game
- As soon as either of the referees notice an injured player, the game will be stopped and a playover will be called
- Any player may reach across the net to set a pass providing the ball has not fully penetrated beyond the vertical plane of the net
- Legitimate protests will be denied if they are not lodged before the first service following the situation being protested

1981

- The captain of the protesting team may be the only one to protest; the referee sees that the score, players, positions, substitutions, timeouts, and the situation is recorded on the scoresheet prior to the next service. The scorer, captains, and first referee sign the protest to agree that the facts are correct

1982

- If there is an illegal substitution the team is penalized with a time out and the substitution refused

- When the wrong player serves the scorer interrupts the play and a sideout is called
- Once the lineup is submitted the only way to make a change is through substitution

1983

- When a backcourt setter jumpsets to a teammate and the ball is legally touched by a blocker, the ball remains in play. This used to be a back row player violation

1984 (After the Los Angeles Olympics)

- Players can serve anywhere behind the backline
- In order to be considered a blocker the player must have some portion of his body above the net
- A ball may be double hit if it is played in one motion without using the fingertips

Effects of International Rule Interpretations

Use of the overhand pass to serve in power volleyball is rare. At recent championships over 99 percent of the serves were passed with the forearms. Coaches no longer teach the overhand pass for service reception, and players only practice this technique for passing slow-moving balls and setting. Before and during the 1964 Olympics, international referees called overhand reception of the serve very tightly. When Olympic players representing the United States returned home, they used the forearm pass exclusively to prevent the officials from calling a thrown ball. Leading coaches reasoned that officials would closely scrutinize the overhand pass but rarely call a rule infraction on the "bump" or forearm pass. For good percentage plays, the forearm pass and moving players deeper into the court so that they can bump every serve is recommended.

The overhand service reception is legal. However, players have perfected the forearm pass until it is possible to bump the ball with such accuracy that there is virtually no advantage in using the overhand pass. The spectators have benefitted also because the referee's whistle is noticeably quieter during service reception.

Upon returning from the 1964 Olympics, United States players, coaches, and referees were astonished at the officials' leniency during the set. At the Olympics, the foreign officials had automatically called every overhand service reception a thrown ball, and then ignored the manner in which the setters delivered the ball. The international setters had learned to set the ball from any body position in any direction. Blockers from the United States were confused by the setters' maneuvers and seemed to be continually late in reaching their blocking assignments.

American setters had been taught to stand with their shoulders at a right angle to the net and to set the ball directly forward or backward. Since the USVBA referees had not yet incorporated the interpretations of the International Volleyball Federation, American setters also had been taught to release the ball with a flick of the wrist, which meant that when they contacted the ball, they released it immediately. Although American players had a good "touch" on the ball, they had not learned to keep the ball in contact with their fingers as long as the foreign setters.

The obvious advantages of a prolonged contact of the ball are increased options of direction and greater accuracy of the set. The foreign setters could maintain prolonged contact by keeping their elbows closer to the sides of their body and by relying on greater arm and hand action to deliver the set. After exposure to the advantageous international style of setting, the better setters from the United States worked to master international techniques, and United States National Officials became more liberal in their interpretations of what constituted a thrown ball.

In the 1963 Pan American Games, 1964 Olympics, and subsequent international competition, players representing the United States were exposed to half-speed spikes and open-hand dink, or placement, shots. As the international spikers were confronted by opponents reaching over the net to block, they developed these alternate methods of attack to complement the hard spike. These off-speed shots caught the American backcourt players flat-footed because they were interpreted as thrown balls in national competition within the United States. Returning Olympians developed these shots as techniques of attack and used them frequently enough to force opposing players to learn to dive and roll to the floor to retrieve off-speed shots.

National officials who would have whistled lesser-known spikers off the court for using open-hand dinks and half-speed spikes with prolonged hand contact, gradually liberalized their interpretation of what constituted a thrown ball during the attack, and these methods soon became accepted practice. Before these techniques of attack became popular, a player went to the floor to retrieve a ball only if he were out of position or had tripped. In the 1980s our USA teams and referees travel all over the world and are kept up to date on current international rule interpretations.

Figure A-1 *The Antenna.* If the spiker hits the ball into the antenna, the ball is declared dead and awarded to the defense. If the ball rebounds into the antenna after touching the block, it is awarded to the offense. (Norm Schindler)

The Last Twenty Years

The time-consuming ritual of having five players form a screen in front of the server to hide the ball from the receiving team was outlawed in 1965. At one time, screening players were actually allowed to wave their arms in a distracting manner to confuse their opponents. Often the receiver could not see a small server at all—nor could he see the flight of the serve until it came into view just before crossing the net. Naturally, the accuracy of the pass was impaired, which proved to be a great handicap to the few teams that needed a precise pass to use their three-hitter offense.

It was not unusual for a server to change his position from the right to the middle or left of the serving area. Until 1968, this serving area extended across the entire backline. The server often moved the screen about in a comical parade until the chosen receiver was isolated behind a wall of players. After the 1984 Olympics the serving area will once again extend beyond the entire backline.

Today's rules call for the server to put the ball into play without undue delay when the referee blows his whistle and calls for the serve. Players are not allowed to screen or raise their arms to confuse the receiver. Advanced passing techniques allow players to receive the serve with greater accuracy. This allows the setters to arrive under the ball in position and to watch the approaching spiker and the blockers. Thus, the skilled setter can deliver a variety of "play sets" to deceive the opponents' block.

Allowing the blockers to reach across the net to contact the ball after the offense has attacked it has significantly changed the game. It forces opposing setters to pull the sets back from the net to prevent the blockers from forming a "roof" around the set and stuffing the spike to the floor. Since the spikers must contact the ball farther away from the net, the spike has to travel in a flatter trajectory instead of being hit straight down into their opponents' court. Spikers can no longer jump up and hit the ball as hard as possible to attempt to overpower the block.

Successful spikers learn to place the ball past the blockers using a variety of spiking angles and a change of pace dink shot and/ or off-speed spike. Every good player must learn to dive to recover dink shots and half-speed spikes that fall in front of him.

Individual blockers are now allowed to contact the ball twice in succession instead of standing helpless as their blocked ball drops to the floor. Long rallies are common with the liberalized blocking rules, and the dive and roll have become a common defensive fundamental. Players are no longer cheered when they hit the floor to retrieve a ball; they are expected to do so.

Figure A-3 *Front-Row Blockers.* Any or all of the front-row players are allowed to block. In top competition, it is tactically sound to use three blockers to stop a strong spiker. (Norm Schindler)

Figure A-2 *Dink Shots.* Referees have become increasingly lenient in monitoring open hand dink shots during the last few years. Usually, this shot is called strictly at the high school level; loosely at the college level, and rarely ever in international play. (Norm Schindler)

Emphasis on overall conditioning and increasing the vertical jump through jump training have become popular with serious volleyball athletes.

The four-man block that hindered the three-hitter attack was abolished in 1969, and only front-row players are now allowed to block. Teams that can pass the ball accurately usually experience one-on-one blocking situations against their three-hitter attack.

When a backcourt player was allowed to join three frontcourt teammates at the net to block, it was difficult, regardless of the play, for a spiker in a three-hitter attack to isolate himself in a one-on-one situation. Four blockers spaced evenly across the court always enjoyed a tactical advantage at the net. It was feared this rule change would legislate against the small player who, under the previous rulings, could switch to the backcourt to dig and allow a taller player to take his place at the net.

This rule, however, has forced players to become skilled in all defensive aspects of the game. The tall and clumsy player who switched to an end blocking position in all three backcourt positions had to learn to play backcourt defense. The small setter who switched to the backcourt had to learn to block. Smaller players have not vanished from the sport; they have increased their vertical jump by better techniques, weight training, or a combination of both. The tall and slow spiker has either improved his defensive skills or has been relegated to the middle-in position on the middle-in defense where fewer digging skills are needed.

The spiker is allowed to reach over the net when following through after contacting the ball. This relieves the referee of stopping the play every time an offensive player's hand inadvertently flicks across the net.

The referees' whistles were further silenced in 1975 when the defending team was allowed three contacts to return the ball after it was touched or deflected by the block. This rule gives the serving team a better chance to score and shortens the length of the match. In the past, the referee had to call the play dead when a blocker's teammates did not realize that their blocker had contacted the ball and continued to dig, set, and spike for a point or side out.

After the 1976 Olympics, the USVBA converted their court dimensions to metric measurements and round net posts without cable started to be used in our nation's schools to replace dangerous cable and the breakdown-prone A frames shown in Figure A-4. The six substitutions a game rule was immediately used by college men and USVBA men and women in 1977, but the high school and college women still use the old twelve substitutions a game rule. That

Figure A-4 *Snafu.* The USVBA recommends the use of round net posts with no supporting cable to prevent injuries and the classic breakdown of the net during the middle on a match. (Richard Mackson)

same year, the three ball system was adopted by most major colleges and the lapse between serves was shortened noticeably. The 1977 ban on "deliberate coaching" during the game was largely ignored and unenforceable, and by 1980 coaching during the game was allowed if "not done in a disruptive manner." In 1978 the serve could be blocked over the net. This rule changed receiving formations and led to tactical changes such as a block of the blocked serve. After the 1984 Olympics a rule that allows the player to serve anywhere behind the backline will hinder the accuracy of the passer. Coupled with another post 1984 Olympic rule which allows double hits the serving team will score points faster.

VOLLEYBALL ASSOCIATIONS

United States Volleyball Association (USVBA)

The USVBA, formed in 1928, is recognized by the United States Olympic Committee as the governing body for volleyball in this country. The association has a full-time, paid executive director, assistant director, and full-time head and assistant coaches for the USA Men's and Women's program.

The YMCA has traditionally supplied integral leadership in this organization. Many volunteers in the association are retired players who wish to stay close to the game and do so by accepting committee or officiating assignments.

The Amateur Sports Act of 1978 gave member organizations affiliated with the USVBA an increasing role in the governing of this organization. The USVBA registers its own players and regulates all eligibility procedures for organizations, teams, and individuals competing in its local, regional and national tournaments. The organization conducts national championship for Open Men's, Open Women's, and Senior Women and Men's divisions at a different site each year. The USVBA Championships are traditionally held in early May.

The USVBA has a membership of over 22,000, which is small in comparison with East European and Asian volleyball associations.

The USVBA publishes an *Official Volleyball Rules and Reference Guide* annually. The association's rules are adopted by the NCAA, NAIA, NJCAA, AAU, and almost every other organization that sponsors volleyball competition in the U.S.

The USVBA sends teams abroad to play major international volleyball events. Due largely to the efforts of the USVBA, volleyball has become the greatest participant sport in the U.S.

National Collegiate Athletic Association (NCAA)

The NCAA conducts 41 national championships in 19 men's sports for over 800 colleges and universities in three divisions. These championships are open to all member institutions. Four teams are invited to the NCAA Men's Championships: the champion from the West; the Midwest; the

Figure A-5 *NCAA Volleyball.* NCAA Championships consistently draw the largest volleyball crowds in the United States. (Stan Troutman)

East; and one at-large entry. The California Intercollegiate Volleyball Association (CIVA); the Midwest Intercollegiate Volleyball Association (MIVA); and the Eastern Collegiate Volleyball League (ECVL) are the strongest regional leagues.

The NCAA conducted 31 women's championships during the 1982–83 academic year; championships are held in fourteen sports and three divisions in volleyball. The first NCAA Women's Volleyball Championships were held on December 20, 1981. Twenty-four teams were selected for regional play in a single elimination tournament at four different sites. The four regional champions met at UCLA's Pauley Pavilion with USC defeating UCLA 3 games to 2.

The NCAA maintains more than 80 full-time staff members in its national headquarters in Shawnee Mission, Kansas.

Division for Girls and Women's Sports (DGWS)

The DGWS is a division of the American Association for Health, Physical Education, and Recreation.

The first intercollegiate national volleyball championships for women were held at California State College at Long Beach in 1970 and were sponsored by the DGWS. Twenty-eight top-ranking teams from states such as California, New Mexico, Oregon, Florida, Ohio, Mississippi, Missouri, Illinois, Utah, and Texas were represented.[2] Several former Olympians and USVBA All-Americans competed on their college teams. Sul Ross State University in Texas emerged as the DGWS champion.

Association for Intercollegiate Athletics for Women (AIAW)

The AIAW was established in 1971 by the DGWS to provide leadership in women's intercollegiate athletics. The AIAW conducted the collegiate women's volleyball championships in four-year and two-year college divisions from 1971 to 1980 with all major collegiate volleyball institutions participating. In 1981, the NCAA initiated Women's Volleyball Championships and most of the major Division I volleyball powers opted for NCAA participation. The AIAW ceased to function in 1983.

National Association of Intercollegiate Athletics (NAIA)

The first intercollegiate volleyball tournament sponsored by a national collegiate governing body was hosted by George Williams College in Downers Grove, Illinois, in 1969. The seven-team double elimination NAIA volleyball championship "was won by Earlham College, Richmond, Indiana, with Indiana Tech, Fort Wayne, Indiana, finishing second."[3]

National Junior College Athletic Association (NJCAA)

Kellogg Community College won the first NJCAA Volleyball Championship in 1974 at Schoolcraft College in Livonia, Michigan.

Amateur Athletic Union (AAU)

The AAU usually holds tournaments a few days before the USVBA Championships and

[2]Lyndee Dossey, Publicity Chairman for DGWS National Intercollegiate Volleyball Championships, personal correspondence with the author.

[3]Jerre McNamara, "Earlham College Wins the National Association of Intercollegiate Athletics National Volleyball Championships," 1970 *Official Volleyball Guide*, p. 128.

Figure A-6 *International Protocal.* After the introductions at an international match, players and coaches exchange gifts. (Norm Schindler)

chooses a location near the USVBA site. The AAU tournament attracts a number of teams that desire a final tune-up before the USVBA championships. Teams in this tournament are usually at partial strength because many players are not willing to take the additional expense and time away from their jobs or schools to compete in both championships.

The AAU sponsors a Junior Olympic Volleyball Program.

High School Associations

The National Federation of State High School Athletic Associations Sports Participation Surveys usually indicate that high school sponsored girls interscholastic programs have about 800 percent more participants than the boys programs. Girl's volleyball is popular over the entire country, and that is reflected in the recruitment of athletes from various sections of the United States for our USA Women's Team. Texas

leads the nation in participants, although the competitive season is short, leaving very little time for pre-season preparation. Boys volleyball is particularly popular in Southern California and that is also reflected in the selection of players for our USA Men's Team.

United States Olympic Committee (USOC)

There are about 130 nations with membership in the International Olympic Committee; this varies slightly with the current political climate.

The USOC funds Olympic sports, such as volleyball and channels the money through the USVBA. The women were considered to have an excellent chance for a medal in the 1980 Olympics had they been allowed to participate, while the men did not qualify.

In the past, United States Pan American and Olympic Volleyball teams have never achieved their full potential because key members cannot afford to support themselves or their families while training with the U.S. National team. Under a revised eligibility code, the U.S. Olympic committee can reimburse expenses incurred while training for national or international competition.

Our women are currently rated in the top three in the world with Japan and China. Our men have the potential to win a medal and are also ranked in the top three. Eight of the ten berths for the Olympic Men's Volleyball competition are filled at least one year ahead of the competition. The host country and the last Olympic champion qualify automatically. The winner of the World Championship and representatives from the continents of Africa, Asia, South America, North and Central America, and the winner of the European championship also qualify. Two nations qualify in a Special Olympic Qualification Tournament held a month before the Olympics. The United States Men's Team must defeat Cuba in the North and Central American zonal qualification to ensure Olympic participation. The United States Women's Team must compete in the same North and Central American Zonal Tournament as the men. Historically the women can qualify by winning the Pan American Games, but The International Volleyball Federation is controlled by the Communist voting block, so changes in Olympic qualification are always possible and could fluctuate every four years. In 1988 twelve men's teams will qualify for the Olympics.

International Volleyball Federation (FIVB)

About 145 countries maintain membership in the FIVB. Volleyball is a major sport in at least 25 of these countries. Olympic Games, Pan American Games, World Games, international matches, and all competition conducted outside of the United States abide by the playing rules of the International Volleyball Federation. In 1977, the USVBA made several rule changes to bring its rules into alignment with those of the FIVB. In both USVBA and International Rules, the only exception for women is a lowering of the net.

The Federation International Volley Ball (FIVB) competitions are more competitive than the Olympic Games. Since ten men's teams and eight women's teams are allowed to enter the Olympics, many of the world's better teams are eliminated in tough zone competition and fail to earn a berth in the Olympics.

United States Collegiate Council (USCSC)

In 1967 the USCSC was founded by the following organizations:

National Junior College Athletic Association

United States National Student Association

National Association of Intercollegiate Athletics (NAIA)

The National Collegiate Athletic Association (NCAA)

American Association for Health, Physical Education, and Recreation

The primary purpose of the Council is to promote international collegiate sport through increased participation of American student athletes in the World University Games. The World University Games is a major biennial competition sponsored by the IUSF. Volleyball competition is held every two years during the summer for full-time students. The USA Men's team competed for the first time in 1973 in Moscow. There were 24 entries and the USSR won 21 straight games to win the championship. Cuba was second, Korea third, Poland fourth, East Germany fifth, Brazil sixth; and the United States finished eighteenth.

RECORD OF TOURNAMENT WINNERS

For more information concerning the following tables, the reader is referred to Harold T. Friermood's "Cumulative Record of Volleyball Championship Winners," in the *1969 Official Volleyball Guide.*

Table A-1 *Olympic Games Men's Volleyball Championship Winners**

Tournament	Year	Place	Participating teams	Winner	Runner-up	USA
1	1964	Tokyo	10	USSR	Czechoslovakia	9th
2	1968	Mexico City	10	USSR	Japan	7th
3	1972	Munich	12	Japan	East Germany	**
4	1976	Montreal	10	Poland	USSR	**
5	1980	Moscow	10	USSR	Bulgaria	**

*Volleyball was not included in the Olympic Games from 1896 to 1960.
**USA team defeated by Cuba in Zonal Qualifications for Olympic Games.

Table A-2 *Composite Medal List—Men's Competition*

Country	Gold	Silver	Bronze	Total
USSR	3	1	1	5
Japan	1	1	1	3
Czechoslavakia		1	1	2
Poland	1			1
East Germany		1		1
Bulgaria		1		1
Cuba			1	1
Romania			1	1

Source: Los Angeles Times, July 11, 1983

Table A-3 *Olympic Games Women's Volleyball Championship Winners**

Tournament	Year	Place	Participating teams	Winner	Runner-up	USA
1	1964	Tokyo	6	Japan	USSR	5th
2	1968	Mexico City	8	USSR	Japan	8th
3	1972	Munich	8	USSR	Japan	**
4	1976	Montreal	8	Japan	USSR	**
5	1980	Moscow	8	USSR	East Germany	***

*Volleyball was not included in the Olympic Games from 1896 to 1960.
**Did not qualify.
***USA Boycott.

Table A-4 *Composite Medal List—Women's Competition*

Country	Gold	Silver	Bronze	Total
USSR	3	2		5
Japan	2	2		4
Poland			2	2
East Germany		1		1
North Korea			1	1
South Korea			1	1
Bulgaria			1	1

Source: Los Angeles Times, July 11, 1983

Table A-5 *Past National Results for Women Championship Winners*

Tournament	Year	Place	Winner	Runner-up
1	1970	Cal. St. College, Long Beach	Sul Ross St. Univ., Alpine, Texas	UCLA
2	1971	University of Kansas	Sul Ross St. Univ., Alpine, Texas	CSULB
3	1972	Miami Dade CC	UCLA	CSULB
4	1972	BYU	CSULB	BYU
5	1973	College of Wooster	CSULB	Texas Women's University
6	1974	Portland St. Univ.	UCLA	University of Hawaii
7	1975	Princeton	UCLA	University of Hawaii
8	1976	Texas-Austin	USC	UCLA
9	1977	BYU	USC	Hawaii
10	1978	Alabama-Tuscalooga	Utah State	UCLA
11	1979	So. Illinois	Hawaii	Utah State
12	1980	UCSB	USC	U. of the Pacific
13	1981	Los Angeles	USC	UCLA
14	1982	Stockton	Hawaii	USC
15	1983	Lexington	Hawaii	UCLA

Table A-6 *National Collegiate Athletic Association Men's Championship Winners*

Tournament	Year	Place	Winner	Runner-up
1	1970	Los Angeles	UCLA	CSULB
2	1971	Los Angeles	UCLA	UCSB
3	1972	Muncie, Ind.	UCLA	SDSU
4	1973	San Diego	SDSU	CSULB
5	1974	Santa Barbara	UCLA	UCSB
6	1975	Los Angeles	UCLA	UCSB
7	1976	Muncie, Ind.	UCLA	Pepperdine
8	1977	Los Angeles	USC	Ohio State
9	1978	Columbus	Pepperdine	UCLA
10	1979	Los Angeles	UCLA	USC
11	1980	Muncie, Ind.	USC	UCLA
12	1981	Santa Barbara	UCLA	USC
13	1982	University Park	UCLA	Penn State
14	1983	Columbus	UCLA	Pepperdine
15	1984	Los Angeles		

Won-Lost Records in NCAA Tournament Play

Team (Years Participated)	Years	Won	Lost	Pct.	1st	2nd	3rd	4th
Army (1973)	1	0	5	.000	0	0	0	1
Ball State (1979–71–72–73–74–79)	6	7	17	.292	0	0	4	2
Calif. Santa Barbara (1979–71–72–74–75)	5	8	11	.421	0	3	1	1
Long Beach State (1970–73)	2	7	3	.700	0	2	0	0
Ohio State (1975–76–77–78–80–81–82–83)	6	6	11	.353	0	1	5	2
Penn State (1981–82–83)	3	2	4	.333	0	1	1	1
Pepperdine (1976–77–78–83)	4	5	3	.625	1	2	1	0
Rutgers-Newark (1977–78–79–80)	4	1	7	.125	0	0	1	3
San Diego State (1972–73)	2	7	3	.700	1	1	0	0
Southern California (1977–78–80–81–82)	5	7	3	.700	2	2	1	0
Springfield (1971–74–76)	3	0	9	.000	0	0	0	3
UCLA (1970–71–72–74–75–76–78–79–80–81–82–83)	12	30	3	.909	10	2	0	0
Yale (1975)	1	0	2	.000	0	0	0	1

Table A-7 *United States Volleyball Association Winners Since 1968 Men's Championship*

Tournament	Year	Place	Winner	Runner-up
39	1969	Knoxville	Los Angeles YMCA	San Francisco Olympic Club
40	1970	Honolulu	Chart House of San Diego	Balboa Bay Club, Newport Beach
41	1971	Binghamton	Santa Monica YMCA	Chart House of San Diego
42	1972	Salt Lake City	Chart House of San Diego	Santa Barbara Volleyball Club
43	1973	Duluth	Chucks Steak House of Southern California	Ski Mart, Long Beach
44	1974	Knoxville	Univ. of California, Santa Barbara	Balboa Bay Club, Newport Beach
45	1975	Reno	Chart House of San Diego	National All Stars
46	1976	Schenectady	Maccabi, Los Angeles	ANVA, Los Angeles
47	1977	Hilo	Chuck's Steak House, Santa Barbara	Maccabi, Los Angeles
48	1978	El Paso	Chuck's Steak House, Los Angeles	Outrigger Canoe Club, Honolulu
49	1979	Dayton	Nautilus Pacifica, Long Beach (CA)	Outrigger Canoe Club, Honolulu
50	1980	Portland	Olympic Club, San Francisco	Chuck's Steak House, Los Angeles
51	1981	Arlington	Nautilus Pacifica, Long Beach (CA)	Chuck's Steak House, Los Angeles
52	1982	Hilo	Chuck's Steak House, Los Angeles	Olympic Club, San Francisco
53	1983	Memphis	Nautilus Pacifica	Outrigger Canoe Club, Honolulu

Table A-9 *FIVB Men's World Volleyball Championship Winners*

Tournament	Year	Place	Participating Teams	Winner	Runner-up	USA
1	1949	Prague	10	USSR	Czechoslovakia	-
2	1952	Moscow	11	USSR	Czechoslovakia	-
3	1956	Paris	24	Czechoslovakia	Romania	(6th)
4	1960	Sao Paulo	14	USSR	Czechoslovakia	(7th)
5	1962	Moscow	19	USSR	Czechoslovakia	-
6	1966	Prague	22	Czechoslovakia	Romania	(11th)
7	1970	Sofia	24	East Germany	Bulgaria	(18th)
8	1974	Mexico City	24	Poland	USSR	(14th)
9	1978	Rome	24	USSR	Italy	(19th)
10	1982	Buenos Aires	24	USSR	Brazil	(13th)

Table A-8 *United States Volleyball Association Winners Since 1968 Women's Championship*

Tournament	Year	Place	Winner	Runner-up
21	1969	Knoxville	Long Beach Shamrocks	Hawaiian Women
22	1970	Honolulu	Long Beach Shamrocks	Sul Ross State Univ., Alpine, Texas
23	1971	Binghamton	Los Angeles Renegades	Long Beach Shamrocks
24	1972	Salt Lake City	E. Pluribus Unum, Houston	Region 13 Seniors
25	1973	Duluth	E. Pluribus Unum, Houston	Los Angeles Renegades
26	1974	Knoxville	Los Angeles Renegades	Wilt's Little Dippers
27	1975	Reno	Adidas (Cal.) Volleyball Club	Santa Monica (CA) Dippers
28	1976	Schenectady	Pasadena, Texas	Adidas (CA)
29	1977	Hilo	So. Bay Spoilers	Adidas (CA)
30	1978	El Paso	Nick's Fish Market, Los Angeles	King Harbor Spoilers, Redondo Beach (CA)
31	1979	Dayton	Fireside Mavericks, Los Angeles	Adidas (CA)
32	1980	Portland	ANVA, Fountain Valley (CA)	Los Angeles Renegades
33	1981	Arlington	Utah State	Palo Alto YMCA
34	1982	Hilo	Monarch (Hon.)	Gym Master
35	1983	Memphis	Snytex	The Fish Market

Table A-10 *FIVB Women's World Volleyball Championship Winners*

Tournament	Year	Place	Participating teams	Winner	Runner-up	USA
1	1952	Moscow	7	USSR	Poland	-
2	1956	Paris	17	USSR	Romania	(9th)
3	1960	Sao Paulo	10	USSR	Japan	(6th)
4	1962	Moscow	14	Japan	USSR	-
5	1967	Tokyo	4	Japan	USA	(2nd)
6	1970	Varna	22	USSR	Japan	(11th)
7	1973	Montevideo	10	USSR	Japan	(6th)
8	1974	Mexico City	23	Japan	USSR	(12th)
9	1978	Leningrad	24	Cuba	Japan	(5th)
10	1982	Lima	24	China	Peru	(3rd)

Table A-11 *Pan American Games Men's Volleyball Championship Winners**

Tournament	Year	Place	Participating teams	Winner	Runner-up	USA
1	1955	Mexico City	6	USA	Mexico	(1st)
2	1959	Chicago	9	USA	Brazil	(1st)
3	1963	Sao Paulo	8	Brazil	USA	(2nd)
4	1967	Winnipeg	9	USA	Brazil	(1st)
5	1971	Cali, Colombia	11	Cuba	USA	(2nd)
6	1975	Mexico City	8	Cuba	Brazil	(4th)
7	1979	San Juan	8	Cuba	Brazil	(5th)
8	1983	Caracas	6	Brazil	Cuba	(4th)

*Volleyball was not included in the first Pan Am Games (1951).

Table A-12 *Pan American Games Women's Volleyball Championship Winners**

Tournament	Year	Place	Participating teams	Winner	Runner-up	USA
1	1955	Mexico City	4	Mexico	USA	2nd
2	1959	Chicago	4	Brazil	USA	2nd
3	1963	Sao Paulo	3	Brazil	USA	2nd
4	1967	Winnipeg	6	USA	Peru	1st
5	1971	Cali, Colombia	9	Cuba	Peru	6th
6	1975	Mexico City	7	Cuba	Peru	6th
7	1979	San Juan	8	Cuba	Peru	4th
8	1983	Caracas	7	Cuba	USA	2nd

*Volleyball was not included in the first Pan Am Games (1951).

Table A-13 *North Central and Caribbean Zone Men's Championship*

Tournament	Year	Place	Participating teams	Winner	Runner-up	USA
1	1969	Mexico	4	Cuba	Mexico	3rd
2	1971	Havana	6	Cuba	USA	2nd
3	1973	Tijuana	7	USA	Cuba	1st
4	1975	Los Angeles	5	Cuba	Mexico	3rd
5	1977	Santa Domingo	9	Cuba	Mexico	-
6	1979	Havana	7	Cuba	Canada	6th
7	1981	Canada	4	Cuba	Canada	-
8	1983*	Indianapolis	5	USA	Cuba	1st

*Canadian Men's Team qualified for the 1984 Olympics by taking third because the USA and Cuba had qualified previously.

Table A-14 *North Central and Caribbean Women's Zone Championship*

Tournament	Year	Place	Participating teams	Winner	Runner-up	USA
1	1969	Mexico	3	Mexico	Cuba	-
2	1971	Havana	4	Mexico	Cuba	3
3	1973	Tijuna	7	Cuba	Canada	3
4	1975	Los Angeles	5	Cuba	USA	2
5	1977	Santa Domingo	8	Cuba	Canada	3
6	1979	Havana	5	Cuba	USA	2
7	1981	Canada	4	Canada	Cuba	4
8	1983*	Indianapolis	6	USA	Cuba	1st

*Canadian Women's Team qualified for the 1984 Olympics by taking third because the USA and Cuba had qualified previously.

Diagram A-1 *Point or Side Out*

Diagram A-2 *Ball In Bounds or Line Violation*

Diagram A-3 *Ball In*

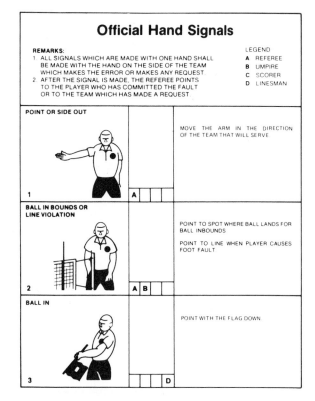

Official Hand Signals

REMARKS:
1. ALL SIGNALS WHICH ARE MADE WITH ONE HAND SHALL BE MADE WITH THE HAND ON THE SIDE OF THE TEAM WHICH MAKES THE ERROR OR MAKES ANY REQUEST.
2. AFTER THE SIGNAL IS MADE, THE REFEREE POINTS TO THE PLAYER WHO HAS COMMITTED THE FAULT OR TO THE TEAM WHICH HAS MADE A REQUEST.

LEGEND
A REFEREE
B UMPIRE
C SCORER
D LINESMAN

POINT OR SIDE OUT

MOVE THE ARM IN THE DIRECTION OF THE TEAM THAT WILL SERVE

1   A

BALL IN BOUNDS OR LINE VIOLATION

POINT TO SPOT WHERE BALL LANDS FOR BALL INBOUNDS

POINT TO LINE WHEN PLAYER CAUSES FOOT FAULT

2   A B

BALL IN

POINT WITH THE FLAG DOWN.

3   D

Source: United States Volleyball Association 1984 Rule Book (Colorado Springs, Colorado: United States Volleyball Association, 1984). Used with permission.

Official Hand Signals (continued)

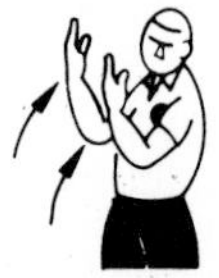 **BALL OUT** 4 A B		RAISE THE FOREARMS IN A VERTICAL POSITION. HANDS OPEN. PALMS FACING UPWARD
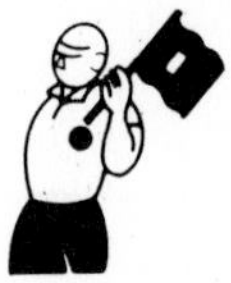 **BALL OUT** 5 D		RAISE THE FLAG
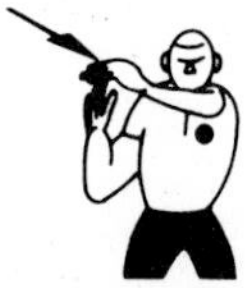 **BALL CONTACTED BY A PLAYER** 6 A B		BRUSH ONE HAND WITH A HORIZONTAL MOTION OVER THE FINGERS OF THE OTHER HAND THAT IS HELD IN A VERTICAL POSITION.
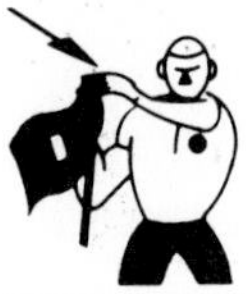 **BALL CONTACTED BY A PLAYER** 7 D		RAISE THE FLAG AND BRUSH IT WITH THE OPEN PALM OF THE OTHER HAND
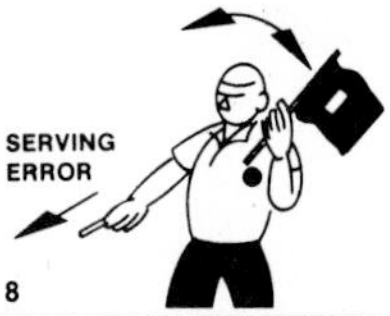 **OUTSIDE THE ANTENNA** SERVING ERROR 8 D		WAVE THE FLAG AND POINT THE ARM TO THE VERTICAL NET MARKER OR THE ANTENNA. WAVE THE FLAG AND POINT TO THE SERVING AREA.
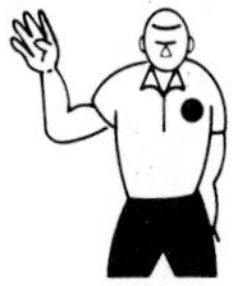 **FOUR HITS** 9 A B		RAISE FOUR FINGERS.
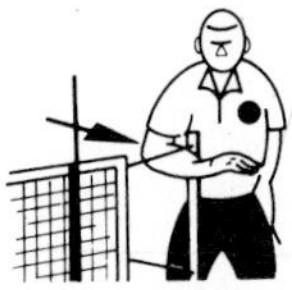 **CROSSING CENTER LINE** 10 A B		POINT TO THE CENTER LINE AND AT THE SAME TIME INDICATE WITH THE "SERVICE" SIGNAL TO THE OPPONENTS' SIDE; POINT TO THE PLAYER WHO COMMITTED THE FAULT.

Diagram A-4 *Ball Out*

Diagram A-5 *Ball Out*

Diagram A-6 *Ball Contacted by a Player*

Diagram A-7 *Ball Contacted by a Player*

Diagram A-8 *Outside the Antenna Serving Error*

Diagram A-9 *Four Hits*

Diagram A-10 *Crossing Center Line*

Diagram A-11 *Held Ball*
Thrown Ball
Lifted Ball
Carried Ball

Diagram A-12 *Double Hit*

Diagram A-13 *Ball Contacted Below the Waist*

Diagram A-14 *End of Game or Match*

Diagram A-15 *Time Out*

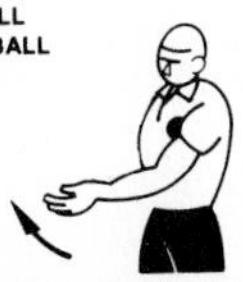

Diagram A-16 *Substitution*

Diagram A-17 *Ball Not Released at Time of Service*

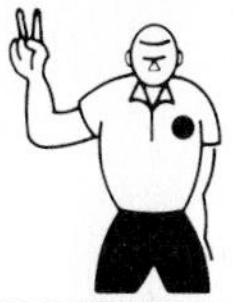

Official Hand Signals (continued)

HELD BALL THROWN BALL LIFTED BALL CARRIED BALL			SLOWLY LIFT ONE HAND WITH THE PALM FACING UPWARD.
11	A		
DOUBLE HIT			LIFT TWO FINGERS IN VERTICAL POSITION
12	A	B	
BALL CONTACTED BELOW THE WAIST	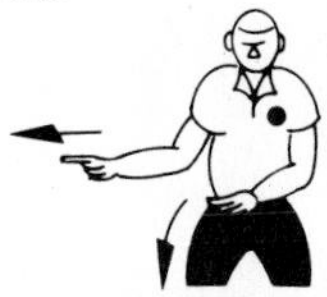		POINT TO THE PLAYER WHO COMMITTED THE FAULT WITH ONE HAND AND MOTION WITH THE OTHER HAND FROM WAIST DOWNWARD
13	A		
END OF GAME OR MATCH	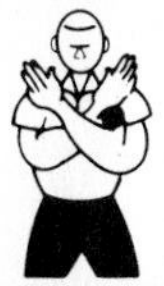		CROSS THE FOREARMS IN FRONT OF THE CHEST.
14	A		
TIME OUT	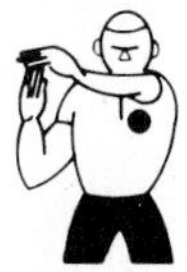		PLACE THE PALM OF ONE HAND HORIZONTALLY OVER THE OTHER HAND, HELD IN VERTICAL POSITION, FORMING THE LETTER "T" FOLLOW BY POINTING TO THE TEAM REQUESTING THE TIME OUT
15	A	B	C
SUBSTITUTION	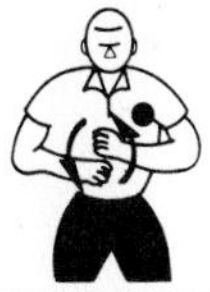		MAKE A CIRCULAR MOTION OF THE HANDS AROUND EACH OTHER.
16	A	B	
BALL NOT RELEASED AT TIME OF SERVICE	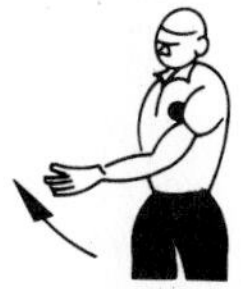		LIFT THE EXTENDED ARM, THE PALM OF THE HAND FACING UPWARD.
17	A		

Official Hand Signals (continued)

DELAY OF SERVICE

RAISE FIVE FINGERS IN A VERTICAL POSITION.

18 | A

Diagram A-18 *Delay of Service*

BALL IN THE NET AT TIME OF SERVICE

PLAYER TOUCHING NET

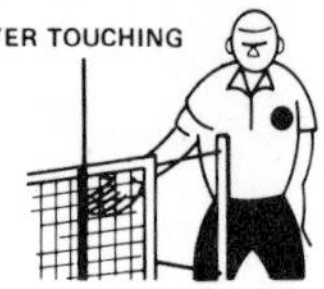

TOUCH THE NET WITH THE HAND.

TOUCH THE NET WITH THE HAND AND POINT TO THE PLAYER WHO COMMIT— TED THE FAULT.

19 | A

Diagram A-19 *Ball in the Net at Time of Service Player Touching Net*

DOUBLE FOUL OR PLAY OVER

RAISE THE THUMBS OF BOTH HANDS

20 | A

Diagram A-20 *Double Foul or Play Over*

BACK LINE BLOCK OR SCREEN

FOR SCREEN. KEEP HANDS BELOW TOP OF HEAD

FOR BACK LINE BLOCK RAISE HANDS ABOVE TOP OF HEAD

POINT TO PLAYER(S) COMMITTING FAULT

21 | A | B

Diagram A-21 *Back-Line Block or Screen*

OUT OF POSITION

MAKE A CIRCULAR MOTION WITH THE HAND AND INDICATE THE PLAYER OR PLAYERS WHO HAVE COMMITTED THE FAULT

22 | A | B | C

Diagram A-22 *Out of Position*

OVER THE NET

PASS THE HAND OVER THE NET AND POINT TO THE PLAYER WHO COMMITTED THE FAULT.

23 | A

Diagram A-23 *Over the Net*

BACK LINE SPIKER (ATTACKER)

MAKE A DOWNWARD MOTION WITH THE FOREARM AND POINT TO THE PLAYER WHO COMMITTED THE FAULT.

24 | A | B

Diagram A-24 *Back-Line Spiker (Attacker)*

Diagram A-25 *Ball Touching Object*

Diagram A-26 *Warning-Penalty-Exclusion*

Diagram A-27 *Point*

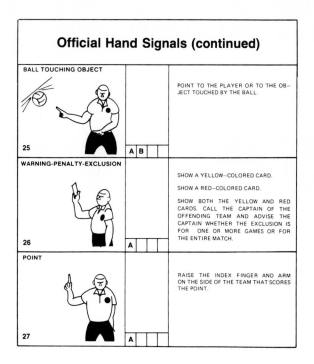

Official Hand Signals (continued)

BALL TOUCHING OBJECT			POINT TO THE PLAYER OR TO THE OB-JECT TOUCHED BY THE BALL.
25	A	B	
WARNING-PENALTY-EXCLUSION			SHOW A YELLOW–COLORED CARD. SHOW A RED–COLORED CARD. SHOW BOTH THE YELLOW AND RED CARDS. CALL THE CAPTAIN OF THE OFFENDING TEAM AND ADVISE THE CAPTAIN WHETHER THE EXCLUSION IS FOR ONE OR MORE GAMES OR FOR THE ENTIRE MATCH.
26	A		
POINT			RAISE THE INDEX FINGER AND ARM ON THE SIDE OF THE TEAM THAT SCORES THE POINT.
27	A		

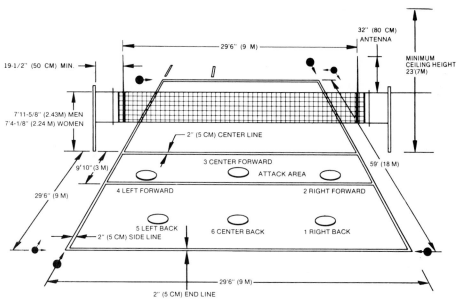

NOTE
INDICATES POSITION OF LINESMAN WHEN FOUR ARE USED
INDICATES POSITION OF LINESMAN WHEN TWO ARE USED

Diagram A-28 *Court Layout (unlabeled)*

COLLEGE VOLLEYBALL QUESTIONNAIRE

If space is insufficient for full answers, please use the reverse
side of form.

Name_____ Nickname_____

Campus Address _____ Campus Phone _____

Home Address_____ Home Phone _____

Height _____ Weight _____ Age _____ Date of Birth_____

Married _____ Spouse's Name _____ Children Age(s)_____

Shoe Size _____ Waist Size _____ Jersey Size_____

Month and Year Entered This School _____

College_____ Major _____ Class _____

Organizations _____

Business or Professional Objectives _____

Years of eligibility remaining, including present season _____

When will you graduate? Quarter_____ Year_____

List volleyball experience in high school, clubs, open teams, Armed
Services _____

_____

How many seasons of college volleyball have you played?_____

Colleges, universities, and/or junior colleges attended _____

List names, dates, and athletic achievements_____

_____

Prominent relatives in athletics _____

Your biggest thrill in sports _____

_____

Who is the greatest volleyball player you ever played against?_____

_____

_____

Who is the greatest volleyball player you ever saw?_____

Why did you choose this college?_____

_____

Chart A-1 *College Volleyball Questionnaire*

Bibliography

VOLLEYBALL PUBLICATIONS

Official Volleyball Guide. Richard E. Smith, editor. Published annually by the United States Volleyball Association. Price $5.50. Address: United States Volleyball Association, 1750 East Boulder Street, Colorado Springs, CO 80909. Presents a summary of the past USVBA season, and includes the coming season rules. Much information about the organization of the USVBA is included.

Volleyball Rule Book. A publication of the United States Volleyball Association. Price $3.50. Address: USVBA, 1750 East Boulder St., Colorado Springs, CO, 80909.

USVBA Case Book. Richard E. Smith, editor. Published annually by the United States Volleyball Association. Price $3.00. Address: USVBA, 1750 East Boulder St., Colorado Springs, CO, 80909. This is the book of official USVBA rule interpretations and is a necessity for officials.

Volleyball USA. A publication of the United States Volleyball Educational Foundation. Published four times annually. Annual subscription included in USVBA registration is $2.00. Non-membership subscription is $5.00, U.S.: $6.00 elsewhere. Volleyball, USA, 1750 East Boulder Street, Colorado Springs, CO 80909.

Volleyball Monthly. Published by Straight Down, Inc., Post Office Box 3137, San Luis Obispo, California 93403. (805)541-2294. Subscription price is $9.95 for one year. This is the best source for current volleyball information in the country.

Volleyball Technical Journal. Dr. Lorne Sawula, editor. Published four times yearly by Canadian Volleyball Association. Subscription price: $18.00/yr. Address: CVA, 333 River Road, Vanier City, Ontario K1L 8B9, Canada. Excellent resource for those interested in international volleyball and current research on training. Has many practical articles for coaches.

VOLLEYBALL TRAINING FILMS

The six training films below are individual super 8mm color, silent filmloops. Unless otherwise specified, Technicolor cartridges will be shipped with the order; Kodak cartridges are also available however. The loops are the Serve, Forearm Passes, Overhand Sets, Spikes, Blocks, and Dives and Rolls. All six are available for $149.70, but I would recommend purchasing individual cartridges for $24.95, as I authored the films in 1969 and two are outdated. The best loop features Toshi Toyoda demonstrating dives and rolls and still technically sound. Spiking is demonstrated by our 1968 Olympic Men's captain, Larry Rundle, and is a very good technical film. Serving is good, and it includes an excellent demonstration of the round-house serve by Toshi Toyoda. Overhand setting is still good. The passing loop features an elbow snap technique that I no longer recommend, and the middle blocking segment of the blocking film contains technical errors. The six film loops are available from Champions On Film and Video, Box 1941, 745 State Circle, Ann Arbor, Michigan 48106. The film is also available in 16mm sound and color in two parts. Part One includes the Serve, Forearm Passes, and Overhand Sets for $79.00. Part Two includes Spikes, Blocks, and Dives and Rolls for $79.00. Part parts are available in ¾ in. U-matic video for $107 or ½ in. Beta/VHS for $89.

Films

This is Volleyball. 16mm, color and sound, twelve-minutes long featuring male and female highlights from the 1976 Olympics. Price $180.00. Excellent film for any level.

Volleyball 76. 16mm color and sound; thirty-minutes long featuring explana-tions of techniques and tactics employed by male and female teams in the 1976 Olympics. Price, $360.00. Very good instructional film for beginners.

World Cup Matches. 16mm color and sound from 1978 World Cup. Shows each play in normal speed and slow motion. Price, $300.00. This is a film for advanced players. It contains a lot of repetition on combination spikes using men only.

Basic Skills Slide Series. Sixty-five excellent slides of male and female players in the 1976 Olympic Games preforming basic techniques. Price, $90.00.

The four films listed above can be ordered from: Volleyball Publications, P.O. Box 286R, Huntington Beach, CA 92648.

Power Volleyball For Women. 16mm, color and sound, twenty minutes featuring our outstanding U.S. Women's National Team. For rental information contact: USVBA Films, 1750 E. Boulder Street, Colorado Springs, CO. 80909 or phone 303/632-5551.

JUMP TRAINING

Vertec. Manufactured by Questek Corporation, 19145 Parthenia Street, Northridge, California 91324. Phone 213/992-4048 or write for current price and shipping charge. The Vertec is a natural jump training device explained in Chapter XII, Conditioning and Training.

VOLLEYBALL CAMPS

Al Scates Instructional Volleyball Camps. Write to Al Scates, UCLA Athletic Department, 405 Hilgard Ave., Los Angeles, CA 90024 for a current brochure.

Volleyball Terms

I. OFFENSIVE MANEUVERS:
Serving, passing, setting, and attacking

A. Serving

Crosscourt Serve: A serve landing near the opponent's right sideline.

Line Serve: A straight-ahead serve landing near the opponent's left sideline.

Overhand Serve: A serve performed with an overhand throwing action.

Overhand Floater Serve: The overhand floater serve has no spin and moves in an erratic path as it approaches the receiver. The ball is hit with only a momentary point of contact and very little follow-through.

Overhand Spin Serve: The server contacts the lower mid-section of the center of the ball; he or she uses the heel of the hand to initially contact the ball, and then uses the wrist snap to roll the hand over the ball, imparting topspin.

Round-house Serve: The arm moves in a windmill action, and the ball is contacted directly over the hitting shoulder.

Sky Ball Serve: An underhand serve that is hit so high it looks like it is falling straight down. It is used for play at large arenas or outdoor courts.

Underhand Serve: A serve performed with an underarm striking action. The ball is usually contacted with the heel of the hand.

B. Passing:
The reception of the serve or first contact of the ball. It is an attempt to control the movement of the ball so that the ball reaches another player. A pass of a hard-spiked ball is called a *dig*.

Bump Pass: See Forearm Pass

Elbow Lock Pass: Arms remain locked before and during contact. Movement of the arms is directed in an arc from the shoulders.

Overhand Pass: A pass executed with the hands held higher than the elbows with the palms facing outward.

Forearm Pass: A ball played off the forearms in an underhand manner. It is the best way to pass a serve and dig a spike.

One-Arm Pass: See One-Arm Dig (Digging).

C. Setting: Passing to place the ball in position for a player to spike. The setter is the player who sets the ball to the spiker.

Back Set: A set made over the head, behind the setter, and usually executed with two hands.

One-Set: A vertical set delivered from 1 to 4 ft. above the net. The spiker contacts the ball while the set is rising.

Slow One-Set: A vertical set that travels about 2 to 4 ft. above the net. The spiker attacks the ball after it reaches its peak.

Two-Set: This set usually travels from 3 to 5 ft. above the net. It does not require the same split-second timing as the one-set and can be mastered by any good spiker.

Three-Set: A play set delivered low and fast about 10 ft. from the left sideline to the spiker. It is designed to beat the middle blocker.

Slow Three-Set: A play set lobbed 10 ft. from the left sideline to the attacker. It is most effective when the attacker can "freeze" the middle blocker with the threat of a quick hit.

Four-Set: A play set placed close to the sideline at a height of 1 to 4 ft. above the net. This play is very difficult for the middle blocker to cover when the ball travels a distance of 15 to 20 ft. from the setter to the spiker.

Five-Set: A back lob to the setter on the right sideline is called a five-set. It is low enough to create a one-on-one situation for the off-hand spiker.

Regular Set: A ball delivered in a high arc that is not quick enough to defeat the middle blocker.

Shoot Set: See Four-Set

Lateral Set: A set made to either side of the setter.

Normal Set: See Regular Set

One Hand Set: Many setters jump-set passes that are going to travel over the net by intercepting the ball with the fingertips of one hand. This works particularly well in the one-set to a middle attacker.

Punch Set: When the ball is going to be passed over the net and it is impossible to set the ball with two hands, the backcourt setter may elect to punch set the ball with the knuckles rather than risk the chance of throwing the ball by contacting it with the fingertips.

Jump-Set: The player setting the ball jumps to confuse the block or to place himself in a better position to save a long pass that will drop over or hit the net.

D. Attacking: Hitting the ball into the opponents's court.

Crosscourt Spike: A spike directed diagonally to the longest part of the court.

Dink: Usually a one-hand hit in which the tips of the fingers are used to hit the ball to an area of the opponent's court.

Deep Dink: A dink that lands in the opponent's backcourt.

Follow-through: The attacker reaches over the net contacting the ball on his side first.

Line Spike: A spike directed down the sideline closest to the spiker.

Off-Hand Side: The side of the court on which the spiker would contact the ball with the predominant hand before the ball crosses in front of the spiker's body. For example, the right-front corner would be the off-hand side for a right-handed spiker.

Off-Speed Shot: A ball that rapidly loses momentum because of the reduced speed of the striking arm just prior to contact. The off-speed shot is most effective when used infrequently and directed toward a definite weakness in the defense.

On-Hand Side: The side of the court on which the spiker would contact the ball with the predominant hand before it crosses in front of his body. For example, the left-front corner would be the on-hand side for a right-handed spiker.

Pre-Jump Takeoff: The spiker hops and lands both feet simultaneously with the heels parallel; next he shifts his weight to the balls of his feet, bends his legs, forceably contracting them, and thereby forcing himself to leave the floor.

Round-House Spike: A spike hit with an extended windmill action of the arm. The ball is usually contacted with the body perpendicular to the net.

Spike: A ball hit forceably with one hand. Backcourt players cannot spike the ball unless they take off from behind the 10 ft. spiking line.

Spiker: A player who performs a spike, dink, or off-speed shot.

Step-Close Takeoff: The spiker takes a long last step by jumping forward, contacting the floor with the heel of one foot and then with the heel of the other foot; his weight then rolls from both heels to the toes as he takes off.

Tip: *See* Dink.

Wipe-Off Spike: A conscious effort to spike the ball laterally off the block into the out-of-bounds area.

II. DEFENSIVE MANEUVERS:
Blocking and Digging

A. *Blocking*

Block: A play by one or more players who attempt to intercept the ball over or near the net. Blocking is permitted by any or all of the players in the front line.

Attack Block: An attempt to intercept the ball before it crosses the net.

Double Block: Two players blocking at the net.

Down Block: Blockers drop their arms when they judge that the ball will not be hit by the spiker at a downward angle.

Key: A term used to describe close observation of opposing players' habits or actions in order to gain a clue to their next moves. For example, many blockers watch or "key" on the setter to see if he arches his back prior to contacting the ball, which usually indicates a back set.

Key on the One Play: The middle blocker jumps with the middle attacker to stop the quick one-set.

One-Hand Block: A technique used when the blocker is out of position. This maneuver gives the blocker greater lateral coverage above the net.

One-on-One Block: Used when only one blocker can reach his assignment.

Single Block: One player blocking at the net.

Soft Block: The forearms are held parallel to the net and the hands are held either tilted backward or parallel to the net.

Triple Block: Three players blocking at the net.

Turning the Ball In: A technique used by the end blocker to prevent the spike from hitting his hand and going out of bounds. He reaches over the net with his outside hand between the boundary line and the ball.

B. *Digging:* Passing a spiked ball while standing, diving, rolling, or jumping.

High Dig: Arms are held parallel to the floor—when the flight of the ball permits—to enable the dig to travel high into the air on the digger's side of the net.

Backhand Dig: Hitting the ball with the back of the hand. During the dive, this technique allows the player to field a low ball and keep his palms close to the floor in anticipation of a quick landing.

Cushioning the Ball: Digging the ball with a backward movement of the arms or body.

Dive: A technique used to recover a ball by going to a prone position on the court.

One-Arm Dig: Used when the ball cannot be contacted using the forearm pass. The ball can be effectively contacted anywhere from the knuckles of the closed fist to the elbow joint.

Roll: A movement that allows a player to go to the floor without injury and return quickly to his feet.

III. TEAM DEFENSE

Area Block: Blocking a designated area of the net. Frequently used by small blockers.

Blue Defense: See Off-Blocker Defense.

Free Ball: When the defense sees that the offense will hit the ball over the net with an upward flight or weak spike, it calls, "Free!" and assumes a normal serve-reception pattern.

False Weakness: A play used to lure the opposition into spiking to an area that they think is weak. For example, a blocker may leave the area above the net open for a crosscourt shot and then quickly move his arms to the middle of the net just prior to the spiker contacting the ball.

Middle-Back Defense: A defensive formation that uses the middle-back player to recover deep spikes.

Middle-In Defense: A defensive formation that uses one backcourt player to recover all short dink shots.

Off-Blocker Defense: A defensive formation that uses the off-blocker to recover short dink shots.

Red Defense: *See* Middle-In Defense

White Defense: *See* Middle-Back Defense

Blue Defense: See Off-Blocker Defense

Zone Block: *See* Area Block

IV. TEAM OFFENSE

A. *Combination:* A play that involves two attackers penetrating into a single blocker's zone of the net.

Double Quick: The middle attacker approaches for a front one-set and another attacker approaches for a back one-set. This play usually isolates the middle blocker who must defend against two attackers.

Right Cross: The middle attacker approaches for a one-set and the right attacker crosses behind him for a two-set.

Tandem: The middle attacker approaches for a one-set, and another attacker follows right behind him for a two-set.

Four-Man Reception: Four-man receiving formations are very efficient if four superior passers are receiving the serve. The advantage of this system is that the player at the net can block the serve.

Five-One Offense: This offense uses five hitters and one setter. Consequently, in 50 percent of the rotations, the offense runs with three frontcourt hitters and in 50 percent of the rotations, it runs with two hitters at the net. One player sets all the good passes.

Multiple Offense: A two- or three-hitter system that uses play sets.

One-on-One Situation: This refers to one attacker spiking against one blocker. Most offenses run their patterns with one-on-one situations as their goal.

Percentage Play: Certain sets can be hit with a better spiking percentage in certain situations. For example, when the ball is passed about 20 ft. from the net, the best percentage set is a regular set. The attacker would have a poor spiking average if the setter delivered a quick set on a bad pass.

Play Sets: Sets used to create favorable attack conditions. Plays are called by the setter or the attacker to avoid the block. Play sets vary greatly in height and distance from the setter to the attacker.

Six-Two Offense: An offense that uses three hitters at the net and a back-row setter. Four players are spikers and two are setter-spikers.

Three-Hitter Attack: The offense used when a backcourt setter is used.

Two-Hitter Attack: The offense used when one of the frontcourt players is a setter.

V. MISCELLANEOUS

Antenna: A pole extending vertically from the bottom of the net to a height of 32 in. above the net at the sideline.

Contacted Ball: A ball that touches or is touched by any part of a player's body or clothing.

Foul: A failure to play the ball properly as permitted under the rules.

Gather: The act of squatting just prior to jumping.

Netting: Touching the net while the ball is in play. This act terminates play when seen by the referee or umpire. In doubles, the player calls his own nets.

Out-of-Bounds: The ball is out-of-bounds when it touches any surface, object, or ground outside the court; touches the net outside the markers on the sides of the net; touches a net antenna; or passes over the net not entirely within the net antennas.

Scoring: A team can only score points when it is serving

Screw-Under Step: A technique used by a player to put himself in a more favorable position to play the ball by taking a long step with his lead leg and squatting. His trailing leg is extending as he pivots toward the ball. This technique is used to pass, dig, or set the ball.

Seam: The area directly between two serve receivers, diggers or blockers.

Side Out: When the serving team fails to score a point, the ball is given to their opponents; the exchange of service is called a side out.

Thrown Ball: When, in the opinion of the proper official, the ball visibly comes to rest at contact, the player has committed a foul.

Index